PENGUIN BOOKS
ORCHIDS OF THE RAINFOREST

Ram Anand is a Malaysian journalist, filmmaker, and author of *Orchids of the Rainforest*.

He wrote and directed the Indian short film *Dusk*, and has also worked on Malaysian television episodes and stage plays.

He holds an MA in Film Direction from Bournemouth University, UK.

Ram has spent the past decade writing extensively about Malaysian affairs in various local and regional publications. He currently writes for *The Straits Times*.

He lives in Kuala Lumpur, having conceded that he would never resolve his identity crisis as a third-generation Malaysian Telugu, and because there's no substitute for Malaysian food.

T0124653

ORCHIDS OF
THE RAINFOREST

A Novel

RAM ANAND

PENGUIN BOOKS

An imprint of Penguin Random House

PENGUIN BOOKS

USA | Canada | UK | Ireland | Australia
New Zealand | India | South Africa | China | Southeast Asia

Penguin Books is part of the Penguin Random House group of companies
whose addresses can be found at global.penguinrandomhouse.com

Published by Penguin Random House SEA Pte Ltd
9, Changi South Street 3, Level 08-01,
Singapore 486361

First published in Penguin Books by Penguin Random House SEA 2021

ISBN 9789814914031

Typeset in Adobe Garamond Pro by Manipal Technologies Limited, Manipal

www.penguin.sg

For my Mom, Dad and cousins,

I hope you don't notice the resemblances.
If you do, please don't disown me.

For Rathi and Loshana,

Thank you for validating me as an author.
Here's your payment, but I'll always be in debt.

CONTENTS

1. Schadenfreude   1
2. Karthiga A/P   9
3. Kunyit   27
4. Sungai Keling   43
5. Catharsis   56
6. The Fifteen Minutes   67
7. Red   81
8. Samarahan   84
9. City of Clouds   91
10. Wallflower and the Easy One   116
11. Intan   136
12. Entropy   143
13. Dramaturgy   164
14. Love Is a Dream   185
15. Equality & Chivalry   192
16. Day of the Universe   220
17. Heterodoxy   238
18. Home   253
19. Muhibah   267
20. Mangalyam   280

Chapter One

SCHADENFREUDE

June 2018.

Malaysia does not have an official summer per se, but every year, the sun shows its might; the water reserves shrink in fear, and its citizens ramp up their electricity bills and air-conditioning units in order to avoid breaking into sweat in their own homes—even those who can barely afford to do so.

No one quite knows how long this particular season tends to last every year—its timing is a little erratic, much like the blanket of haze that pays a recurring annual visit—but its duration has gradually prolonged. It had gone on long enough this time that the government had bought out television advertisements and larger-than-necessary highway billboard spaces to remind people that the country does not have an infinite supply of water.

There are people who are truly oblivious to these facts and there are those who choose not to see it or acknowledge it, especially when it means drastically changing the way they live. Geetha Rao belongs to the latter category. As she opened the sliding door to the balcony of her unit at Tropicana Heights, she noticed that copious amount of rainfall had happened while she had been soundly asleep at night. The trees on the golf course were still dripping wet; the pavements and her balcony floor were wet and slippery. Her house maid was quickly aware of the situation; she brought out the in-house slippers before Geetha took a second step into the balcony.

'It's slippery,' Maria said in her Filipino accent. Geetha—decked in her loose t-shirt and shorts—put on the slippers, and collected her cup of morning coffee from Maria's hands, before turning her attention to the view from her balcony. Maria scuttled inside and returned with a pack of cigarettes and a lighter, which she placed on a small tea table on the generous third-floor balcony. She smiled as she closed the sliding door, and Geetha turned around and nodded with an appreciative smile.

Geetha took her phone out of her shorts pocket, and placed it next to the cigarettes, glancing at the amount of WhatsApp messages that had come in this morning. She swiped through all the notifications without unlocking her home screen, and noticed a couple of messages from some middle-class folks pointing out that the night's rainfall should ease their water concerns. Geetha knew rainfall did not immediately mean treated water for consumption, but she normally did not engage in any discussions in these groups. In fact, she did not know why she even bothered to stay in these groups. Reading all the messages and unverified forwarded videos that her neighbors, colleagues, former classmates, extended family members, and her bridesmaid dabbled in on a daily basis made her feel like she was living a more purposeful life compared to most, if not all of them. It made her feel less miserable about the fact that the only time she felt true to herself during the day was in the silence and solitude of the balcony, or the fact that she didn't feel at home in this place. In fact, she had never felt at home anywhere in her life.

She placed her coffee on the small table, and picked out a cigarette from the box before lighting it up. She took an inordinately long puff, and exhaled out into the moist air.

The rain is a gift—a sign that water reserves might recover, and that the prolonged heatwave might be over, at least for this year—but it also almost always means a traffic nightmare. Geetha realized that the traffic situation might demand a prolonged commute to work, and gradually picked up her pace of smoking. Finishing the cigarette was rapidly turning from an empty-minded act to a chore she was powering through, so she abruptly dropped the half-finished butt on the balcony, darted back into the house, and reminded Maria to remove the butt before her husband got back home. Smoking a cigarette was the closest Geetha would ever come to infidelity. As she stepped into the shower, she realized she didn't know where he had been the whole night.

Prakash was a surgeon, but she always compared him to a biscuit when discussing her marriage with her friends. 'He's like those chocolate chips, Chipsmore,' she told her cousin once, albeit with a smile, like she had never cried about it, scrolling through an old crush's pictures. 'Sometimes, he's around too much. Sometimes, I don't see him at all.'

Yesterday and today were empty biscuit days. He had an extensive on-call at the hospital, slept in the doctors' rest room, and headed over for locum work. At the end of such an extensive work cycle, he gathered his team and headed over to Puchong to spend the night at one of its several dimly-lit pubs. Some days, he would head back home, but most days, he would crash at a friend's place. Today was one of the latter. Geetha had never met this friend. She had been married to him for five years.

She stepped out of the shower and headed for her room's oversized, overcompensated walk-in closet. She had spent 10,000 ringgit on the closet five years ago when they had moved into this condominium in an upmarket neighborhood.

She thought it would make her feel at home. It didn't. The only attire that excited her was her white shirt, dark blazer and dark skirt. It's what she had been wearing to work every day for the past decade. She had tried to be so many things before—but the best version of her had always been this—a lawyer. She walked to her shoebox and picked one out of many identical looking shoes as Maria prepared her lunch and office bag on the living room table. After two reruns that saw her forget her car keys and her charger, Geetha finally got into her car with everything that she would need for the day. She buckled up, turned on the ignition, and picked up her phone to finally disable the silent mode on it. Her day starts now. Before she could accelerate, her phone chimed incessantly. She noticed missed calls, messages and WhatsApp notifications. Before she had the time to check them, the phone rang again; a landline number, and she answered. As she listened to the voice on the other side of the line asking a series of ominous questions in Malay, she stared at the rain, and thought about how the rain felt like a gift this morning.

The rain was a gift for her, but it had not been very kind towards her husband, who had been driving through empty stretches of road at three in the morning. He had also been inebriated, so she couldn't blame everything on the rain. Her husband didn't survive to see the sunrise, or the blanket of haze. Biscuit has left the building. She froze, phone still in her hands, moved her hands ever so slowly to kill the engine, and stared blankly at the dashboard. Her mind was still functioning rationally. She typed in a name on her phone's address book, albeit with shivering hands, and made a call.

* * *

Anu's morning had not been going according to plan. She had gone to bed at 10 p.m. but had struggled to fall asleep. The end result wasn't very different from the countless times she had woken up with a hangover. She snoozed a little too generously before she realized that it had rained profusely the night before, which normally results in unspeakable acts of road congestion. As she left the corridors of her walk-up apartment towards her car, she noticed that the road adjacent to her house in Puchong—some thirty kilometers from Kuala Lumpur— was already having an early onset of vehicular paralysis. She shuddered at the thought of having to join the parade in full knowledge that she would be late for work. Luckily, she had a respite. She kept her car keys in her bag, hauled her things and walked to the metro station some 100 meters away. She settled in the train, which was more crowded than usual, after finding a seat facing two teenagers who sat on priority seats without a care in the world.

Her phone chimed. She knew it was her boyfriend with a routine good morning message. He called it 'checking in on you'. She found it repetitive, monotonous, and on some days, downright pointless. But this was not something worth complaining about. She couldn't pick a fight with him just because he cared a little too much. She decided not to reply to his message until she got to office. As the train hovered slowly on its elevated tracks above a suburban city that housed almost half a million people, she realized that the traffic paralysis was very bad, even by Puchong's already notorious reputation.

'Schadenfreude,' she whispered to herself. She had just learned the word very recently from one of her colleagues— which meant taking joy in someone else's misery. Anu wrote for the lifestyle section of a major newspaper, though she was always cautious in identifying herself as a writer. Her fellow commuters started to crane their necks to peer at the traffic and road below, and she realized they weren't seeing something that occurs regularly. She joined the crowd, and felt further vindicated for having used the train this morning. She saw a major crash on the expressway, blocking three lanes of traffic, with rescue workers still trying to sort out the wreckage. Her phone rang. She hoped it wasn't her boyfriend calling just because she had decided not to reply to a good morning message. It was not him. Instead, it was his sister.

'Geetha?' she answered the call, without as much as a hello. Their girls' night wasn't until the weekend, and they never called each other unless it was absolutely urgent. As she digested the news, she looked back at the scene of the crash, as the train slowed down for its next stop. She picked up her things, and rushed out of the train.

'Hang on, Geetha, I'll call you back,' she said. She rushed down the escalator, excusing herself past the few people who were stationary on both sides of the steps, and worse, those who stood dead in the centre. She started running clumsily—the floor of the oversized overground station seemed slippery under feet—before tapping out her commuter card and taking another escalator down from the station. The staff and other commuters in the station stared at her with bewilderment, but she was past the point of caring. She exited the station and evaluated her distance from the crash site. Panting, she continued walking speedily. She could make out that the mangled car a short distance away from her was a Mercedes, and a fairly new one at that. She picked up her pace and went back to running—by now, she was sweating through her dress. Traffic policemen managing the site prevented her from going any closer, but she didn't need to go any closer to realize that the mangled vehicle, which Geetha occasionally borrowed in order to fetch Anu during their dinner dates, belonged to Prakash.

'Fuck me,' she mumbled, hands on her head, and sat on the pavement by the side of the four-lane expressway. 'Is that your family?' an onlooker asked her. He had several people around him, equally curious to know more about the accident, and they all suddenly looked at her for some answers. She did not reply. The police officer asked her to leave the scene as she was attracting attention. Not wanting to waste a lengthy explanation, she produced her company name card and found out where the body had been sent for a post-mortem. Her phone rang again. This time, it was indeed her boyfriend. She looked at her screen for a good few seconds, and decided against answering. She allowed the phone to continue ringing, until it didn't anymore. She was in no state to speak. Instead, she texted him curtly:

'Your BIL Prakash had an accident. In Puchong. Didn't make it. Meet me at Serdang Hospital. Body is there. Don't call.'

Similarly, she pieced together a brief message for her boss as well. She walked back to the train station, and got into a train heading towards the direction of her home. None of the major hospitals in the entire Klang Valley, except one, had acceptable public transport connectivity. She had no choice but to drive. As the train hovered over the crash site, the markedly smaller crowd in the train craned their necks to see the wreck being towed away. The crowd of onlookers were huge. Some of them did nothing but stand on the sidelines and speculate about the possible causes of the crash, while powering through boxes of cigarettes that seemed to go around in circles. They were there before she had arrived at the scene, they stood there while she processed the news, and they were still there after she had left the place. She regretted not asking for a cigarette from them. She had quit smoking years ago, but to her, smoking seemed like it was invented for days like these.

'Schadenfreude,' she said, whispering a little loudly. A couple of people, who presumably understood the meaning of the word, stopped looking at the crash site.

Chapter Two

KARTHIGA A/P

August 2018.

Karthiga Krishnamurthy had gotten her new car over the weekend. It wasn't much, but it meant a great deal to her. She finally owned something purely out of her own hard work. She had the option of taking a loan against her now secure salary and getting a nice, pimped up, new ride, but instead she went for something that was preloved—something that didn't require her to take on a bank loan.

She rolled in her ten-year-old red Mitsubishi into the school gate and could immediately sense the curiosity of the guard. She rolled down the passenger's window, and Ismail, who was missing his front teeth, peered in. He didn't quite recognize her, and she allowed him to take his time, staring at him with a broad smile.

'Eh,' he said, laughing, snorting, and raising a salute. 'I couldn't even recognize you, teacher,' he added, 'you looked like a completely different person last Friday.'

She maintained her smile, and raised her half-full cup of Starbucks coffee. 'Do you want coffee?' she asked. Ismail brought a flask from his small, non-existent station, and handed it over to her. She gave him a generous portion of her latte.

'What happened over the weekend?' he asked.

'The new car arrived. And then I decided I wanted everything to look new,' she beamed back. 'You do,' he said warmly. 'Thank you,' he waved his flask, and Karthiga rolled up her windows as the heat was beginning to get to her. She drove to the teachers' parking lot, before proceeding to sit in her new car's old air conditioning system for a further five minutes.

Karthiga had had an existentially transformative weekend, but it was by no means as abrupt as it would have appeared for Ismail. When she got the car, she whipped the one dress she always wished she would wear to her school when she was truly happy, a bright red colored saree with golden borders, given as gift to her three years ago. She spent the weekend fitting her new car as well as fitting her blouse to go with the saree. But she wasn't entirely satisfied with her endeavors towards transformation, so she walked into one of the few salons open in the town of Rawang on a Sunday and got herself a haircut, before adding a dash of blonde and red coloring to it. She looked every bit like an oxymoron—a gas-guzzling Lancer, her glowing saree, and her short blonde-red hair that seemed to thematically match the saree. Individually, all three elements demanded attention, and mixed together, Karthiga's very presence in the school was louder than her voice could ever be.

The moment she got down from her car, she became the centre of attention. Half the people did not recognize her and clearly mistook her for a newcomer. Another half did, but a million questions popped in their head. Starved of the time required to ask all these questions, they expressed their surprise and went on to tend after their usual business. The lunchtime teachers' gathering was going to be a cauldron of curiosity.

Karthiga, who wore Karthi on her name tag, put down her things on her desk and was preparing for her first class of the day when one of the teachers, who had been giving her an uncomfortable look which she had put down to her strikingly bold appearance for the day, told her that she was needed in the principal's office.

Armed with just her phone, she showed up at the principal's office, where she expected to engage in a short yet meaningful conversation. She knew her expectation was misplaced when the principal, a stout man named Edward, asked her to close the door behind her. Edward and Karthi never had much to say to each other; they were neither friends nor enemies. She helped herself to a seat after ten seconds of silence, as it dawned on her that Edward was not going to start conversing with her until she made herself comfortable in his office.

'Good morning,' she said, with a straight face.

'Good morning,' Edward said, and started rummaging the first drawer of his desk, looking for something. Both the air-conditioning and the fan in the room were turned on, and it didn't take long for Karthi to feel cold, even under her thick saree cloth. Edward, despite his build and his age, which Karthi estimated would be in the late forties, had a very childlike look. He was always clean-shaved, and had a delightful smile about him. She couldn't remember anyone having a negative thing to say about him. He had been the principal in this school for the past four years, and this was the first time Karthi had been in his office longer than a minute. She looked at the clock ticking, the decorations in the room, and finally gave up on her feeble attempt at staying silent.

'I'm sorry. Am I being punished for looking awesome today?' she said, starting off her question with a little bit of irritation which then somehow morphed into a light-hearted joke. Edward found what he was looking for, looked back at her, and started paying attention to her appearance.

'I just noticed. You look really nice and bright. Like a shiny apple!' he said, giggling childishly to himself. For a moment, she considered if she should laugh at the joke.

'At least now I have company, since I look like a potato,' he laughed further with his low, endearing tone. The innocence of his joke made her giggle, but it soon subsided as Edward gently pushed across a letter.

Karthi reached out for the letter, pulled it close to her. 'Before you open that, I would like to explain something to you,' Edward said. She nodded, her palms on the letter, and her eyes fixed on him. She had never seen him so serious before.

'I'm not married, Karthi. And there's a good reason that never happened. Some people have speculated on the "why" for years, both at this school and the previous schools I have been in. I know why, and I think you do, too,' he said, and paused.

Karthi grabbed the letter and laid back on her seat, resting her chins on her fingers. She thought about what he had said for a little while, and then started to get his drift.

'This is not something I usually discuss with anyone, because I don't think it's anyone's business. But unfortunately, there's a certain reality of the country we live in, the society we live in, and the government that employs us,' he cleared his throat.

Karthi broke into a small acknowledging smile, and put the letter back on the table. She was beginning to understand what the content was about after all.

'They are transferring you,' he concluded.

'To where?' she asked.

'I don't know. You have to read it yourself. But I'd hazard a guess and say it's somewhere across the sea. But you are only going to start there in the next schooling year,' he said.

'In the meantime?' she asked.

'In the meantime, they have suspended you.'

She buried her face in her palms. She was exasperated, tired. She had overdone her weekend celebrations. She wanted to feel like a new person, like the person she had always felt like on the inside, but as long as she was part of a society, she did not get to make all the rules.

'Is there a particular someone who started this fire?' she asked, as she opened the letter and looked at the location of her next school—two and a half hours across the sea to Samarahan, located in the state of Sarawak, one of the two Malaysian states in the island of Borneo, which is also shared with Brunei and Indonesia.

'I'm just going to ask this—why did you post it so publicly?' Edward asked.

'Why shouldn't I?' she retorted.

'Because, like I said . . . realities,' he stammered. Edward seemed to realize the folly of his own argument the more he tried to explain it.

'I don't see what I did wrong, sir. You may have resolved to live your life a certain way without publicly acknowledging who you are, but you can't expect me to do the same. And that's surely not what I would tell the kids I am teaching,' she said.

'That's exactly what they fear—that you will influence the kids,' Edward said.

'Influence them to do what, to be themselves?'

Edward let out a big sigh and took off his glasses.

'I'm not them. I'm not defending them. Your fight is not with me,' he said, taking a handkerchief to wipe off the sweat dripping from his face. Despite how air conditioned his room was, the temperature within the room seemed ramped up. Karthi, too, felt she was sweating just as badly as she did during her walk from the carpark to her desk.

He offered her a box of tissues. She gave him the daggers.

'But you are not defending me either,' she said, took the letter and walked out of the room. She grabbed her car keys and her bag from her desk, the opened letter still within her grasp, and walked out of the school compound as gracefully she had entered less than an hour before. She got into her shiny new car, ramped up the air-conditioning, took off her shiny new saree which was beginning to weigh on her, and drove back home wearing just her blouse and petticoat. It wasn't until fifteen minutes later that she stopped at a traffic light halfway towards her house, and a bike rider waiting idly beside her car looked in and spotted her half-dressed, turned around, and couldn't resist the temptation to look again.

She flashed him the middle finger as he shot one last look towards her when the light turned green. She heard him shout, but she had enough anger in her to sprint away from him and give him a run around if he ever thought she was worth chasing all over town. Banking on her adrenaline, she drove towards her home with an abandon, hoping that the man on the motorbike, or worse, some police officer, wasn't following her. She drove into her housing estate—a row of terrace houses—half of them on the brink of falling apart, and drove into the barely-adequate porch of her house. She parked as close as possible to her front door, and sat quietly in the car, looking at the rearview mirror and making sure no one had followed her. Five minutes later, she decided that the coast was clear. As she stepped out of the car, she was grateful she did not live in an apartment, which would have meant walking past security guards and sharing lifts with strangers who would have seen her walking without a saree on. She opened the door, and made sure that her two housemates were not in the house. She closed the door behind her, and then screamed at the top of her lungs, but quickly changed her mind after realizing that her neighbors would easily interpret her screams as a sign of an ongoing robbery, given the reputation of this neighborhood. Instead, she sat down on her living room sofa, grabbed one of the sofa pillows, drew a deep breath, and buried her head in the pillow. And she screamed as hard as she could, in a way that only she could hear.

Over the weekend, Karthi had committed to doing the three things that she had always wanted to do as part of her self-expression since she was fifteen years old. She cut and colored her hair, she decided to finally wear a saree of her own volition, and not-so-subtly declared her sexuality on her social media account. The first two did her no harm, but her last action did not only ruffle feathers—it clearly shook someone's belief systems so much that the Education Department became aware of it and swiftly hatched a plan to send her packing to the other part of Malaysia.

They knew Karthi was unlikely to use family as an excuse— she was raised in an orphanage and had no immediate blood relations. She opened the letter again and read the subject, before looking at her name, Karthiga A/P Krishnamurthy, with Krishnamurthy denoting her father's name. She never knew who Krishnamurthy was. Or if he even existed.

* * *

Karthi's first memory came much later compared to a lot of other children—she could only recall her first memory from the age of four, and one of her earliest memories was that of her standing beside a woman that she couldn't remember, as the latter filled out her name in a series of registration documents, while she sat on a cranky chair that remained even, thanks to a folded paper plane placed below one of its edges.

The column denoting her father's name was left blank until the very end, before the woman started an animated discussion with another man as to what name should go into the blank space. The man made a couple of phone calls outside of the house they were in, as several other kids made plenty of noise with their incessant running around in circles. He came back, crouched over the woman, and whispered something to her.

The woman nodded, and turned her attention to Karthi. She stared at Karthi's eyes, smiled, and gently tugged Karthi's chin.

'Krishnamurthy it is then,' she said.

Maybe if she was older, she would have had the freedom to choose any name she wanted for her father. After all, how many people in life would have that privilege, naming their father?

Karthi never knew if she was named by her biological parents or people in the orphanage, or by some visitor. The person that took her to the orphanage never visited her as she got older, and she never had the opportunity to ask these burning questions. Like many of her peers, she yearned to run away from the home shortly after attaining puberty, but while some girls had a starting point—a name, an address, a landmark—she had none. She didn't know where to start. The woman at the orphanage later told her that her name represented the month of Karthigai, an auspicious month that is celebrated as a festival of lights in the Hindu calendar.

As her body formed, boys started whistling at her in school; some tried to touch her without her permission, and some sat next to her on school buses and tried to inch their fingers closer to hers to hold her hands. She gave them the daggers but hardly reacted to these approaches. It's as though she wasn't feeling what the other teenage girls around her were feeling; they all were like goddesses who were amassing a small legion of devotees, and the girls basked in that attention. They picked the clumsiest boy in that group of devotees and had trysts.

Karthi had no interest in such things, but she also did not belong to the other group—girls who were so intent on their studies that they refused to even look at boys no matter how much their hormones raged. There was this chasm among the girls she grew up with. All of them wanted to get out of the house and find their own rightful place in the world; half of them believed a boy would help them find their place, while another half saw academic excellence as their only way out. Karthi belonged to neither. She wanted to get out as well, but unlike the others, she didn't see education or men as her lifeboats.

It wasn't until she was seventeen that Karthi understood how she was different from the others. During a school trip, a group of girls were comfortable enough to sit on each other during the hour-long bus journey and then slept next to each other harmlessly while discussing their acts of sexual rebellion. But Karthi didn't feel comfortable when Thurga partially sat on her lap on the bus, or when she held her hands as the girls giggled while telling mindless stories to each other before sleeping. Karthi wasn't comfortable, but at the same time, she didn't want Thurga to stop touching her. The problem was, she wanted more. She saw the way Thurga looked at guys. And she looked at Thurga.

After the trip, Thurga was all Karthi could look at and think about. Thurga had a family, and came from a comfortable upper-middle-class background. She was an above-average student who buried herself in books when it came to examinations. She had a boyfriend and didn't hesitate stealing some school time to spend time with him. She rebuked attention from all other guys; she had no interest in taking in more attention than necessary. For a seventeen-year-old girl, Thurga seemed calm, mature, and very centered, something that Karthi had only ever seen in adults.

Karthi tried getting inducted into Thurga's social groups so that she could spend more time with her. She eventually became Thurga's study partner as they prepared for the crucial high-school leaving examination, SPM, and spent an increasing amount of time together at Thurga's house revising for the exams.

Thurga had had a lot of adolescent sexual curiosities, and discussed watching lesbian pornography with Karthi. Karthi listened, pretending to be straight, pretending as if lesbians are people she didn't understand. She listened as Thurga threw around theories about "curing" non-heterosexual people. For a while, Karthi considered herself problematic—that she needed to be cured.

After writing her SPM papers, she spent the excruciating months of emptiness that ensued waiting for her results by going out with one of Thurga's male friends who had been trying desperately to hit on her. He was a sweet, good-looking boy, raging with desire, but always being gradual in his attempts to establish physical contact. He started by holding her hands in the cinema, and then waited for weeks before he picked her up one night in his mother's car to make a move on her. Karthi accepted his overtures. This was going to cure her. She let him kiss her, she let him fondle her, she allowed him to take a peek. It was the first time she had made out with anyone in her life, yet she came back home feeling empty, indifferent. She had broken curfew and the caretaker, already having opened his occasional bottle of bootleg whiskey, had begun using his colorful vocabulary on her while threatening to report her behavior to the manager.

But none of that bothered Karthi. The next day, she hung out at Thurga's place. The two of them were alone in the room. She checked the time on her rundown Casio digital watch—8.55 p.m. She needed to go back to avoid another shelling by the caretaker, and to avoid being thrown on to the street. She looked at Thurga.

'Remember the videos you spoke about? Can we watch them? I'm curious,' she said. Thurga's jaws dropped, but soon she giggled. She opened an incognito window in her father's heavyset laptop and surfed to a porn site, and set it to mute.

'Does it look disgusting to you?' Karthi asked.

'No, it just makes me curious,' Thurga said, with a guilt-ridden smile on her face.

'Do you want to try it? Just the two of us?' she asked, and immediately regretted her decision. She had probably ended any friendship with Thurga there and then.

But Thurga's guilty-yet-curious look did not wane.

'Okay, but don't make a sound,' she said, as she touched Karthi's hands, with the video continuously playing in the background. This time, Karthi did not resist the urge to have more intimate physical contact. She leaned forward and kissed Thurga. Thurga seemed indifferent as Karthi planted her lips on hers. She remembered the way Arun had kissed her the night before. She teased her tongue a little, and went for a deep, passionate kiss. Fifteen minutes later, Karthi was on top of Thurga. Her hands were inside Thurga's shirt, and also her bra. Thurga paused the increasing intensity of their session, and looked Karthi dead in the eye.

'What is happening? This does not feel normal anymore,' she said. Karthi moved her hands away from Thurga's breasts.

'Sorry . . . I thought you liked it.'

'I do, but not the way you are liking this. Not the way you kissed me. You were better than him,' she said.

Karthi dropped her head, just beside Thurga's; her body still on top of hers, and her fingers gently going across the latter's knee.

'I've always liked you. This is who I am,' she said.

Thurga turned her face to her right.

'But this is not who I am. I was just curious . . .' she said, holding Karthi's hands, removing them from her knee.

'I'm sorry,' Karthi said.

'No, I'm sorry,' Thurga said, kissing her forehead. 'I should have never called it a disease.'

They resolved to stay friends despite what happened that night, but the awkwardness prevailed in the long run, and they didn't really keep in touch after they officially left school.

The SPM results came out a month after their tryst. Karthi didn't regret the amount of time she had spent with Thurga at the expense of other girls from her own home or other classmates who had wanted to hang out with her. As a result of their revision, Karthi surprisingly scored As in six of the ten subjects she had taken, even one more than Thurga.

Of the three girls from the home who sat for SPM that year, she was the moderate one—Christina, who was the caretaker and the manager's favourite, scored eight As, with those around her claiming she could have done even better were it not for biased marking systems. They never appealed. Lakshmi, who was eighteen years old at the time and had gone through a 'transition' class for one year between primary and secondary after failing her primary exit examinations, UPSR, had failed her SPM too. She had scored decent passing marks in most subjects, but failed Bahasa Malaysia, the Malay language paper. The advisors offered to let her re-sit SPM the following year, but saddled with guilt, she decided to quit schooling and opted to start working at the local McDonalds to somehow eke a career for herself.

Karthi received a placement at a state-owned teachers' training institute in the northern state of Kedah later that year, and duly took the offer. She received partial funding and a partial loan from the government, which she undertook to repay once she had started earning a salary.

Being in Kedah was a different universe for Karthi. She made new friends quickly, and took to the new environment like a fish to water. Her home managers and donors stopped following up on her progress after a year, in large part due to Karthi not participating in any conversations unless initiated by them. She knew Christina had received a placement to do her matriculation, but soon she no longer cared how the latter was faring in life. Karthi felt like she belonged to this place, more than she had ever felt at the home or her old school for years. She was surprised at how much she felt at home while being surrounded by people of different faiths; there were very few Indians in this part of the country.

Karthi stayed in an all-women's dorm and soon discovered that she wasn't entirely alone; there were others who shared her sexual orientation. Being one of the few Indians in the college, she received plenty of attention and interest from other non-heterosexual women in the hostel. She received so much attention that when Karthi came across the word 'promiscuous' while reading a novel three years later, she felt it best described her own self.

However, the good days did not last very long. Her lovers lived in their own closets. Most of them had boyfriends; some were ready to be married to men, while those who were single did not dare proclaim their sexual identity, fearing backlash from the local community, the conservative lecturers, and also the local religious departments who had enforcement powers. She didn't understand how they could pretend being someone they were not.

'Because,' said Zarina, a Pakistani-Malaysian whom Karthi regarded as the most beautiful woman she had ever seen, 'we are used to suppressing our wants so that our basic needs are provided for by society. It's easier to suppress your wants when you have been told since your childhood that a woman's wants are always a bad thing.'

Zarina did not succeed in suppressing herself for very long. She quit the institute without completing her course, and instead went to a private university and did finance. She ended up working for an investment bank in Kuala Lumpur, and gradually changed her look. She wore shirts on most days and rocked a pair of trainers. She had streaks of auburn on her shoulder length hair. She still remained the prettiest woman Karthi had ever known. They hadn't communicated much over the years but Karthi didn't need validation to know what Zarina was feeling—liberation. The freedom of being herself.

* * *

Her rusty house grill creaked at half past five, indicating her housemate had returned from work, as Karthi created a Jobstreet profile to look for opportunities in the private sector. The letter was still open, laid out beside her laptop on their plastic dining table near the makeshift kitchen. Laskhmi dropped her keys in the key bowl and showed up with several plastic bags of banana fritters. She placed them on the table, grabbed a plate, served almost half of it and handed it to Karthi.

'This is too much,' she said.

'It's okay. Eat, eat until you figure out what to do next,' Lakshmi said, before crouching over Karthi and hugging her by the shoulders.

Unlike others from her home, Lakshmi had never given up on being in touch with Karthi. Karthi had never thought much of Lakshmi as a friend, but when the adrenaline and the vigour of youth cleared a path to level-headedness, she realized Lakshmi was probably the most consistent person in her life. She had been consistent in keeping in touch throughout the years, and immediately opened up her rented home to Karthi once she was posted back to Rawang for her first teaching gig.

Laskhmi lived with her younger sister in a relatively poor neighbourhood, occupied mostly by blue-collar factory workers. The house rent was cheap because it was falling apart at its seams, but Lakshmi always maintained a respectable appearance about the place. She earned half of what Karthi earned, yet she never hesitated in buying food for all three of them. The fritters were not an exception; they were the norm. This was in large part due to Lakshmi acting both as an elder sister and a mother to Kasturi, who was five years younger than her. Kasturi lived in the same home as Karthi and Lakshmi, and it was not until years later that Karthi realized that Lakshmi could not handle protecting her younger sister and dealing with her own education and adolescence at the same time. She was strong for her sister, but fell apart in finding an escape route for herself. Lakshmi had long accepted, despite being only twenty-six years old, that she would be a blue-collar worker for the rest of her life. But she never doubted her ability to provide for the people who depended on her, and somehow, she saw Karthi as someone who needed protecting when the latter returned to Rawang.

'I'm going to make us some dinner,' Lakshmi said as she headed to the kitchen and started rummaging the fridge for vegetables and took stock of cooking items that were available. Lakshmi was visibly exhausted from work, but Karthi knew nothing she said would have stopped the former from cooking dinner for Karthi tonight.

Being in Kedah over the years, Karthi thought she didn't need any more friends and was now capable of making friends at will, but several months after living with Lakshmi, she finally understood what she had missed out in her life—family. Lakshmi took care of Kasturi and Karthi so much that Karthi feared Lakshmi would never try and find a partner for herself or have her own little family.

Lakshmi disappeared for a short while to change into a more comfortable pair of home clothes, and when she returned to the kitchen area, Karthi looked at the visible scars on Lakshmi's knees, something that they had never spoken about. Laskhmi collected a tray of vegetables from the fridge, along with a knife, and joined Karthi at the dining table.

Lakshmi had had her share of boyfriends over time. She dropped out of school with no prospects and was surrounded by men who seemed to be enjoying very simple lives, but often gravitated on the precipice of alcohol and drug addiction. Aside from her knees, there were also marks on her back and arms that indicated some form of abuse, but Karthi could never bring herself to ask questions about them in fear of evoking an unwanted memory. She never saw Lakshmi being vulnerable in her whole life, and she feared she wouldn't know what to do or how to react if Lakshmi broke down in front of her.

Karthi gobbled down the banana fritters while trying to contain her own anxiety.

'I don't want to go to Sarawak, but I'm not sure if I have a choice,' she said.

'Can they just do that to you?' Lakshmi asked.

'They are the government. They can do anything they want,' she replied.

Lakshmi, who had started dicing the vegetables for their collective dinner, chuckled.

'Karthi, people can say anything they want. They said you must like a boy; you must be with a boy. Did you listen to them just because they said so?' she asked. Karthi allowed a small smile to escape from her lips.

'Try and find out at least, if they can do that to you.'

'How?'

'Lawyer,' a loud voice travelled from across from the house hall, taking them by surprise. Karthi's other housemate, Kasturi, had just returned from her gig as a clinic's receptionist for a slightly perverted, aging doctor who spent more time napping in his office rather than treating patients. Kasturi managed to pass SPM, and subsequently obtained a diploma in nursing. She was only twenty-one, but she was the firecracker of the house. She had a very colorful Tamil vocabulary, the kind that scared away even the most self-appraising rowdy in town. If they took digs at her or her sister or the fact that they had no parents, she had the ability to name, shame and smear three generations of their family within three lines. The motorbike gangs that used to hover around the house to catch a glimpse of Karthi would drive off if Kasturi was spotted at the house. Once, when two guys attempted to brave through her barrage of insults and try to speak to Karthi anyway, Kasturi raised enough noise that even the most uncaring of neighbours had no choice but to make sure that the house with the three single girls was not disturbed by jobless, love-struck young men.

Kasturi wore ankle bracelets at all times, and there was always a sound in the house no matter where she went. She walked briskly into the kitchen.

'You are the most educated one among the three us, Ka. Do I have to teach you all this?' she snarked and went off to change her clothes in her room.

'I rely on you to protect me from guys, so of course, you have to teach me,' Karthi said. She stood up, walked towards Kasturi's room, and stood outside the creaking brown door. Kasturi pulled open the door with an inordinate amount of force and Karthi stood in her way, arms crossed.

'But I have to teach you how to keep your room tidy,' she said. Kasturi smiled and hugged Karthi. For a while, everything seemed alright. Karthi had always wished she would get out of this former tin-mining town that had come to encompass both the old and the new Malaysia. Bespoke villas and suites built around the Templer Park forest reserve sold for millions, while the displaced former estate workers from the fringes around Rawang ended up in poorly maintained, largely unguarded housing areas. This urban poor was finding it difficult to figure out its place in a town that was becoming an extension of the capital while trying to retain its own innocence and adolescent flaws. But with the transfer order, she was going to fight to stay in Rawang, to be able to come back home to these two women, because family is where home is.

Chapter Three

KUNYIT

July 2018.

Sabitha rummaged through her handbag, attempting to find a single one ringgit note in it, without much success. She was exasperated enough that she took two steps back and sat down in the seemingly endless row of blue chairs in the dimly-lit hospital hallway. She stared at the vending machine with contempt and resignation. She had too much money on her for a simple drink. She decided she was not going to give up. She took her coat and placed it on the chair next to her, and took out her phone from her bag. She was going to message the only person who could rescue her from her current predicament.

Anand appeared at the corridor a few minutes later, rushing through as though he was tending to something urgent. She looked at him with relief and extended her palms.

'Please tell me you have small change?' she asked.

Anand, who was already short of breath, having jogged through the corridor, looked at the vending machine and realized what Sabitha's emergency was. This time, he looked at her with contempt.

'You made me come all the way here for this?' he said, and handed her several small change notes and some coins, emptying out his right pocket.

'The cafe is two blocks away. I have no energy to walk that far,' she said. She stood up, adjusted her knee-length floral patterned yellow kurta, walked to the vending machine, and picked a blackcurrant juice box.

'Only kids would make a man rush through three blocks so they can get a Ribena,' he said. 'Now I need a drink as well. Get something else with all that balance money.'

'Where were you?' she asked, unpacking her juice box while slotting coins at a leisurely pace into the vending machine in order to get Anand a Coca-Cola.

'Pediatrics,' he said, still panting. She handed him the can, but did not let go.

'Do you want to have lunch together?' she asked.

'It's 3 p.m.,' he looked at the screen of his phone.

'So, are you telling me you had lunch without me?' she asked.

'No. I mean we are way past lunchtime . . .'

'Okay, do you want to have food together once we finish?'

'Yes. Where?' he asked.

'My cousin is coming to pick me up later. Join us for the meal, and then he will bring me to the condo so I can get my luggage. So, you get a free ride today,' she smiled.

Anand and Sabhita intern at Kuala Lumpur's busiest public hospital. Although it is one of the few public hospitals that has relatively better public transport connectivity, they both have to walk for twenty minutes before and after work to and from the nearest Light Rail Transit (LRT) station.

They were both in their penultimate year of a medicine degree at one of the many universities that offered medical courses in the country, mainly focusing on Indian students whose parents were obsessed with the idea of making their children doctors.

Anand hated being a part of any norm or stereotype, and similarly had come to hate the fact that he was brown and was going to become a doctor saddled with six-figure loans that would take years to pay off.

However, having taken such a huge financial commitment along with his family, he begrudgingly decided not to drop out of the path he had inadvertently agreed to go on. One more year, and Anand would be out with a medicine degree and the approved right to have everyone else address him as 'doctor'. That seemed to be the highlight of the seven years he would have spent studying medicine, in the eyes of his parents.

'Everyone will call you a doctor, there will be a certain respect,' his father said every time he asked why it was so important to him that his son become a doctor. Forget saving lives or job stability, the prefix was worth its weight in gold. Anand scoffed at the idea of respect. Hardly anyone acknowledged the amount of respect doctors like him get from their seniors, medical officers, surgeons, or patients who thought the hours spent reading Wikipedia entries made them more qualified than him, and patients who simply refused their suggestions based on their seniority.

He might endure another two years of this under the name of housemanship, but he had long decided he was not going to practise as a doctor in the long run; the remaining length dependent upon how his entrepreneurship venture pans out in the next year or two.

Sabitha was not like Anand. She enjoyed problem-solving; she basked in the stress, and was truly confident that she was going to make some lives better with her skills. She skipped meals, practised a ridiculously unhealthy diet for a doctor, constantly had eye bags due to inadequate sleep, yet remained pint-sized. She was on the course to perfection, her parents loved what she had chosen to do, she loved what she had chosen to do, and she could do no wrong in the eyes of her family—except for the secret that she had been harbouring.

* * *

Sabitha and Anand waited at the hospital lobby adjacent to the emergency drive-in lane, as accident victims with horrific lacerations and profuse bleeding were wheeled in on several stretchers. Once the ambulance driver finished helping the nurses and doctors bring the patients into the emergency room, he stepped out with a white washcloth, trying to get the blood stains off his hands. He reached for his left chest pocket and took out a box of cheap cigarettes, before feeling up his trouser pockets. Looking at Sabitha and Anand holding on to their white coats, he approached them.

'Do you have a lighter?' he asked Anand, after almost absent-mindedly asking Sabitha before deciding against it. Anand merely shook his head. He was not a smoker, but he almost understood, and shared, why that man would need a cigarette at the time. The driver continued to ask other strangers before he finally received a lighter. Having lit up his fix of nicotine, he needed someone to talk to, and he came back around to stand beside Anand and Sabitha.

'It's bad. A four-car pileup on the highway. It's been raining incessantly and the roads are so bad, yet some people insist on driving as though their fathers owned the entire stretch,' he said, taking deep puffs.

Anand nodded as the man recounted the horrifying accident scene that he had just attended to. Malaysians loved baulking at the driving systems in many neighbouring Asian countries, as a large part of the country is connected by a four-lane expressway, yet it has one of the worst road fatality rates in the world. Anand had long concluded that Malaysians were just bad drivers. Maybe they would drive better if they didn't have four-lane expressways to casually weave in and out of to jump ahead of traffic, as though some eagle-eyed person was watching their skillful manoeuvres through barely-functioning highway cameras, waiting to give them individual awards later on.

Having ranted about broken bones, severed limbs, and wailing relatives, the man finished his long drag of nicotine and excused himself to perform his Asr prayers, the third of five Islamic prayers in a day. As his eyes trailed on the driver disappearing past the corridor, Anand missed the fact that Yuvaraj, Sabitha's cousin, had already arrived, and that she was calling out his name. Anand headed for the back seat of the brand-new Honda Civic, but Sabitha nudged him to sit in the front. Anand obeyed, took the seat, and introduced himself to Yuvaraj, before Sabitha went on to give a lengthy justification as to why she was dragging Anand along for lunch. He immediately knew that Sabitha was not completely comfortable with Yuvaraj, who introduced himself as Yuva.

The three of them didn't converse during their journey to the restaurant. Yuva drove to a busy Asian restaurant that had an extensive menu and average food, and when they found a table, Sabitha waited until both men were sitting opposite each other, before sitting beside Anand. Their orders didn't take long to arrive, but Sabitha and Yuva seemed intent on having a silent meal. A part of Anand wished he had had lunch on his own, ideally sitting in front of the television in his home, watching one of his favourite shows. Anand had ordered a lamb chop, and was struggling to cut through the stubborn meat. Yuva, who ordered simple fried rice, finished his meal almost as soon as he started it. Sabitha was pacing herself with her noodles, but was constantly checking her phone in between eating. Yuva knew she wasn't normally this distracted at a dining table.

Anand decided it was now up to him to break the tension at the table, so he could eat in relative peace. 'Do you guys generally not talk to each other or is it because I am here?' he had to ask.

Both Yuva and Sabitha chuckled at the question.

'Don't worry, it's not you,' Yuva said immediately. He was an exceptionally good-looking young man—everything from his polo t-shirt to his shades to his car screamed upper middle-class comfort. Sabitha looked up with a smile, but it became clear she was not going to tell the reason behind their awkwardness.

'We have not spoken to each other for several years. Maybe five, six,' Yuva said, after much hesitation and loud whispering if he should discuss the matter.

Anand had to take long pauses before asking questions, because he was still trying to finish the meat. 'Problem? You don't see each other at family functions?'

'We see each other, but we don't talk. I know what she's up to, and she knows what I am up to. We are . . . updated about each other,' he said. 'Don't know if she's going to continue being that quiet for the three-hour drive we have after this, though,' he added, not-so-subtly, probably hoping for a response from Sabitha. She let out an awkward smile, and once again feigned getting a message on her phone after taking a mouthful of noodles. Anand could see from the corner of his eye that she was only checking her Facebook.

The awkward evening continued on for a while, before Sabitha and Yuva dropped Anand off at his apartment and headed off to Ipoh, Perak together.

Later, in a series of messages to Anand, Sabitha explained the origins of the tension between her and her cousin.

Sabitha and Yuva were both second-generation born Malaysian Telugus. Their current lifestyle and urban dwelling was a stark contrast to how their grandparents had migrated to Malaysia from the eastern coast of India as labourers, barely sixty years ago. The cousins belonged to the first generation in their family to have attained higher education, and also the first generation to have completely migrated and live in urban landscapes. Their grandparents and their parents spent a substantial part of their lives living in self-contained communities in plantation estates managed by the British, in both colonial and post-colonial times. Up until their parents' generation, the idea of marriage among cousins—marrying the offspring of the opposite sex sibling of the father or mother was kosher—very much normalized.

Sabitha and Yuva were earmarked for each other by their parents, in all their half-seriousness, when both were in their early teens. What was supposed to be a harmless tease for Yuva, his other cousins, and his parents did not sit well for Sabitha, who had spent her teenage years feeling increasingly awkward around Yuva, his parents or her other cousins. Being repeatedly teased to marry her cousin, Sabitha revolted, refusing to be defined only as Yuva's marriageable cousin. As both of them turned into adults, the family made it clear that they did not have any intention to carry on the practice of marrying off children within the family—but the awkwardness between Yuva and Sabitha never really went away. By the time she was a young adult, Sabitha had stopped speaking to Yuva altogether. Yuva never asked why, but it was also apparent to her that he never really understood why the whole charade had annoyed the living daylights out of her. Today, due to a series of coincidences that could only be pinned down to universal conspiracy, they had to travel with only each other as company, for three hours.

Sabitha spent the first hour of the 300-kilometer journey serializing the history of her tension with Yuva over text messages with Anand. Yuva tried to drown in his decidedly questionable taste of music, but could no longer maintain the curtain after an hour, as they entered the national expressway that stretches for hundreds of kilometers with an almost identical view from both the windows.

'Did you just introduce me to your boyfriend?' Yuva asked. Sabitha paused texting Anand.

'Erm, no. He's a very close friend. We study together. We work together. We live in the same building,' she said.

'Sounds like all the ideal conditions for him to be your boyfriend. Why not, then?' he asked, with a chuckle that Sabitha was not fully comfortable with. It reminded her of the years when he egged on cousins who used to tease them as being a couple with little or no regards to her feelings.

'I really don't know how to answer that question. Love doesn't work that logically, I think,' she said.

'I think there's a certain logic to it. I think there's an element of logic as to why me and my girlfriend are together. I mean, it's not all superficial. I made some logical arguments, and asked why not, and guess what, she ended up saying yes . . . It's not like you expect love to be like in the movies we watch, don't you? I know you are only twenty-three, but I can burst the bubble for you and tell you it doesn't work that way,' he said, almost with a smug and self-proclaimed wisdom.

Sabitha retreated into her phone, as Anand responded to her series of whiny messages.

'Throw him off. Tell him about you,' Anand told her, with a mischievous emoticon. She looked at the time, and realized they had not even covered half of the journey.

'I don't expect it to be like in the movies, because I don't think my kind of love stories happens in the Indian films we watch,' she responded to Yuva after a prolonged silence between them.

Yuva thought Sabitha's earlier non-response was an indication that the conversation topic was over. He did not expect her to think and come up with a response. She was no longer reacting to his prodding, she was responding to them. He looked at her inquiringly, but she did not offer further explanation.

'So you do have someone?' he asked.

'No, I don't.'

'So how are you sure that yours will be different?'

'Have you seen *Brokeback Mountain*?' she said as she placed her phone inside the compartment between her and Yuva. She was now fully involved in the conversation.

'No, but I've heard about it. Why are we talking about it all of a sudden?'

'What is the movie about, do you know?' she asked.

'It's about two gay guys or something like that, right?,' he said.

'Yes, you are right. That's my kind of love story.'

She folded her arms, and smiled at him, as he looked confused, trying to keep his concentration on the road.

'Oh,' he said, and looked at her. '*Oh*,' he became louder. This time, she chuckled and smiled. She enjoyed his apparent discomfort. The car drifted to the left, to the slow lane, and the speed dropped.

'You should keep your eyes on the road,' she said. Yuva had plenty of questions that he was dying to ask, and it showed on his face. He stayed silent for the next thirty minutes, until they reached a rest area by the expressway.

'When did you know? Are you sure?' Yuva asked suddenly, while drinking coffee, and rubbing his eyes.

'I think in some way, I have always known. Probably started being honest with myself at sixteen. I'm just going to ignore the fact that you asked if I'm sure about my own sexuality,' she said, sipping her black tea. Yuva tried to retort but decided against it. The silence on their table, in a food court brimming with humans and rows of hawkers and traders catering to hundreds of travellers at any given time, was noticeable.

By the end of their three-hour journey, Yuva was attempting to maintain the silence between them. He no longer wanted the walls between them to be brought down. Sabitha enjoyed how uncomfortable she was making him. Yuva got easily agitated with the evening traffic at Ipoh, the picturesque capital of the state of Perak, as the last rays of dark orange filled up the skies. Sabitha felt it was rude to end the journey on such a bitter note.

'Am I making you uncomfortable with all this?' she asked.

He cleared his throat.

'No, it's not that . . . I just disagree. But we can agree to disagree on this,' he said.

Her jaw dropped. She was not tempted to respond to what he had just said. They parked at the corner of a quiet neighbourhood before walking five minutes to a spacious house with a tent out front, and rows of cars parked either side, cramping the road.

'Thanks for driving me, by the way,' Sabitha said, carrying her bag of clothes. Yuva gave a sombre smile as they neared the distinct sound of some women crying, some louder than the others. Yuva walked in and greeted the men at the porch while Sabitha froze at the entrance. Drowning the sound of the grieving women was that of a priest performing prayers. Yuva glanced back at her, and disappeared into the blanket of smoke emanating from inside of the semi-detached bungalow lot. Sabitha tiptoed her way past the watchful relatives, some that looked familiar and some who looked like complete strangers, looking for someone that would make her feel more comfortable. She realized she was in an alien environment— she had barely been to this house; she did not know most of the people who were in the house, and she showed up only for the sake of one person. She helped herself into the house and stopped on her tracks to acknowledge the priest's prayers, glanced at the laminated picture of the departed, and continued her way towards the kitchen. She saw the outline of a woman in a simple white top and black jeans, with a familiar voice, barking orders at Yuva, and relief washed over her face. She dropped her bag by the fancy built-in kitchen cabinet, and hugged the woman from behind.

'Hey!' Geetha exclaimed, as she turned around and kissed Sabitha on her forehead.

'I feel like a stranger here,' Sabitha smiled with a sense of guilt. She shouldn't be complaining in a funeral house, but she knew Geetha would understand.

'I feel like a stranger in my own in-laws' house, so trust me, I've got it worse. That's why I needed you.'

Geetha was wearing her specs, and her face was devoid of any spark or elegance. Sabitha was not used to seeing her favourite cousin being in such a state. She wasn't used to seeing her cousin reduced to kitchen work, or playing the role of a traditional wife. She found it ironic that Geetha was carrying out these duties after her husband had passed away.

Geetha grabbed Yuva by his shirt as he passed by both of them. 'Can you loiter around here and help with whatever that is needed?' she asked.

'Why, what are you going to do?' he asked.

She stared at him quietly, with a gradually increasing display of contempt.

'Yuva, my husband passed away, not yours. I need my space too. It is bad enough that everyone here thinks I answer to them. I don't need my own brother piling on,' she said, all the while trying to maintain her volume so that the other half-strangers walking in and out of the kitchen would not realize that she was low-key flipping out at her brother.

'Man, calm down, I was just asking,' he said. She let go of his shirt, grabbed Sabitha and walked to the exit gate of the house. As expected, around five people, including her mother and her father-in-law, all asked her where she was headed to. She walked as fast as she could, faking an emergency store-rush.

'I need to buy something, I'll be right back,' she said. She did not bother to offer more explanation, and did not give them enough time to ask another question. Sabitha followed her cousin's footsteps all the way until they both got in her car and drove her BMW to a nearby lake garden. Geetha parked illegally in a spot from where the water and the garden path were visible, but she was beyond caring for such details by now. She took in the fresh air, put on some melancholic music, and sat crouched on her driver's seat, hugging her knees. Sabitha was quiet, and she was sure that was the best thing she could have done for Geetha right then.

'It's only been sixteen days. They are already talking about properties, insurance money, all that shit,' Geetha said.

'Who's "they"?' Sabitha asked.

'It feels like everyone. Including my parents,' she said, paused, and wiped off tears that were starting to appear in her eyes.

'Do you miss him?' Sabitha asked.

'No one ever asks me that,' Geetha said, as she stopped fighting the tears. 'You know something Sabi, don't do what I did . . . Don't do this settle-down-bullshit for the sake of it. Even if it gets you a nice BMW,' Geetha said, with a small, almost rueful chuckle. She was now mindlessly looking at the receipts and monies near the armrest and the dashboard.

Sabitha looked at her cousin with despair. She recognized a woman hiding a pain that she could not quite express out loud. Geetha might be straight, but was also struggling in being honest with herself.

The sixteenth day prayers signified the end of the mourning period for the family of the departed, but Geetha had barely confronted her own emotions regarding the death of her husband of five years. She never knelt and wailed the way her mother-in-law or other women in the family did on the day of the funeral. Instead, she stood by his lifeless body, stoic, unmoved, almost confused.

Geetha Rao lived life in a straight line—she studied well, she went to do a course approved by her parents, dated a couple of Tamil men but never allowed the relationship to turn serious because she always knew she was not going to battle her parents when it came to choosing a life partner, and then allowed her parents to embark on their due process of finding her a partner once she was called to the bar. She came from a middle-class family, but was fair-skinned, well educated, and had had a job in a respectable law firm by then. This allowed her parents to pin her marriage prospects with her own upward mobility in terms of economic class. Prakash wasn't visually striking, but he was a financially comfortable man with some odd repetitive habits, nothing which were considered harmful. Geetha carved out the mobility she wanted, moving to an upscale neighbourhood, living near a golf course, opening up her own law firm. Prakash said he did not want kids too soon after marriage; they used protection at all times. When Geetha opened her own firm, she did not want pregnancy and motherhood to get in the way, so she told him she was not ready this time around. They continued using protection, but the frequency reduced. After their fourth anniversary, the conversation never happened. They gave contradicting answers during family visits that clearly showed they were no longer discussing if or when they would want to have children.

'I just followed on this path set before me, and now suddenly I don't even know what to do. I feel like nothing here is mine. Again, people are trying to make decisions for me and I'm just going to let them,' she said.

Sabitha held Geetha's hands, and calmed her down.

'You had a good five years with him,' she said. 'Let's think about that, maybe?' she added, feeling both wise and naive at the same time.

Geetha held Sabitha's chin and stared right into her eyes.

'So, no one has told you about the fact that he wasn't alone in the car? There was someone next to him. So, no, I don't think I ever had him,' she said.

Sabitha fell silent. Geetha alternated between sobbing and silent contemplation for the next hour, before they headed back home. Geetha sat quietly in the car for a few more minutes once she parked it several lots away from the house.

'You know, I always knew he had a secret, and somehow, my worst nightmare came true. I thought the secret would come out some day, but I was hoping it would not be about an affair,' she said.

'What did you want it to be?' Sabitha asked.

'Anything. Gambling addiction. Alcoholism. He could have been gay, even. That would have explained a lot, really. But just not another woman. Now I have so many questions and he's six feet under. She's dead as well, so I can't storm into her house either,' she said, half-smiling ironically.

Geetha's phone buzzed.

'We need more kunyit,' her mother's message read. Indian funeral rites almost always need an endless supply of turmeric. But the message's timing left Geetha laughing and snorting uncontrollably. Geetha's mother was unable to remember what turmeric was called as in English, hence reverted to its Malay description.

'Seriously, kunyit, at this moment?' Geetha exclaimed, as Sabitha struggled to get in on the joke that was leaving her cousin in splits.

Kunyit had another meaning in their schooling years— faggot. The irony of the timing of the message was not lost on her. Sabitha chuckled along mildly, and was tempted to come out to her cousin whom she had always looked to as an elder sister, but decided against making the moment about her.

'Oh man, I'm so tired after days of eating nothing but vegetables and no drinks,' Geetha said as she started the car again to make an actual store-run, referring to the sixteen-day family fast where the deceased's relatives who took part in the funeral process are barred from eating meat or consuming alcohol.

'Tomorrow, when this is over, I want to do something drastic,' she said.

'What would that be?' Sabitha asked.

'Eat beef,' Geetha said, with both mischief and clarity. Sabitha's jaw dropped for the second time in the day, and she cupped her mouth.

Now she knew she had found a moment to come out to her cousin. Geetha can rebel with her choice of meat, and Sabitha can rebel with her sexuality.

Chapter Four

SUNGAI KELING

September 2018.

Most Malaysian Telugus invariably tend to trace the roots of their heritage or that of their extended family to a village, nook, or cranny along the Perak River, which branches out of the western coast of Malaysia. This little cul-de-sac surrounded by water does not have much to offer to those seeking adventure, but it does offer one of the best sunsets at sea level across Malaysia. Following the 2004 Boxing Day tsunami, large boulders and rocks were neatly arranged on a stretch that lasted kilometres—as far as the eye could see. In the subsequent years, the boulders became makeshift viewing docks on a bay that overlooked the Straits of Malacca.

As Sabitha watched the sun begin to dip across the horizon in front her, she could not help but relate to her ancestors from several generations ago who were the first in her lineage to call this small potpourri of villages their home. They left behind families, parents, and in some cases, spouses and children in an attempt to seek a better life in what was then called Malaya. Some of them made the journey because they did not feel they had the liberty to say no to their colonial masters, who ruled both their place of origin and this strip of land some hundred years ago.

They got on boats at the eastern coast of India, from villages in and around the port town of Vishakhapatnam, and made their journey past the Bay of Bengal and the Andaman Sea before reaching Penang. Eventually, most of them found their way to this collection of estates and villages called Bagan Datoh.

But that was not what this town was known as prior to their arrival. In the late 1800s, probably owing to the number of economic migrants from Andhra Pradesh who had set up their homes and roots here, this little cul-de-sac had a very literal description of its populace—Sungai Keling. 'Keling' was a bygone term that was used to described the Indian diaspora in Malaysia, while 'sungai' simply meant river. Travelling on uncharted territory, these pioneer settlers made this town their home amidst the uncertainties and doubts that would have lingered at the back of their heads when they boarded the British vessels over several decades. Sabitha was about to enter uncharted territory, and it was important that she claim this place as her home, regardless of what happened next. She was going to be seen as an outsider or an oddity, at least for a fleeting moment, but she was not going to allow herself to feel like one.

Sabitha had long planned for this day, but the unexpected death of Geetha's husband meant that she decided to wait for three months before making this trip, as she wanted to make this as easy as she possibly could for her family.

That evening, Sabitha called her parents to the dinner table, haphazardly made a few idlis—Indian rice cakes—which she had just learned how to make several months ago, waited till they had finished their meal with minimal complaints, made a cup of tea for everyone, and joined them in the living room, sitting in front of the television as they watched one of the litany of badly-made Indian television shows, made available in their home via an illegally procured satellite dish from India. She had been delaying the inevitable, and she no longer had the courage to pretend like she had nothing pressing to say.

She grabbed the remote control in the living room table and muted the show. 'I have to tell you both something,' she said, her cup of tea in her right hand, one of her feet up the single seat sofa, and her phone tossed to a side. Her parents were already looking inquisitively at her for muting the old and small television set in their house. They merely nodded their heads at her, and she could distinctively hear the sound of the crickets chirping at night near the house, which was situated some 100 yards from the nearest neighbours, and barely had anyone passing through its narrow roads on any given day.

'Promise you won't react,' she said, but she knew as soon as she said it that they will never live up to that promise.

'Tell first,' her father shot her a look of disapproval; he was not going to promise a calm reaction without knowing the subject she was about to open. She continued being silent for a few seconds, stuttered and had several false starts, cleared her throat twice, put her tea aside, put her feet down, and leaned forward, her elbows on her knees. Her palms were trembling.

'I can't ever get married. I won't ever . . . get married' she said, her eyes fixated on the black and white, unevenly cut marble squares on the floor.

'Then what do you want to do?' her mother asked, exasperated. Her father looked a little relieved in contrast; he was probably expecting her to say that she had fallen in love with someone, and if that was the case, there were always going to be very long odds that she would fall in love with another Telugu man, given how small their population was in Malaysia.

But her parents had long held on to the ideal that the continuity of their heritage and identity depended on their children and nephews getting married to other Telugus. They were convinced, with various examples to be used as evidence, that any non-Telugu spouse or partner would not make an effort to ensure their language and culture is passed on to the next generation.

'You want to end up like this for the rest of your life?' her mother asked. Sabitha started seething within. Like most Indian parents, her parents could not help but to equate a productive life with marriage, kids, and being comfortable. They would spend thousands to educate their children so they can live comfortable lives—but they don't really consider their jobs done until their child is legally partnered off with someone, and is continuing the cycle of having kids.

'I am pretty sure I will be a doctor for the rest of my life. I'm sure that counts for something?' she said, looking directly at her mother and struggling to hide her anger, before calming herself down. She did not want to start the conversation with an argument before she had even come to the core subject of the discussion, and she realized a prolonged conversation would just create flashpoints that would expose the ideological chasm between her and her parents—the reason why they were capable of spending substantial amounts of time together without having a fluid conversation with each other.

'I do not like guys,' she said in a mellow tone, almost like a whisper. She was not looking at her parents, her head hung low, and for a moment, she felt like a child who had lost something valuable and was confessing her sins to her folks. But this wasn't a sin.

Both her parents looked at her, perplexed, having seemingly caught part of her confession. She straightened her body a little, and repeated herself with more conviction. 'I am not attracted to guys. I just . . . can't be with them. I have no interest,' she said.

She looked at her parents now, and calculated, with some curiosity, if they were sensing where she was headed with her confession.

'What is she trying to say?' her mother looked at her father instead. His eyes were initially fixed on Sabitha, but slowly turned away to stare blankly into the darkness outside their home. She sensed that he had some understanding of what she was trying to say, though that by no means meant a stamp of approval.

'So, you will not have kids or a family of your own?' her mother asked.

'No,' she said, looking at her dad, as he took off his spectacles and rubbed his forehead.

'I will have a family if I'm with someone I like,' she said to her mother.

'If you don't like guys and you don't want to get married, how will you have a family all of a sudden?' her mother asked.

Her father cleared his throat. 'So,' he mumbled, 'you are trying to say you are . . . gay . . . or lesbian?' he asked. He was still rubbing and holding his head, as if he was nursing a headache. It was difficult for her to get a read on his reactions. She's known this man all her life yet she could not anticipate how he was taking her coming out.

'Yes, both words can be used, but . . . yes.' There was pin-drop silence in the house, but Sabitha held her head high. A part of her wanted to hug them, or be hugged, but her feet were frozen. She was not going to move until she knew whether her parents could accept what she had just told them.

'So, we are supposed to just accept that our only daughter wants to be with women and does not want to get married or have kids? We won't be having any grandchildren? We spend everything we have on your education, and this is what you come back with—after watching all those English shows?' her mother, as expected, brought up her education.

'How is this my fault? I am telling you I don't feel like that for men. I wish I would; I wish I can make things easier for all of us, but I can't, because that's just not who I am,' Sabitha said, gradually raising her voice, but stopping short of being confrontational.

'I will do really well in my career. That is the direct reward you would get for educating me. And I will be there for us until the end. But I can't change my sexuality to please others or just to give you grandchildren,' she added.

'Oh my god, you need some prayers,' her mom stood up briskly from the creaky sofa she was sitting on, and walked as fast as Sabitha had ever seen her walk, and disappeared into the prayer room, and later into the kitchen. Her dad was still holding his head. His silence was unsettling Sabitha.

'This is all because of her shows,' her mom was still mumbling to herself, but she was loud enough for everyone to hear. If she had amped up the volume just a little more, Sabitha was sure her mother could drown out the peaceful chirping of crickets at their neighbours' and alert them to the travesty that was ongoing in her house as well. Sabitha had hundreds of things to say or even shout from the top of her lungs—for every little remark her mom was making about sexual minorities or personal liberties or her own gratefulness as a child. But when her thoughts collided furiously with each other, struggling to form a coherent, legible argument, she decided to stay silent and let her parents deal with her truth in their own ways. She was asking them to reconcile her sexuality with all the musings of culture and society that had been fed to them for over five decades. One night of ideological discourse, no matter how valid, was not going to change that.

Her father eventually stood up and disappeared into the kitchen as well. He looked disappointed, like someone had punched him in the guts. His muted reaction was stronger than her mother's incessant grumbling and moaning, which continued for some time further. She asked Sabitha more rhetorical questions, all of them voiced from the kitchen—what will they tell the relatives? What about the neighbours? Is she willing to become an outcast in the family? Is she willing to turn her parents into outcasts as well? Is this what she wanted to be remembered for? Why can't she overcome her desires and feelings and prioritize the family instead?

The silence of her husband and her daughter eventually exhausted Sabitha's mother, who went to sleep soon after without as much as a good night, something that had never happened in Sabitha's entire life. Her father reappeared a while later, after her mother had retired to bed. He locked the doors, without saying a word, prayed at the altar, and headed towards the stairs to go to his room.

'Will you turn off the rest of the lights?' he asked her, the first thing he had said to her since she came out. His tone was different, but he was trying to make things feel as normal as possible, at least for now.

'Yes, nana,' she said, feeling slightly relieved, having tracked his movements the entire time while expecting a word from him. 'Good night,' she said, while she had the chance. He did not reply. As he went up the stairs, she turned her attention to her phone, feeling both proud and lonely at the same time. Having fought it for hours, she allowed tears to roll down her cheeks, but resisted from sobbing. She knew she was not going to get any sleep that night.

* * *

After a sleepless night, Sabitha woke up groggy, put on one of the few salwar kameez that she had in her collection, and reluctantly followed her parents to the neighbourhood temple, which was also built primarily for the surrounding Telugu populace. As she walked into the vast fields and courtyard surrounding the temple, she feared her parents would make her come out to other community members, but her fears were misguided; they were earnest in seeking divine intervention on her behalf. She prayed mindlessly to please her parents, who oscillated between being confrontational towards her to treating like she was terminally ill and was in need of all the prayers in the world to stay alive.

'Do you feel any differently?' her mother asked, as she tidied the edges of the sacred ash on Sabitha's forehead while walking back to their house. With the mid-morning sun screaming onto her face, all Sabitha could do was yawn, which seemed to make a complete mockery of the seriousness with which her parents were treating the situation. She was dreaming of her bed back at her room in Kuala Lumpur.

Sabitha knew her parents were not going to stop at divine intervention alone, and thus was not surprised when she saw the outlines of several cars parked alongside the narrow street near her house as she headed back. There were people already waiting at the front porch, and these were not people she had wanted to see at this point in time. A couple of aunts and uncles greeted her, and were restless to start the inquisition before she could settle herself in the house. Sabitha didn't have time to get changed. Her mother implored her to sit down and entertain guests, and told her that she could change later.

'They've come all the way to see you,' her mother said when Sabitha tried to tell her mom that she was going to her room for a little while. Her mother probably knew that Sabitha was just going to buy time; if she went to her room, it was unlikely she would be back in the living room anytime soon. Sabitha told herself that the worst part was already over. She went to the living room and greeted her elder relatives, and found a quaint corner in the hall. She expected the questions and intervention to start soon. But she wanted to see if they were going to be subtle in broaching the topic.

They were not very subtle. They went straight to the point, but none of the questions seemed to be directed to her in particular—the elders discussed the situation as though they were oblivious to her presence in the house. She did not have the energy to ask to be heard and then to string together a cohesive argument for herself. She feigned interest and tried to stay awake as long as she could, until a BMW passed by the house, gingerly, looking distinctly out of place in these surroundings. The elders in the house watched on curiously, but Sabitha felt like she had just found a jolt of renewed energy. Minutes later, after finding a parking space wide enough for the car, Geetha walked into the house, smiling at a motley of family elders who greeted her with mumbles and silence. Sabitha, who happened to be sitting closest to the entrance of the house, stood up, and exchanged warm pleasantries with her cousin. The elders were still trying to make sense of her presence in the house.

Sabitha's mother greeted Geetha, offered to make her a cup of tea, and gestured Sabitha to follow her into the kitchen. The elders gingerly shuffled around to make space for Geetha at the sofa, and she ended up sitting next to her own mother.

'Did you call her here?' Sabitha's mother asked the moment they got into the kitchen.

'Yes, ma,' Sabitha experienced the relief of trodding on the cold cement floor on the kitchen.

'Why do you have to involve her in this? She is already in grieving, as it is. You could have told me,' her mother said, as she furiously whipped a hot cup of sugar-laden milk tea.

'If you could invite all those people over without asking me, putting me in the spot like that, I am sure I can invite someone who can see things from my side as well,' she said.

'So what, she's supporting all this now? Is that why you've become so brave?' her mother retorted.

Again, Sabitha stayed silent and refused to engage in a repartee.

'What are you doing here?' Geetha's mother, who had come over to help counsel her niece out of her pronounced sexuality, asked, looking at her own daughter.

'I've come to drive Sabitha back to Kuala Lumpur,' Geetha, said, clearly trying to take up as little space as possible on the sofa.

'But, why?'

'Because I need her for something. It will be nice to have company because, as you know, I'm going through some tough time,' she said with a straight face. Geetha didn't look like someone who was going through a tough time, not at that very moment, at least. Everyone in the room knew Geetha was lying and that she had come to get Sabitha out of the house, but stopped short of raising an argument out of respect for a grieving widow.

Sabitha reappeared in the living room with a cup of tea for Geetha, followed by her mother. 'Sabitha, please pack your bags as soon as possible. I am hoping to be in Kuala Lumpur by evening,' she said as she received the cup of tea. They both had a three-hour drive back to the city. No one protested. Within half an hour, they were hitting the twenty kilometer single-lane straight stretch lined by palm oil and coconut trees on either side, well on their way out of the small town where their collective ancestors had started their Malaysian journey.

Both of them were quiet in the car for the first hour, before Geetha pulled up next to a McDonald's so that they could get something to eat. They browsed the menus, but food was the last thing on Sabitha's mind. She took a window seat and rested her head against the glass panel as Geetha returned to the table minutes later with a burger for herself and a large drink for both of them.

'I wasn't sure if you were going to come,' Sabitha said. 'It was a toss-up between calling you and Anand,' she said, taking a sip of the drink and yawning again.

'Who's Anand?'

'He's my best friend. He would not have hesitated to come and get me, but I know everyone in the family would have been hostile towards to him. And he has to drive all the way to these boondocks,' Sabitha said. 'Thank you, for coming and for not reacting badly to this like the others.'

Geetha chuckled. She opened her burger box, took a good look at it, and then pushed the box cover to Sabitha. The latter coughed as she took another sip of her drink, taking a good look at the cover—that of a Big Mac. 'That's . . . beef.'

'I told you I am going to do this,' she said, and took a big bite of the burger, curiosity and wonder written all over her face.

'So . . .' she continued, her mouth full with the forbidden meat that she was clearly enjoying, 'I was never going to judge your choices. I know you are not going to judge this.'

Sabitha smiled, and took a few French fries, a sign of her returning appetite. 'What was your reaction when you got to know, after I messaged you? Were you shocked?'

'No, Yuva told me weeks ago, when we were in Ipoh,' Geetha said.

'I thought that was private. Does that mean . . .'

'Yes, he also told my parents,' Geetha continued enjoying her burger.

A new realization washed over Sabitha's face.

'Yes, your parents knew after that as well. That information travelled long before your coming out party. You know you haven't really spoken to my brother much over the years, so don't let that exterior of his fool you into thinking he's a cool person. He's a blabbermouth.'

'Why did everyone act so surprised, then?'

Geetha shrugged. 'First, you have to tell me, in detail, what actually happened last night,' she said. And as Sabitha started narrating, Geetha continued enjoying the burger without having to pause to speak.

As soon as Geetha was done with her meal, they resumed driving, but Sabitha was still replaying events from the previous night and adding her musings.

'All their reaction was fake, then,' she said.

Geetha smiled calmly, and tapped Sabitha's hands. 'You don't know this family well enough yet, then. No, they were not feigning their reaction. What they did was to pretend they never heard the information that Yuva passed down, and they just hoped a day like yesterday would never happen.

Because they had warning, it does not mean they were prepared for it.'

An hour later, they stopped again. Geetha rummaged through a small bag she had at the backseat of her car and took out a cigarette, lighting it up. Sabitha looked at her, jaw dropped.

'That's such a judgmental look,' Geetha said, as the wind from the other cars whistling past them blew in her face.

'I'm a doctor, I'm never going to encourage that,' she said. Geetha scoffed, and then stumbled upon an idea.

'You know what you should do? Post a filler somewhere, and look for another Telugu lesbian in Malaysia. Then one of you can get pregnant by surrogacy. The whole family would jump out of joy if you did that. You will be ensuring cultural heritage continuity,' she said, half smiling, and realizing the irony of her own suggestion.

'So that will turn me into an acceptable gay?' Sabitha asked.

'Yes, so, is there anyone in our community that you find hot?' Geetha asked, realizing that she was now capable to diffusing any tense or serious situation with her newfound sarcasm and ironic statements.

'Right now . . . you,' Sabitha smiled mischievously.

And they both knew they would be okay.

Chapter Five

CATHARSIS

September 2018.

On the day she was supposed to return to office after a two-month long absence, Geetha opted to finally put on the expensive Michael Kors watch her late husband had bought for her, which had remained in storage for a long time. Having been so used to wearing black coats and skirts her whole adult life, she thought a rose-gold coated watch was going to needlessly stand out compared to the rest of her outfit. But having realized she didn't have many material possessions to remember him by, this seemed like a good day as any to put on the watch given to her by her cheating, dead husband. She walked into her office building, tapped her entry past the security lobby, looked at the twenty people waiting at the lobby to get up the lift, and was suddenly overcome by anxiety. She froze the same way she had when she had first heard about Prakash's passing, seated in her idle car. The bright sun outside suddenly seemed gloomy, and a heavy sorrow washed over her, as though someone had just died. Prakash had indeed died, but despite being a Chipsmore husband for over five years, he seemed to have managed to bring a part of her with him as well. She felt a little dead inside. No part of her wanted to go to the office she owned, or start doing the work she had done for the past ten years of her life. She turned around, and tapped out the same way she had tapped in. She scanned the building lobby and headed for the row of comfortable waiting chairs by the glass panels. In the four-odd years that she had had an office here, she had never bothered to sit on these chairs.

She watched people come and go, trying to close her eyes to escape from the sudden weight of the world she was feeling in her mind. In the midst of doing that, she felt someone tap her shoulder. She jolted back into consciousness, expecting to see a security guard or a colleague hovering above her. Instead, she saw Jason, an old acquaintance, or to be more precise, the closest anyone would come to being considered an ex in her rather uneventful youth before her marriage. She had long lost touch with Jason, but she had regularly updated herself about his life by following his Facebook account. Jason was exactly how she had remembered him all these years. He was good-looking, clean-shaved, and dressed to kill. The only difference was his age was starting to show on parts of his face, and a stubble of a beard was slowly growing on his chin, although she was pretty sure it would not grow much thicker than it already was. Jason had always tried to grow a beard or a moustache, but even his strictest attempts at a no-shave Movember ended up with him looking like a clean-shaved man from a distance.

'Hey there, Geetha?' he asked.

Geetha mumbled back an introduction, unsure if she wanted to catch up with an old acquaintance in her current state.

'What are you doing here?' he asked. She wanted to tell him she was losing her mind, and losing control of her life.

'My office is up here,' she said, not knowing what to say if he were to ask what she was doing looking distraught at the building lobby. But he didn't.

'I'm sorry, I saw on Facebook what happened. I wasn't sure about what to say, or if there's anything to say,' he paused. He was going to ask if she was doing okay, she was sure of it. But again, he stopped short of asking the obvious.

'Can I buy you coffee? If you are not in a rush, that is,' he said. The questions continued racing through her mind. Was he asking her out, within minutes of seeing her after almost a decade?

'Sure,' she said, quietening her mind. She needed any distraction she could get. For the first time in her life, Geetha stopped analysing a situation and instead allowed the sequence of events to determine her next action. Bumping into him after all these years couldn't just be a coincidence. It had to mean much more than that. But sitting across from him at the building's only cafe, she knew the meaning didn't need to be romantic— she noticed his engagement ring, and she calmed down.

'So, what are you doing here? What are you doing nowadays?' she finally strung together a coherent sentence as she took a sip of the coffee he had brought her. She did know what he was up to. Contrary to his appearance, Jason was an activist–lawyer, and was constantly in the media for taking up cases with huge social and political implications. He loved his David-versus-Goliath battles, and she was sure there would be political payoff somewhere in the horizon for him.

'My office is also here,' he said, with a chuckle. 'Funny I never ran into you here in all these years,' he added.

She always thought that there was no money in taking up such social cases and doing the human rights work that he was doing, but Jason not only had a unit in the same expensive building as hers; he had a bigger floor space, and also operated from a much higher floor.

'The view must be good from up there,' she said.

'It's something to be experienced. If you have time to spare after this coffee, you can have a look for yourself,' he said.

Less than an hour later, she was standing in the common area of Jason's office—looking out at a view that encompassed most of Petaling Jaya, the most famous and developed city in the state of Selangor, just a few kilometers away from Kuala Lumpur.

'It's pretty nice, right?' he asked, with a warm smile. She merely nodded in approval. His office looked more refined than her own, even though he did more pro bono work than her. In fact, she had never done pro bono work before in her career. She had questions, but she decided she had no business knowing how Jason runs his firm.

'I hope you are feeling better now,' he said. He had never once asked if she was doing okay throughout the morning. He was a charming man and had a way with words. She smiled at him and nodded. Her vivid memories of her college trysts with him were coming back to her. She had slept with him numerous times because she had liked him, and it had taken her a ridiculously long time before she realized that he was never going to reciprocate her romantic feelings towards him. But even after she had realized he was never going to take their relationship seriously, she had continued to allow herself to be charmed by his words and his not-so-subtle invitations for nightcaps.

'Do you want to come over for a drink, tonight, maybe? At my place, I mean,' he said, as she made herself comfortable on his office reception's sofa. Jason sat close to her, leaving a small gap between them. Geetha thought she was vividly remembering an invitation from the past, and it took her some time to realize that she was actually hearing him make advances towards her.

'Aren't you engaged?' she asked him, and the pleasant experience was wearing off. She was sure of it because of the ring and because she had seen the pictures on Facebook. Jason never uploaded any pictures that showed him having a partner, but his fiancée was always more than happy to tag him in pictures and posts whenever they were together.

Out of the corner of her eye, she saw three women ring the doorbell to the firm. One of them, an Indian woman with colored hair and a saree, caught Geetha's attention; although she wasn't sure whether it was a positive or a negative feeling. The receptionist attended to them, and they engaged in an animated conversation. One of Jason's legal assistants appeared and started taking notes, listening to the three women while sitting them on a transparent round table near the entrance of the office.

Her attention shifted back to Jason shuffling uncomfortably as he sat right next to her on the sofa, albeit slightly on the edge and awkward.

'Why, that doesn't matter. We will be having a drink, that's all. She doesn't live with me,' he said, with a nervous laughter and a muffled voice, as if making sure no one else is listening to their conversation. Jason started the conversation thinking that he was going to talk to the same Geetha he used to know in college, but by now he was realizing that while he had stayed the same over the years, Geetha was now a completely different person.

'That is exactly the problem,' she said, with a strong look of disapproval. She had been charmed by his gestures and words up to this point, but she was in no mood to let another man into her pants so soon after Prakash's demise. It had very little to do with Prakash himself—she was now second-guessing all the qualities she used to seek in a man, and she wondered if everything that she had found attractive in men was the right choice for her all along.

'This is not law school, Jason. I'm not twenty-two, and I know a drink often tends to lead to other things. I have a great place in Tropicana Heights, and I have a great collection of expensive wines at my home. And I have my own family members with whom I can share a drink. So, I fail to see the appeal of having a drink with you, unless I want to participate in this little game that you are trying to play,' she said, her takedown punctuated in parts as she continued being distracted by the three women, who had been moved to a small sofa just by the door. Jason's legal assistant interrupted Geetha and Jason's conversation, so that she could explain to him the case that the women were looking to pursue. It was the perfect excuse for Jason to pause the conversation without having to respond to her rejecting his advances. He stood up, walked to the other side of the office, and conferred with his assistant.

He spent five minutes listening before he nodded and returned to the seat, looking even more fidgety. He stared at her quietly, and grabbed a cookie from the welcome table, offering her one. She declined.

'I'm sorry I offended you, I just tried . . .' he said.

'Your luck?' she finished the sentence for him.

He nodded with guilt.

'What is that about?' she changed the topic, helping him end the awkwardness, pointing to his legal assistant and the three women.

'It's someone who has come in after reading about the pro bono work we do. One of the women is a teacher who has been transferred because of her sexuality. So, I guess they are looking to see if they can bring the government to its knees?' he said.

Geetha felt a conviction that she had not felt in ages. 'I have never taken a pro bono case before,' she said.

'You should. It's very rewarding,' he said.

'Politically, or is it something more substantial than that?' she asked, as her eyes continued to be fixed on the women and their interactions with each other.

'Both. It does help me sleep well, too,' he said, avoiding the sarcasm in her question. 'But I am not sure if I can help them,' he added.

'The famous civil liberties lawyer can't help them?' she asked, her sarcasm prevalent.

'I don't see how. If she was sacked, maybe I can bring it to an industrial court; that's all I can see myself doing right now—off the top of my head. I need to study before I can decide what to do,' he said.

'You know, I think there might be a way we can put this awkward advance you just made, behind us. Pass them on to me. Let me do this case,' she said, armed with a surreal conviction which she could not quite place her finger on. But having already lived this morning as a complete antithesis to all the decisions she had made in her life up until that point, she was convinced this was the completion of her morning's purpose—to find these three women. And although Jason was not sure which of them was going to be the plaintiff, Geetha had a very strong instinct that it was the woman with red-colored hair. She had a look about her, a look that said she was going to take on the world.

Jason hesitated momentarily, but he was never going to object. 'Sure, let's do that,' he said, and stood up. 'I'll make the introduction,' he added. Geetha followed him, and they both soon stood in front of the three women who were in animated discussion with each other.

'Hi, I'm Jason,' he introduced himself, offering a handshake to which all three of them obliged. 'This is Geetha Rao, she is an experienced lawyer who owns a firm which is also in this same building. She just happened to be here for a discussion and she heard about your case and is very interested in taking it up as part of her pro bono portfolio. Provided, of course, we can find a legal remedy for your case,' he said, repeating himself again in Malay, as it became clear that the two other women accompanying the plaintiff were not particularly well versed in English.

'Shall we go to my office and continue this conversation?' Geetha asked the women in Tamil. The comfort of familiarity that washed over their faces was priceless. They were clearly not familiar with the environment of a law firm and were intimidated by all the legal terms that were being thrown at them earlier by the legal assistant, who was merely doing her job. The women nodded enthusiastically, and immediately stood up. Geetha walked them out of Jason's office, but asked them to wait for her at the lift lobby as she circled back and pushed open the plush glass doors of his office before it closed and locked her out. Jason was just about to head back to his room when he noticed Geetha's return. She was still holding the door.

'You know what else would help you sleep well at night?' she said, and Jason came close to her knowing he did not want her shouting the answer across the reception area. He knew she was not going to say anything kind, and he merely mumbled, waiting for the answer.

'Just don't be a cheating scumbag,' she said, her look laced with daggers. She returned to the lift and escorted the three women ten floors below to her much more modest, less spacious, cramped office. Instead of the reception, she had all three of them seated in the comfortable client meeting room. The pervasive appearance of black dresses and shirts in her office continuously reminded her of mourning, so she picked the three most colorful mugs she could find in the pantry—red, blue and orange, and got hot tea made for the women. By the time she sat in front of them, deciding to take the case notes down herself, she had got rid of her coat, rolled up the sleeves of her white shirt, unbuttoned the top of her shirt, lost her heels, and had replaced them with comfortable slippers that she kept stashed in the reading room. She looked at her phone and realized she had had her phone on silent for several weeks now. She stared at her phone screen for a few seconds, reflecting, as the women opposite the curved rectangular table looked on in anticipation. She put her phone back on ring mode, and pushed it aside.

'Hi, I'm Geetha,' she said, reintroducing herself.

'I'm Karthiga, and I'm the plaintiff,' said the woman with the red hair, looking as sure as ever.

'Kasturi,' said another woman, who was wearing a nurse's top and had her name tag pinned. She didn't really need to introduce herself.

'Laskhmi,' said the quietest, and calmest looking of the three.

'They are my sisters,' Karthi said, feeling compelled to offer an explanation. But Geetha didn't need one. Her mind was made up at Jason's office. This was going to be her first pro bono case, and she was going to do it herself. She wasn't doing it for any political mileage or any recognition; she had a healthy client roster. But she would be a fool not to recognize the importance of the media leverage for a case like this. But she needed to find a method.

'If you want to go down this path, Karthiga, you would need to commit. You would need to own that person who did whatever she wanted to during that one weekend that led to this situation. You need to be that person, who wasn't ashamed to be public about her sexuality on her Facebook. This time, this will be much bigger than Facebook. It will be in front of other lawyers, a courtroom full of people, and more importantly, with some media attention. So, you have to ask yourself if this is something you are willing to live with. This battle will take time,' Geetha said. 'I need to study the constitution and whatever little legal precedence there has been for cases like yours. I don't know what I will find and what the options will be. But before I put in my time, I want to know if you are willing to go the distance,' she added.

As she heard Geetha's words, Karthi already felt like she had won half the battle she was about to fight. She had spent weeks seeking out small-time lawyers to take on her case, but many of them turned it down because they had not wanted to attract press attention in an overtly sensitive environment in the country. Be it an issue regarding race, religion, or sexuality, voices claiming to represent the straight majority were painting their bigotry all over town, masking them as offended sensitivities. She had been up and down twenty law firms, and that was without counting the inquiries of independent visits that Lakshmi and Kasturi had made as well. They would not tell her exactly how many offices they had been to, but she was sure they had covered almost all the law offices in Rawang and its adjacent towns. If their issue had been one concerning race or religion, there would always have been race and religion champions who would have come forth and offered to help her. But while she was being seen as an aberration across all the major religions, sexual minorities like her were nothing more than everyone's favourite political punching bags. Those who were not using them as punching bags were busy turning a blind eye and pretending they did not exist in Malaysia.

The three of them showed up at Jason's office, after a round of online research showed them a list of civil liberties lawyers who were well-versed in defending the rights of minorities. They planned to make a strong appeal for their case to be taken on board, and considered using an emergency stash of cash for the same purpose—if no one would fight their case for free. Again, Karthi wore her saree because she wanted to make a statement—to herself more than anyone else. She was now sitting in front of one of the most confident, elegant woman she had ever met, who was offering to take this case up for free, and that too by putting her own personal hours, even though the activity in her office showed she had paying clients that she could attend to. Geetha did not seem to care about the consequences. She had so much to lose, yet acted like she had nothing to lose. Karthi saw a reflection of her own spirit, and if not for what the receptionist told her on her way out of the firm after their first meeting, she would have not known that this woman had just lost her husband and was still grieving.

Chapter Six

THE FIFTEEN MINUTES

October 2018.

Anu hummed along to her only collection of Malayalam songs, which she only listened to in solitude, as she drove under the pouring monsoon rain with low visibility, thanking her lucky stars she wasn't one of the dozens of drivers who got into accidents or car breakdowns in this weather. Relief washed over her as she finally pulled up towards the guardhouse of Tropicana Heights in her maroon Myvi, an extremely popular locally-made hatch. As she stopped by the guardhouse, she realized she was a visitor and needed to roll down the window to convey the unit number and her car plate registration to the security personnel. Seated in his booth, the Nepali guard was in no mood to get wet in the rain taking down her plate number, leaving her no choice but to alight from the car with her purse, run up the slippery three steps that allowed her to stand in the roofed part of the guardhouse and make her registration. The short dart that didn't even last a few metres was enough to leave her soaked from top to toe, and while she took stock of the amount of drying she needed to do later, the guard made three calls to Geetha's unit before verifying her visitor and allowing Anu into the carpark.

Anu walked towards Geetha, with a couple of wine glasses in her hand, her grey t-shirt completely drenched, and her hair disheveled, as the latter waited in the lift lobby, her hands cupping her mouth. Geetha was trying to control her giggle, as Anu sauntered painfully through the lobby, with an equally drenched tote bag on her shoulders.

'Don't laugh. That's mean. It's not like I meant for this to happen. Even an umbrella couldn't have saved me,' Anu said in exasperation as Geetha used her floor-specific access card to escort her guest to her unit. Once inside, Anu headed straight to the dining table in the middle of the house and laid down the wine glasses.

'You have dozens of bottles of wine in the house. Are you seriously telling me you don't have glasses for it?' Anu asked, as she tried to find a way to plant herself on a chairs without making it wet. 'I think I need a cloth,' she said, as Maria brought out an expensive-looking bottle of wine and placed it on the table next to the wine glasses, before taking the wine glasses for a wash. Geetha followed Maria into the kitchen and showed up with a cheese platter, which lit a spark in Anu's eyes.

'Woman,' Geetha, said, looking right at Anu's chest, 'you need new clothes. I can see right through to your red bra,' she said, giggling again. Anu stretched the shirt and looked at her own chest. 'Oh, my fucking god, is this why the guard took a really long time to call you?' Maria thoughtfully showed up with not one, but two towels. Anu stood up as Maria carefully laid a towel on the chair, and handed Anu another towel to wrap herself in.

Geetha reached forward and tried to hug Anu, but the latter blocked it. 'You'll get wet as well, are you mad?'

'This is my house and I have a lot of clothes, for both of us, so stop fretting,' she said. 'And I never drank in the house before, so I wasn't sure where I was going to look for the wine glasses,' she said, before excusing herself to her room to find a pair of comfortable clothes for Anu and also for herself.

Geetha hoarded wine bottles, but always ended up taking them outside to her favourite bar, where she would drink with Anu or any of her other friends and colleagues. Prakash occasionally joined Geetha's drinking sessions with one of her friends, and also with Anu, and Geetha did likewise with his friends. The only times she drank at home was when Prakash would have his friends over and she would be invited to join them. Both of them enjoyed an occasional drink, perhaps Prakash more often than her, but they never made a plan to have a drink between just the two of them in the house. That only happened on vacations, and that was almost always accompanied with silence and a lot of phone browsing. But neither of them acknowledged it as a problem or tried to do something about it. Geetha simply did not want to rock the boat. And now she knew Prakash did not fret over the situation because he was getting his romantic needs fulfilled elsewhere the entire time.

Geetha reappeared from her bedroom after what seemed like an eternity and flung a pair of pyjamas at Anu. 'You are sleeping here tonight. Get comfortable,' she said. Geetha was already in her sleeping shorts, and helped herself to the first glass of wine, which she finished before Anu came out wearing the pyjamas. 'Whoa, slow down, the bottle will finish faster than you think,' Anu said.

'Why worry, I told you, there are at least ten other bottles where that came from,' she said, carefully spreading cheese on shortbreads.

Anu retook her seat at the dining table, across Geetha, and looked at the latter with intent, as if she was trying to coerce a confession out of her.

'I know that look. I am fine. Really. Can't I have a nice Friday night? So what if I overdo it? I have the whole place to myself now, though I am not sure if that is going to remain the case,' she said.

'What do you mean?' Anu asked. She removed the towel Maria had placed on the chair and was now using it as a makeshift blanket to wrap her legs. She was comfortable.

'He paid two-thirds of the mortgage for this place. I have to pay the entire thing myself now. This is on top of the battle for all his other assets. He has three other condominiums and a house in Ipoh that's all under his name. All his assets. But I have been up-keeping them. In fact, for two of the condominiums, I have been bridging the gap between the rental income and the mortgage payments,' she said. 'And now the vultures are circling, trying to get their hands on as many things as possible. This as well, though I am sure they would run away the moment they realize the kind of bill this place comes with,' she added.

Anu reached out her hands, and caressed Geetha's hands. She opted not to say anything, as she did not have a solution to offer to Geetha. She hoped the comfort of her companionship and her qualities as a listener would help make the latter feel a little better, at the very least. She sat in silence, patting Geetha's hands. Geetha smiled back at her, and she felt a gush of appreciation for the relationship she had with her brother's girlfriend.

'I always wonder, why isn't your brother ever invited for these things that we do?' Anu asked. She had asked this question umpteen times, but the answer never tired her.

'Because I think he's a bit of an ass; I don't have this kind of relationship with him, and I think you are the best decision he will ever make in his life,' Geetha said. 'As Yuva's sister, I am really glad he has you in his life. As your friend however, I do find myself wondering—what are you doing with this guy? But I can't make such honest musings if he was around here, he would get all sulky and defensive. So, shut up and drink,' she said.

'And, also,' Geetha paused, looking a little more serious. 'I might need you to conduct an interview with someone and write an article as a favour for me,' she said.

* * *

November 2018.

Anu had been biting her nails as she alighted the lift to her office floor. She did not always see eye-to-eye with her section lead and had spent the past year learning to be content in doing what she called the 'fluff pieces' that allowed her to keep her job and live a decent life. She wrote meaningless interview pieces with celebrities about their lives, the clothes they wore, and new gadgets or malls in the city. But what she had been tasked to do this morning required her to not only engage her own section editor, but also the news desk editor. And there was the small matter of insisting that they let her write the story if they indeed gave a green light to the article. This was a day of battles. Her newspaper, *The Star*, was the most well-known English newspaper in the country, but it often suffered from schizophrenia, as did most of the print publications in Malaysia. The general assumption was that a story like this would have its takers among the editors in the newspaper, but then the decision makers were always armed with only a finite threshold of being a rebel or being bold with their content. Somedays, they just couldn't afford to irk the regulators, ministries and their political owners any more, and on those days, they would go into a 'play safe' mode, where the bosses turn into the stereotypical Asian parents—extremely conservative and afraid to take even a small step that is outside regular formulas.

'How sure are we that she will win this case, ah?' the news desk editor, draped in a purple dress and a matching shawl, asked, when Anu finally bumped into her at the pantry, some five hours after she first pitched the idea to her section head and news of her pitch slowly made its way up the newsroom hierarchy. She stirred her coffee daintily, with a small smile directed towards Anu, who felt her hands tremble in nervousness, and her voice muffle in the weight of it all.

'But this isn't about winning the case, right? It is about the fact that she is bothering to battle at all,' she said.

'Darling, so many people take up battles out of the media limelight every day. We don't even know for sure if she is the first person to take up such a battle,' she said, as she walked out of the pantry, signalling Anu to follow her towards the other end of the newsroom, where the political reporters and the paper production heads sat. They trained their eyes on her—someone from the same organization crossing boundaries and territories.

'After all, it is just a court case. We can report it if she wins it, sure, but I'm not sure we want to write about it before anything substantial happens. Then you will have all these right wing organizations writing press statements about us; so much attention, for what?' she continued, turning around and facing Anu, raising her eyebrows and demanding an answer. Anu cleared her voice, but could only hear a meek 'urm' being meted out. The editor smiled at her mischievously.

'Well, I just think . . .' she tried again, but the editor interrupted Anu by raising her hands. They were standing at the edge of the news editors' cubicle. She walked towards the news editor and the production head, who were in an animated discussion with each other; the production head slouched over the news editor, drawing out page layouts. She whispered something indistinctly to them, something that lasted long enough to make Anu wonder if she was supposed to stay where she was standing, or concede defeat and leave the area. The editor returned after a while.

'So, we have a bit of extra space at some point this week, but it can't be a very long piece. Give her the fifteen minutes, hopefully it will benefit her battle. And make sure she doesn't talk to anyone else until we come out with the story,' the editor said, and disappeared past the corridor. Anu sighed in relief.

* * *

Zamri was busy editing wedding pictures he had taken over the weekend for a couple referred to him by his friends, sitting in a little corner of his photo room, his laptop placed strategically to ensure it was in no one's line of vision. He knew his colleagues would never tell on him doing personal editing work during work hours, but his boss will inevitably have a few choice words should he find out. He was not going to give his boss an opportunity to get on his nerves any more than he already did on a daily basis.

'Zam,' his boss sauntered into the cramped room, with five photographers already sitting in all available corners of the office, with one of them deciding he was better off sitting on the floor. Startled by his boss' presence, Zam half-slammed his laptop close. 'Yes,' he stammered, realizing that closing his laptop entirely in his boss' presence was probably not a good idea after all.

'There's an interview being conducted by one of the lifestyle writers. Just go and take a few pictures of the subject. I forgot putting it on the schedule,' his boss said in a lackadaisical manner, taking his seat in the photo room. He was not apologetic about missing a photo assignment sheet even though news desk editors had notified him about the assignment two days prior. When Zamri looked at his boss, he was reminded of the conflict he had been going through since he opted to become a news photographer six months ago. What promised to be the most exciting job in the world for a newly graduated photographer quickly devolved into a somewhat mundane experience of getting little more than mugshots and candid shots of politicians and newsmakers. His photos caught attention, but he failed to see the depth of the story behind those photos. For him, these people he was documenting were nowhere near interesting and did not possess the kind of personality that made him see them as stories by themselves. He thought of his boss as someone who started out with just as much passion as he did, only to turn into this person who was merely coasting through life.

Zam was an erratic person, and made sure he went on long rides on his 5,000 ringgit Yamaha bike during the weekends to take pictures of vast landscapes, and the people who live and toil in such landscapes. They represented stories to him, but without a reporter next to him and with his poor command of the English language, he was unable to bring these stories to the larger world. They lived in his memory card, and in his mind.

'Okay, chief,' Zamri said, as he grabbed his camera, the basic kit, and walked out of his office past his boss and his fellow colleagues, walking the length of the newsroom, dotted with rows of small cubicles with reporters and editors, glued to their desktops and laptops, before reaching the designated interview room. There were people inside in the room already. He peered in from the outside, trying to make out who the reporter was. When he noticed Anu, he immediately messaged her and asked her to step outside.

Anu excused herself from the interview and stepped outside of the room.

'Chief forgot to put out a sheet. I have no idea what this assignment is about. Can you tell me more?' Zamri asked Anu.

'The story is about that woman inside,' Anu said, pointing towards a woman sitting inside the room wearing a red saree, in his line of vision. 'She is trying to file a suit against the government for transferring her from her job without her consent,' she explained.

'Why did they transfer her?' he asked, picking out the right lens for the shots, and setting up the camera as he spoke. Anu paused for a bit, and cleared her throat.

'Because she's lesbian,' Anu said. Zamri stared at her blankly for a good few seconds, before nodding.

'You have more questions?' she asked, sensing his hesitation. He shook his head.

'I'll ask the rest later,' he chuckled, collecting himself, and putting his game face on.

He entered the meeting room, fully expecting to stay not more than five minutes. But, this subject was different. She had red hair to go with the red saree she was wearing. She had a dark complexion, an infectious smile and laugh, was beautiful, but her voice generated little more than pain and anxiousness whenever she spoke. He could only make out parts of the conversation as he took several pictures of the subject, who kept looking at the camera whenever he trained his lens on her, which was distracting because Zamri was shuffling around different corners of the room, while Anu and her subject sat towards the front of the elongated wooden table in the room. He walked up and whispered in Anu's ears, 'Ask her to stop looking at the camera.'

Anu chuckled, paused the interview for a while, and told her interviewee in English to pretend like the photographer was not in the room. Zamri soon resumed taking photos the way he wanted to—candid shots of the woman as she was fully focused on speaking. With every couple of shots, Zamri went through his memory card to review his pictures. He wanted to take more, a rather unusual instinct when taking mugshots of interview subjects in an enclosed space.

When he finally got a picture of her that he was satisfied of, he wished the story would make it to the front page or a centre-spread—Karthi was glowing, the picture captured so much about her. But he knew the story will probably be nothing but a small or medium-sized column because of the sensitivity of the matter. If the government were to notice an article about lesbian teacher suing them, they would not just harass the interviewee, but would also trouble the paper's owner, editors, and the reporter. He, at the very least, might be questioned at a police station for the grand crime of taking pictures.

He was all for rebels, but he wasn't sure about sexual minorities. He had gay friends and he had fully accepted them for the way they were, but he wasn't sure if they should have been out and loud about their sexual orientation. Why announce it and attract attention to yourself?

Now done with taking pictures, Zamri decided he was going to stick around nonetheless. He helped himself to a seat at the far end of the table, sitting a pretty distance away from Anu and the interviewee. 'Can I sit here?' he asked Anu sheepishly. Distracted from her conversation, she nodded in a rush. He couldn't help but take another picture from where he was sitting, but became all too aware that the sound of the camera shutter was a distraction for the others in the room. He laid his camera gently on the table, and started reviewing the pictures. He turned to his left and noticed the chatter of three other women who were in the same room, but were sitting on the opposite end from where the interview was happening. Zamri had been oblivious to their presence the entire time, partially thanks to the size of the room; due to a lack of availability, Anu had been given a room that normally hosted a large editorial meeting involving staff from all different floors of operations. He saw a lawyer who seemed like the oldest of all the women in the room—and two other women who looked decidedly uncomfortable and unfamiliar with being in a newsroom. They tried their best to suppress their voices, but one of the women, who looked to be the youngest of the three, had a rather loud voice. He was the only man, and the only non-Indian in the room, and that somehow fascinated him.

He stayed silent for the remainder of the forty-five minutes of the interview. He was sure at least two-thirds of the interview will never see the light of day—it was just too long for a news piece. Anu finally turned off her recorder and exchanged pleasantries with her interviewee.

Zamri stood up, gathering his equipment. As he headed towards the door, Anu called him, and introduced him to the interviewee.

'Zam, this is Karthiga,' she said to him. Zamri shook hands with Karthiga. 'I'm sure he has taken some great pictures of you,' Anu said to Karthiga. Zamri merely nodded with a small smile.

'The saree looks nice. Along with your hair, it matches,' he said in Malay.

She responded in almost impeccable Malay, laced with a northern accent. 'It's my favourite one. I try to wear it whenever I feel it is going to be a special day, or when I want it to be a special day,' Karthi said, adjusting her dress after having sat down for so long. Together, the women and Zamri collectively inched towards the door.

'So, has it brought a lot of luck?' Zamri asked.

'I got my transfer letter while wearing this, so . . .' Karthi said. An awkward silence permeated the room for a while. Zamri tried to find something to say, but the words escaped him.

'It doesn't matter whether the events were good or bad, but significant things have happened on the days I have worn this,' she explained further.

Zamri smiled, and nodded. 'You seem to have an accent,' he said.

She chuckled. 'Yes; Kedah. I studied there for a few years, and picked this up. And now it's just stuck.' Zamri nodded, and pushed open the door for all the women.

'Can I take a picture of the rest of you, separately?' Zamri asked, just as he realized that the room was going to be empty soon if he continued merely observing.

'Including mine?' asked the lawyer, puzzled. She had eyebags and looked like she haphazardly put on make-up in the morning.

But Zamri believed the camera lens could capture something beyond all that. 'Everyone,' he said.

For another ten minutes, he profiled everyone in the room and got to know them a little better—the lawyer who had just lost her husband and was taking up the pro bono case for the first time in her life, the teacher who was fighting a seemingly futile battle to be allowed to be herself, two sisters who seemed to act as the teacher's foundation in life, being her squad no matter where she went. And he verbalized how he viewed each of them and their stories.

When they were finally done with the photoshoot, Zamri promised everyone that he would send their pictures back to them. He was the last person to leave the room, after Karthiga.

'Are you single?' he asked, catching her off guard. 'Do you have a girlfriend?' he added, realizing his question could be interpreted differently. Karthiga laughed.

'No,' she said, and he realized she had sweet voice, the kind of voice great teachers often seem to have—the kind of teachers who leave a lasting impression. 'I haven't found time for that yet,' she added, still taken by the casual light-heartedness with which he had posed the question.

'Hope you find someone soon,' he said.

'Thank you,' Karthiga responded with a warm smile. He followed her and her friends in the lift down to the ground floor, and separated from them as they headed to the car park. He stepped out of his office building, found a shaded corner that protected him from the angry sun that afternoon, and lit up a cheap cigarette that he always felt was literally burning his lungs. The packs cost less than three ringgits; he could not have afforded the premium, safer cigarettes with his current salary. He was about to pick up his phone from his jeans pocket when was startled to see a woman in a black office attire stand in front of him with a guilty smile. It was Geetha, the lawyer. 'Can I have one?' she asked. Geetha was slightly taller than him, probably owing to her four-inch heels, and when she lit up her cigarette, her lipstick left a mark on its butt as she took long, hearty puffs.

For Zamri, smoking was a way of emptying his mind. They did not speak to each other for much of the time she stood in front of him.

'What is your name? Sorry, I forgot to ask,' Geetha said, with about a quarter of the cigarette left to burn.

'Zamri,' he said, offering a handshake which she gladly accepted. 'Thank you for all the kind words you said in there, you made my day,' she said just as she put out the cigarette at the corner of the building and tossed it into the general bin. Her Malay was nowhere nearly as good as Karthiga's, which clearly showed that she did not speak the language as often. Zamri muttered his short replies in his broken English, often jumbling up words. There was a gap in their communication; both tried communicating in languages that they were less comfortable in. That was a glimpse of this country, Zamri thought to himself, as Geetha said her goodbyes and started walking under the blazing hot sun towards her car, using the large stack of legal files she was holding to cover her from the solar wrath, before disappearing around the corridor into the basement car park entrance. Zamri took out his phone, put on his twenty-ringgit bluetooth headsets which he knew would fail him sometime soon, and listened to Radiohead.

Chapter Seven

RED

In the middle pages of *The Star*. November 17, 2018.

Seeing Red Over Unilateral Transfer
By Anuradha Nair

Openly lesbian English teacher ready to take government to
court to challenge decision to transfer her to Sarawak.

Karthiga Krishnamurthy loves wearing red, because it's her
favourite color, and also because it is a color that always makes
her stand out. Karthiga doesn't stop with just a red dress; she
colors her hair red, and wears as many red accessories as possible,
as if she is perpetually making a statement.

At first glance, the boldness with which she presents herself
might make people think of her as an activist, or maybe an artist.
But Karthiga is neither. She is actually a public school English
teacher, and she is openly lesbian. And, because of that—she
alleges—the Education Ministry is 'packing her away' with a
transfer across Malaysia.

'They are sending me away, there is no doubt about it. I was
told just as much—that my transfer was the direct result of me
being open about my sexual orientation on my social media,'
Karthiga told The Star.

Karthiga has been transferred from a school near Rawang, Selangor, to the town of Samarahan in Sarawak. She has been told only to report to work at her new place in December, in time for the new schooling year. But since she received her transfer letter in August, she has been told not to come to her school.

'I was deprived of a chance to say goodbye to my students, at the very least. I think a teacher deserves better than that,' she said.

Karthiga will still be travelling to Samarahan as ordered, but that is not stopping her from taking the government to court, in a unique legal challenge that she hopes can set a precedence for the rights of sexual minorities in Malaysia.

Karthiga, last week, filed a civil case against the government at the High Court, where she is going to seek the court's permission to include a tort on privacy and sexual orientation discrimination into the Malaysian legal system—the first such an attempt in Malaysian legal history.

She knows a win is a long shot, but Karthiga believes she has been dealt with poor odds her entire life.

'I was orphaned as long as I remember. I do not know my parents. I grew up in an orphanage. Most people I grew up with ended up in a life of crime, or doing menial jobs, or struggling with some addiction. My sexual orientation shouldn't be the one thing that holds me back from everything I've worked to build in life,' she said.

'The battle is important. Whether we win, that's a different conversation,' says Karthiga.

But her lawyer, Geetha Rao, does not only want to battle. An experienced civil litigation and criminal defense lawyer, Geetha has taken up Karthiga's case pro bono, and will represent her first attempt at raising a constitutional question in court.

'Of course, I want to win. And I believe in this case, and that is why I took it up. Karthiga posted something on Facebook. That should not be used as a reason to transfer her somewhere else,' she says. The dates for the suit are yet to be allocated, and Geetha expects the case to be heard next year at the earliest.

Karthiga, in a Facebook post earlier this year, came out and professed her sexual orientation, while posting about a new car that she had bought. Days later, the transfer order came.

'I don't have parents or family I can come out to. So, I did it on Facebook,' she says, with a chuckle. Same-sex relationships and sexual acts between individuals of the same gender are outlawed in Malaysia, but civil society leaders have long called for better protection being afforded to the Lesbian, Gay, Bisexual and Transgender (LGBT) community so that their basic rights are not encroached upon.

The Education Ministry has not responded to requests for comments.

Chapter Eight

SAMARAHAN

December 2018.

Karthi wheeled a cabin-sized luggage pack and a small backpack on a Saturday morning at the departure lobby of the Kuala Lumpur International Airport, a month after her face and her words were published in the most-read newspaper in the country. Her interview, her story, and part of her story had all been republished since then in several online news outlets who were more than hungry for such content and individuals who rebel against the establishment. She was still entertaining calls from non-governmental organizations and even international pro-LGBT outlets occasionally.

She checked in for her flight before walking around several kiosks in KLIA, looking for the cheapest cup of coffee she could have. She felt a tap on her shoulders. She turned around and saw Lakshmi, drenched in sweat, and still in her work uniform.

'What the hell are you doing here?' Karthi asked. Lakshmi did not respond immediately. Instead, she moved to take a seat in one of the common waiting benches, took out a handkerchief, and wiped off her sweat. Karthi stayed on her feet.

'Someone needed to send you off,' Lakshmi said. Looking at her slippers and her general state of being, it was becoming clear that Lakshmi had opted to ride her aging second hand two-wheeler, which on its best day struggled to make the journey between their home to Lakshmi's workplace, for close to 80 kilometers to reach the airport.

'It really is not that big of a deal,' Karthi said, feeling somewhat elated inside that she was not left alone on a day that seems to be so daunting and numbing for her. She had never been on a plane before. She always imagined that her first journey in the air would leave her feeling thrilled and ecstatic, however, she was anything but.

She wished she could fast forward to a time when she would be comfortably settled in her new home, having overcome any feeling of not belonging to a new land. But time often moves slower just when you want it to move fast.

It took her years to feel comfortable in her own skin and find her voice in one of the most diverse capitals in the region, and now she had to do it all over again across the sea, in a town she knew so little about, surrounded by people with whom she had never spent any time in the past, despite sharing the same Malaysian identity.

She was going away for a presumably long time, but she only packed enough clothes to last her a week; most of her things remained in the Rawang house. It showed the last-minute nature of the decision to accept the transfer, and also her desire to somehow retain the Rawang home as her home even when she was not going to be physically present there.

'That is never going to be enough,' Lakshmi said, looking at her luggage, exasperated. Karthi knew Lakshmi would start nagging her like a mother, but that was not what she needed right now.

'Stop,' she said, kneeling down and placing her palms gently on her sister's knees. 'Stop doing everything. Don't buy anything. Don't rush me anywhere. Just be with me until I go past those gates and wave me goodbye,' she said.

'You know you don't have to go,' Lakshmi said. It was a message that Lakshmi had been repeating time and time again to Karthi over the past week—that she should not take up the transfer and show up at her new school until her legal battle was done. But she knew the legal battle could take months, if not years, and they were not well off enough to afford having her sit unemployed in the house for the duration, even if there was no cost involved in taking up the case. Kasturi had been insisting the same, for her to stay back and allow the two sisters to support her for the time being.

It was only two days ago that Karthi remained unsure if she was going to go through with her plan. She had booked a flight and hotel room for two nights by this point. She realized that not going would amount to quitting. She had started a battle, and she had to go, for her own sake. To prove her strength to herself, before she proved it to the nation or the world.

Not going would mean aborting a journey out of fear of uncertainty, fear of a new place, and fear of leaving home. She needed to leave home, she needed to face the uncertainty that came with it, and she should fearlessly explore another part of the country, even if the idea scared the living daylights out of her. She knew this was something she needed to do—not so much for the world to judge, but so that she could tell herself that she was not a coward when the situation demanded her to step out of her comfort zone.

Thirty minutes later, Karthi gave Lakshmi the longest hug she had given anyone in her life, as the police officers who manned the departure gates watched on. She handed her boarding pass, and everything else that followed was almost automatic, as if she had flown a million times before and she knew by memory what she needed to do next. Before she became conscious of her actions again, she had flown across the South China Sea, flew for the first time in her life feeling like she was on a long bus journey, taken a cab, and made her way to the cheap hotel room that she had booked. She pulled apart the flimsy, almost pointless faded floral curtains in the hotel room, as the air conditioning in the room chugged along loudly, and observed the flat terrain in front of her. Samarahan was a low-lying flat plain, and that made for a very humid and dry weather. Located about thirty kilometres from the Sarawak state capital—Kuching—Samarahan was essentially a university town, housing thousands of students, and almost all of its development was spurred by the presence of the universities and hospitals located in the town. Her stomach grumbled in protest; the physical exertion was finally overcoming her emotional numbness. She sat on her room's bed, picked up her phone, and started googling for food delivery options, feeling uninspired to head out. Her stomach growled even louder. She decided that she could only afford to take a short walk and grab any food that seemed appealing enough within a reasonable distance. She walked sheepishly down the stairs of the hotel, and out into the street, feeling as if she was in a foreign country.

Sarawak was very different from the rest of country. It has the same generic architectural uniformity that makes most of semi-urbanized Malaysia a boring sight to the eyes, but the sense of identity in this state was different compared to the rest of the country. This is the only state in the country that has only state-based political parties. It has its own immigration powers, which have allowed it to refuse entry for many politicians and activists in the past, and the people who hail from Sarawak often wear their identity like a proud badge.

A brown woman walking these streets, she stuck out like a sore thumb. Within five minutes, she was convinced that she was the only brown woman in the entire town. She stumbled past a Chinese eatery, decided it represented her best food option for her first day in an unknown territory. She ordered the signature Sarawakian egg noodle dish—a kolo mee, and found herself surprisingly taken in by the simplicity of its taste. Her mood improved.

Karthi did not talk to anyone over the next two days, and instead spent her time roaming the town on her own, most of the time on foot, and surveying potential rental units in the area that was the closest to the school that she had been posted to. Having initially imagined herself being stationed in a remote school in the interiors of this rainforest-rich state that could only be accessed by helicopter or off-roading vehicles, she felt thankful that she was posted to a relatively urban school instead, which was located within the ambit of the main Samarahan township.

On Monday, she took a cab to the school for the first time, dressed in a baju kurung, a traditional Malay dress, with the same name tag she had used at her previous school. As she walked past the swathes of students loudly fooling around on the school grounds, and the other teachers that were walking around the modestly sized campus, she scanned the place high and low for other Indians in sight, and struggled to spot any.

When she finally reached the teachers' room, an awkward silence fell—the other teachers were either too aware of her arrival or seemed surprised by it. She scanned the room and decided against exchanging pleasantries with anyone, before heading to the principal's room, knocking on the door and introducing herself, letter in her hands. A middle-aged woman sat on the principal's chair, and she seemed equally surprised or perplexed by Karthi's appearance by the door.

'Oh my, you are that girl . . . did they not tell you?' she exclaimed. It became clear to Karthi that unlike her previous school principal, this woman intended to get to the point a lot quicker and was not going to treat her with kids' gloves.

Karthi's thoughts immediately flashed back to the moment where she had sat across Edward, all excited to start a new chapter in her life, only to be told that she was being transferred across the sea to the other part of the country that contributes the most to national resources but gets the least among development investments.

The woman signalled her to close the door, and made sure they had privacy before she handed Karthi a letter which looked identical to the letter Karthi was holding in her hands.

'It came in this morning, and I honestly thought they would have informed you before you made the journey,' she said, as Karthi tried to open the letter.

'Don't bother. They dismissed you, probably over that interview,' she said. 'It was a good article,' the principal said. 'They don't react very well to being fought on issues like these,' she said, matter-of-factly. Karthi was gobsmacked. All she could think of was the amount of time and money she had wasted coming to this town in all that fear only to be told that the job had been taken away from her. She imagined herself broke, lonely and being dependent on others, and her anxiety set in. She should have never colored her hair red. She should never have updated that Facebook status. The fight was being sucked out of her.

Her head spinning, she gingerly made her way out of the principal's office and past other teachers in the teachers' room before her path was blocked by a sprightly man in his forties, wearing glasses. 'Hi, did you just get transferred here?' the man asked, removing his glasses, with a warm smile. Karthi understood the warmth of the smile. He was the brown person she had been looking for all over the town. And clearly, he was equally surprised to see another brown person walk these corridors.

'No, I just lost my job,' she said in a low, hushed tone.

And just like Karthi's stay in Samarahan, their conversation ended before it started.

Chapter Nine

CITY OF CLOUDS

November 2018.

Anu woke up startled and somewhat drowsy on a Saturday morning, wondering why her alarm was going off on a day she normally spent sleeping in until mid-morning at the very least. She tossed and turned, and then stared at the ceiling and the creaky fan in her room for a while, trying to recall the purpose of the alarm. She had gone to bed the previous night as if she had nothing pressing to do in the morning—and she was clearly wrong. She sat upright in a jolt as her memory returned.

'Shit!' she muttered, remembering the appointment she had and realizing she was not even remotely prepared for what would probably be the most important 250-kilometre long journey of her life. She had promised to meet Yuva's parents, a decidedly crucial step in her relationship with him. Her phone pinged. She knew it was Yuva. He was always up when the sun came out, regardless of the time he went to bed. It was as if he had a natural alarm clock. She reached out for her phone which was on the bedside table, still resisting the temptation to slump back into bed, and saw one of his messages without opening and acknowledging that she had read it. There was also a missed call from her mother, but she saw no urgency in returning the call.

'Excited?' he asked. She mumbled nervously to herself, and looked at the three t-shirts she had laid out on her ironing board the night before. Those simply won't do. She had to put more effort if she was going to meet her potential in-laws. She tossed her t-shirts aside, and raided her wardrobe for all the traditional clothes she had—the various kurtis, salwar kameez and that one rare golden bordered saree from Kerala—the piece of dressing that screamed her Malayalam identity more than anything else. Her phone rang; it was her mom. Her mom was more excited about the trip than Anu. She was nothing but a bag of nerves every time she thought about it, and often avoided thinking about it as the date drew closer. All she could think about was the article she had written about Karthi and the impact it was going to have for her case and the subsequent public debate it seemed to be generating.

Anu spent all but five minutes in the shower before clumsily getting into a green salwar kameez, putting on a lipstick that she never used except for attending weddings, and went big on the makeup, before feeling like she may have overcompensated. She checked herself out in the mirror, and decided she was good to go, except for one small element—her room was a royal mess. Anu had an obsessive-compulsive disorder, and she preferred everything in her room to be in an orderly manner—one of the reasons she never invited Yuva to come over and be in her room. She either went to his place, or they took up hotel rooms in the city whenever they felt like they needed to spend time together. She had no option but to leave her room behind a mess for the whole weekend this time; she could take hours tidying up a place, and she would end up delaying the entire journey, which would visibly irritate Yuva.

She was afraid of irritating him, and was increasingly taking pains to avoid upsetting him under any circumstances. He sulked without ever telling the reason, which to her often felt like an eternity of walking on eggshells. The thought of undertaking a three-hour journey with him in that mood was insufferable. Against all of her instincts, she left the room as it was, grabbed her bag, phone, and walked out of the room, closing the door behind her; walking hurriedly down her apartment before making her way to the light rail transit station adjacent to her house. She climbed up the moving escalator, not wanting to miss any trains, and she was relieved to realize that the train that had just left the station was not the one she was supposed to get on. She took a breather and realized that part of her make-up was already melting and she struggled to contain the sweat that was dribbling down her forehead. When the train finally showed up, she found a seat in the half-empty coach, replied to Yuva's messages, and then returned her mother's call.

A row of men sat across her in the train, and she was all too aware of them staring at her and struggling to avert their eyes off her. Anu hardly allowed herself to feel flattered when her looks attracted others, but this morning, she felt the need to be superficial, and allowed a small smile to escape her lips, masking it, as if she was smiling at something her mom was saying on the phone. One particular commuter, who seemed to be in his twenties, seemed to struggle to take his eyes off her. He wasn't particularly bad-looking himself, she thought, but he pretended to look at his phone every time she caught his gaze. She allowed herself to feel a little flattered.

Anuradha Nair was a very attractive woman—she embodied all the mainstream stereotypes about how Malayali girls often looked several times more attractive and beautiful than other South Indian women. When she put on make-up that increased the glow on her already fair face, she often attracted attention wherever she went, though much of that attention had waned over the past couple of years, thanks in no small part due to her own obliviousness to her surroundings. Half an hour later, she got down at the Bukit Jalil station, located a short distance away from the country's most famous stadium, and found Yuva waiting for her in his new ride, looking impeccably flawless. Together, they made an ideal couple, at least on a superficial level. Yuva was a good-looking man as well, and they both seemed well-matched with each other. The problem was, Anu didn't always feel like she was an equal in their relationship. She put her disturbing thoughts at the back of her mind, greeted her boyfriend of four years somewhat awkwardly and then got into the car for a three-hour drive back to his hometown—a place that she had heard about so much before but never had the chance to visit.

'Sitiawan,' Yuva first mentioned his hometown several years ago, way before they had started dating.

'What? Siti-what?' she asked, having very little familiarity with northern towns after growing up in Johor Bahru, one of Malaysia's major cities, which borders Singapore. Yuva pronounced the name of his hometown in two syllables.

'Siti–awan,' he said, pointing to the clear skies above him, as though he was trying to point at some white clouds that he hoped were passing by above them.

'Nice name,' she said, and her brain was already working overtime to find a creative moniker for his hometown. Anu didn't have complete conviction at the time, but she was already gravitating towards writing.

'Nice. Like, a city of . . . clouds,' she said, indicating that she got the hint. He smiled. Yuva had used that term numerous times in describing his hometown since then and it even caught on with some of his hometown friends. There was a reunion event which used the same name. But Anu never insisted that the idea had come from her.

* * *

Janaki stood smack between three stalls in the busy wet market in Sitiawan, the small town on the west coast of Peninsula Malaysia—blocking numerous people who were trying to move freely between the stalls. All three of the vendors were selling mutton, all similarly priced, and although she had done this routine numerous times before, she always contemplated far too long about which stall was going to be her preferred choice. After five minutes of contemplation, and her husband reminding her that she was getting in people's way, Janaki chose the middle stall, which she had chosen dozens of times prior.

Ratha Rao, somewhat relieved at the end of the market experience, quickly got onto his ten-year-old two wheeler, with his wife sitting uncomfortably in the backseat, for a short ride from the wet market to their family home, where only both of them lived now. Janaki had always thought that this was going to be the year her responsibility as a parent would end—she had married off her eldest daughter and all that was left to do was to marry off the son. This was the year that the son promised he would start making marriage plans, so she considered her job half, or maybe even almost, done.

But as she cooked a hearty big meal of mutton biryani for her guests for the day—she never failed cooking up a mean dish regardless of her mood—she was reminded of the fact that her job was far from done. Her son told her that he had been in love all along and that he wanted to marry someone of his own choice—and she was not Telugu. That was a problem. But it was not as big a problem as initially expected; Janaki felt somewhat relaxed because her daughter had married someone chosen by the family, so it didn't sound like a very bad idea to have the younger son marry someone of his own choice. It also helped that her son had fallen in love with a Malayali woman— they were also a minority among the minorities in the Malaysian Indian community—so they would be sympathetic to her and her family's attempts to keep the Telugu culture and language alive through the coming generations. She always dreaded any of her children falling in love with Tamils; she had many great Tamil friends, but she ultimately felt that having an alliance with a Tamil family would result in their family being dominated by the latter and her grandchildren never getting to speak the Telugu language.

But life never goes according to plan. Her daughter lost her husband, and that too before they had any kids, and she was now as good as single again, and suddenly seemed distant from the family. Janaki felt as though Geetha blamed her for getting her married to that cheating dead man, but the latter never had the courage or the energy to say it directly. Instead, she stayed away in a way that she had never done in over thirty years. She had always been closer to her daughter than her son, and Janaki felt the void of not having Geetha around as often as she used to.

She changed to a more vibrant floral top and refreshed after spending hours sweating in the kitchen, as her husband spent the entire time perched on the king sofa reading newspapers.

'Look at this,' he said, approaching her excitedly, as she came out of the master bedroom, all dressed up, with a religious book and her reading glasses in her hands. She put on her glasses as her husband handed a middle page from *The Star* and pointed her to a certain article.

'That's her right?' he said, carefully running his fingers under the bold name print—Anuradha Nair. Janaki nodded as she looked at the headline and the woman pictured beside the article—dark skinned with short brown and red-colored hair, and a red saree.

She looked at the picture and thought about the spirit that belied the seemingly uphill battle that she was fighting—taking the government to court to redeem her personal liberty in a country and society where personal liberty was often seen as being at odds with the natural harmony and state of things. Janaki liked natural harmony and the state of things. This is a country where the word liberal is often frowned upon, treated like it's a cussword that should be removed from all dictionaries. Janaki nodded, quickly brushing away the 'liberal' thoughts and questions that were permeating her mind, as she tried to relate to the experience of her own niece, Sabitha, who unceremoniously decided to come out to her parents months ago. Geetha had backed Sabitha's stance all the way, and she seemed to see her own mother as a villain in a piece of drama that underscored the speed with which the next generation in the family was finding individual voices in a relentlessly transforming world.

Janaki handed the paper back to her husband—who resumed his morning, browsing the newspaper—before proceeding to sit on a wooden chair in their sprawling porch, overlooking the housing street that hadn't had a car pass by since the day started, and started reading the religious book, attempting to find spiritual solace amidst all the uncertainty that life was bringing her at this age. She was convinced that she was too old to be asked to radically change her mindset and worldview about things. She was, for the lack of a better description, settled. Just as settled as the housing street she was living on and the town she resided in. Sitiawan had changed according to the tunes of capitalism, but it never threatened to become a melting pot like other growing urban settlements in the country. Its landmark was still a traffic light junction where four distinct roads merged, each one heading in a specific direction that would take someone out of the town. The whole place could be covered by a fifteen-minute-long drive when there was no traffic. Life wasn't always easy here, but Janaki and her husband managed to make it so; stumbling into one business after another until their attempt at a transportation business took off. Once the money started rolling in, and they found themselves a comfortable place to call home and raise their kids, life never really changed. People came and went, but the trees lined up outside their front porch and the silence of their street had remained the same for decades.

The town was perched by the sea, and hot coastal winds caressed the town both during day and the night, regardless of how high the temperatures soared. Ratha Rao, her husband, knew all too well that this town, while seemingly engulfed in inertia, never really produced people who loved inertia. It generally produced rebels with an anti-establishment angst, or at the very least, ambitious individuals who wanted to go out and make a mark on the larger nation.

At some point in the last decade, more than half a dozen lawmakers in a single Parliament sitting all hailed from this same, seemingly negligible town. This was the home of the communist rebel who was scorned upon by most of Malaysia's political leaders. One of its schools was named after one of the country's most prominent socialist leaders. This town was supposed to be a town of rebels due to its history, Ratha thought, but instead, it was mostly calm and uneventful. Communism and socialism were, just like liberalism and secularism, viewed with a negative connotation by people who controlled much of the political discourse. Greed and capitalism were good, as long as the narrative was able to fit the agenda of race supremacy above all else.

Both Ratha and Janaki retired a few years ago, and spent most of their time being in their homes, surrounded by spiritual musings and the thoughts of life after death. For decades, they had designed their purpose around their children—like many economically struggling Asian parents did—every penny earned was meant to be used to provide the best education and social mobility access for their children. In return for this selfless investment, they expected their children to carry their values, their traditions and give immense weight to their advice. Instead, the next generation has developed ideas of its own and were disregarding the older generation's views and opinions as though they were completely invalid.

* * *

Anu's worst fears had come true despite her trying so hard not to affect Yuva's mood. She made sure she was on time—earlier, she even took the train so that he could pick her up from an area where he did not have to encounter extra traffic, and made sure there were enough snacks so that neither of them would go hungry for the first couple of hours. Despite all of her mindfulness, Yuva barely spoke to her for the first two hours of the journey. She sensed his mood within ten minutes of getting into the car—he had a long face and avoided any form of eye contact, answered her questions by mumbling out words, and had his eyes fixed on the road. Clearly what ruined his mood that morning was the result of something that happened before she got into the car, but she could not figure out if the long face was due to something that she had done or if it was the result of his frustrations with someone else entirely. At the beginning of their relationship, he was temperamental but was always mindful not to take out other frustrations on her, but now everything came under the same umbrella. Seeing him happy in her presence was becoming increasingly rare, and any attempt to make him happy felt like a swim against the current.

She wanted to ask him what was wrong—which would have probably involved her asking the same question umpteen times to get an answer—but never found the right time within the first hour. She preferred the awkward silence between both of them. Just over an hour into the drive, the lack of conversation, the muffled music, and the general awkward tension he created left her so little to do that she fell asleep. She rarely fell asleep during drives, and she was proud of herself about being a good co-driver.

She woke up an hour later as he pulled up for refuelling, just before they were due to exit the monotonous expressway and take the non-tolled suburban and old town routes, which was the only way to get to Sitiawan regardless of the direction anyone was coming from. She had to stay awake for the rest of the journey because Yuva became easily irritable while driving on single-lane carriages, and she was among the few people who could help distract or calm him down from his own temper tantrums. Yuva loved his new car and loved driving it, except when his journey was being slowed down by slow-moving haulages that were tricky to overtake.

But she was not going stay awake and prolong the uncomfortable silence and tension between them. And she knew he was never going to break the silence until she did. 'What's the problem?' she was exhausted, and already seemed miffed in her own right.

'What?' he said, like he did not know what she was referring to.

'We both know there is a problem. You are being annoying right now. We are going to see your parents and I am following you to your home and you are pulling a long face. I am not going to do this for a whole weekend. If you have a problem, say it out now and we will resolve this before we reach,' she said, sitting cross-legged on the passenger seat and tying her hair into a bun. She knew half of her morning make up efforts were now next to useless because she had fallen asleep.

Yuva was startled to be confronted by Anu's irritability. He thought he had the upper hand in the power dynamic between both of them. But sometimes, and lately with increasing frequency, he had the tendency to stretch his silent treatment for such an extended period that it would just end up making her angry.

'It just seems to me like you and Geetha have got some exclusive club thing going on. You wrote such an important article but you never spoke to me about it—before, during or after doing it. And then my sister casually tells me that both of you had been discussing this article for quite some time before the interview actually took place. How do you think that makes me feel?' he said.

'The topic did not come up because you never asked me about my work. And I always inform you when I'm meeting your sister. I even shared the link of the article, as I always do with many things that I write. I don't even know if you read or take interest on things that I write. I always thought my work doesn't matter as much to you,' she said.

'But that's general work that you do. This is not general work. This article is different,' he said.

'How is it different?'

'Because of the subject matter.'

'Because I wrote about a sexual minority?' she asked.

He nodded with a mumble.

'Why does that suddenly make a big difference?'

'You know Sabhi came out recently—to the whole bloody family?'

'Yes, Geetha told me about it . . .'

'Of course she tells you everything . . .'

'Are you jealous of the relationship I have with your sister? I thought you should be happy with the relationship I have with her. I mean, you are driving me to your family house. Isn't the idea of this trip to make your family like me?'she asked, exasperated, and now giving him the daggers. Yuva continued to avoid eye contact, simply because he was now shaken by how she was looking at him.

'Geetha is different. She supported Sabhi. My parents are still reeling from it. And now they are going to read the article you wrote in the paper,' he said.

'I am finding it really difficult to see how you are conflating this argument. Do you have an issue with the fact that I did not share enough about the story with you—or do you have a problem with the article itself? Those are two different things,' she said.

She was making him uncomfortable. He knew what he wanted to say to her if an argument were to break out, but he never thought she would retort with such challenging questions. He simply sighed.

'It's alright. Let's move on from this,' he said, trying to take the high road.

'You can't just go off on me and then expect me to move on. I have been sitting here for the past two hours. And I had to initiate a conversation for you to tell me you have an issue. And when it gets difficult, I am supposed to just forget we are having an argument and move on?' she asked.

'What do you want?'

'I want you to tell me—do you have a problem with the article?' she asked.

'It just sounded sympathetic to the cause,' he said. 'I am not saying she should not have taken up the case. That's her prerogative, and it's her life and her challenge. You could have sounded more neutral. You sound like you sympathize with it,' he quickly added, realizing that his earlier remark sounded homophobic.

'And if I do sympathize with her, what is the problem?' she asked.

'I don't agree with their lifestyle,' he said. 'I don't understand how you can develop feelings for a person of the same sex.'

She grimaced at him but did not say anything.

'Can you understand? Like, how is it even possible? Can you imagine yourself, sleeping with another woman?' he asked.

'No, I can't imagine it because I am straight. But I don't think that because I can't relate to a certain emotion or experience, that experience becomes . . . invalid,' she said.

'But everything has consequences to the rest of us—as a society, as a family, as friends. They do not live in isolation. It affects all of us. If they are given more freedom, where do you draw the line, then?' he said.

Anu was finding it difficult to maintain a discourse with Yuva. She believed in civil liberties regardless of gender or sexuality, and she realized it was a principle that possibly grew on her as she grew older. Yuva did not share some of her more substantial worldview, and she was now having to imagine a married life in which she might choose not to share certain views with him due to his own strong opinions.

'Look, I am not homophobic. I do not disturb them or stop them from living their lives. I just disagree with their choices. And I think man and woman have their roles in life. And we play our roles accordingly,' he said, as if reading what was going on in her head. He didn't help allay her fears.

She thought about saying something in response, but nodded her head instead, realizing she could never know someone well enough. Critical questions circled her thoughts—how had she not seen this side of him before? How did this conversation not come up? Is she okay with this? Can she live with someone who did not subscribe to the same values of civil liberty that she did? Would her consideration of him have been any different if she had known about this side of him before they had gotten together?

She remembered the person she was when she had gotten together with him—that memory was a floodgate she was not willing to open. But deep down, she felt she would inevitably revisit some old memories the more she evaluated everything that had happened during her relationship with Yuva. She wasn't ready for those reflections yet, but she wasn't sure if she would ever be.

* * *

Ratha and Janaki had already opened their rickety sliding gate, which badly needed fixing, to allow Yuva's car to be directly parked in the porch. Anu observed the family home with much fascination—the small-town charm that this particular town contained—and with that, these spacious, aged houses which she was sure had plenty of stories to tell. Ratha and Janaki had racked up a substantial bill renovating their home when they had first moved here more than two decades ago, but they no longer had the energy or motivation to refresh it. Instead, they allowed the once-beautiful furnishings to age along with them—they all still worked and still did their jobs well—but they all took some time to get going.

Anu was quiet as she started her visit, except for a couple of awkward hugs with her future in-laws—partly because she was still reeling from the largely unpleasant journey she had had with Yuva, and also because Yuva mindlessly slipped into his homely comfort by beginning to converse in Telugu with his parents. Anu did not understand a single word. Yuva had tried to convince her to study the language a couple of times if she wanted to fit in his family better in the future, and her reply had always been the same—she will only learn Telugu if he makes an effort to learn Malayalam, her own mother tongue. While Anu had gotten close to Yuva's sibling and had now made a long trip to meet his parents, Yuva was yet to make any concrete effort to meet her parents or her family members.

When they finally got around to speaking to her, Ratha and Janaki spoke a mixture of broken English and Malay with her, and this went on for another hour as they sat on the noisy dining table in the house and had fritters and strong, sweet tea. Despite all her discomfort with the language, and the general awkwardness of meeting people that she was supposed to 'impress', Anu felt this was a town she could always come back to, just find a quiet home and observe the silence. The mixture of language felt dissonant to her. She asked them if they were comfortable speaking in Tamil.

'Yes,' both of them said in unison. It was clear they were just as fluent in Tamil as they were in their own mother tongue. Anu was more comfortable in Tamil, and her command of Malayalam was subpar in comparison. Tamil was the lingua franca among most Indians in Malaysia, although non-Tamils consistently feared that its widespread usage threatened to drown out their own language and cultural traditions.

A part of Anu wondered if Yuva's parents had an equally negative reaction to her article as he did. She was not going to broach the topic on the first day of meeting them, but later that evening, Ratha addressed it subtly. 'I saw your article in *The Star*,' Ratha said, sitting politely in his own home, as she finished her evening shower and came to the living room with only her future father-in-law for company. She took a seat on the same long sofa he was sitting on, leaving space for two people in between. Dressed in her pyjama bottoms, she crossed her legs, and tied her hair, making herself very comfortable. Ratha acted like the guest.

'Thank you, uncle. Yes, it was one of the most important articles I have ever written,' she said.

Ratha merely nodded, seemingly unsure how to prolong the conversation. Janaki came to the living room and instead grabbed an old bean bag and sat on it. She was also fresh after a shower.

'I was just telling her how nice her article in *The Star* was—the one I showed you,' Ratha told his wife.

'Oh yes, I saw that—it was really nice,' Janaki nodded. Janaki felt it was too soon to have this conversation, mainly because she had no idea which direction it was going to go once the ball started rolling. Janaki and Ratha never asked each other what they thought about Sabhi being lesbian—they only agreed that she should have not come out to the family. Janaki's mind has been a storm of conflicting ideologies in recent days, and she did not want to add on to it. She looked at the large Ganesha picture that was in the living room, and cupped her hands in silent prayer for a few seconds.

Anu had an idea that she was hesitating to exercise. But awkwardness was killing her more than the need to avoid conflict, so against her best judgement, she went for the jugular.

'I heard that one of your nieces recently came out as gay,' she said.

Janaki wanted to kill the conversation. But Ratha just wanted to talk—and he was happy there was a topic offered.

'Oh yes,' he said, nodding, seemingly trailing off to end the topic. 'We are all still reeling a little from it. I don't know how her parents are taking it, you know?' he said.

Anu nodded—there was no hate, dislike or homophobia in the conversation so far.

'I don't know. All you youngsters have evolving ideas about sex and marriage, but I think consideration has to be given about where we come from as well. Don't have to see us as enemies all the time,' he said, missing his own daughter as he uttered the words.

Anu smiled warmly—this was not a bad family to get married into—she knew she would get along with both her sister-in-law and her father-in-law. Janaki did not nod along with her husband's comments. It was clear she had a stronger opinion on the matter, but she again opted to keep quiet, given the storm that was now brewing in her head.

Yuva appeared in the living room shortly after, his thoughts preoccupied with his favourite dish—the mutton biryani that his mom had made for dinner that day. He sensed the silence in the hall.

'What?' he asked everyone.

Anu was silent. Janaki was silent.

'We were just discussing about Sabitha,' Ratha said, in his calm, measured voice. It was always very difficult for him to tell how his father felt most of the times because of his calming voice. He reacted with the same poise for almost any issue. By default, the family had come to assume that Janaki's outrage or happiness at a certain subject was also shared by Ratha—because he never spoke about his emotions and did not state his opinion unless repeatedly pressed for it.

Yuva stared at his girlfriend with borderline contempt. She stared back at him with an equal amount of contempt—she was not going to be blamed for attempting to make conversation, after he had done next to nothing to make her more comfortable in his home.

When dinner was done, Janaki quickly wanted to make sure everyone was clear about the sleeping arrangements. She offered Anu the master bedroom and said that she and her husband and son could sleep in the other rooms in the house, but Anu insisted in not taking such a big room by herself. She, instead, proposed a simpler solution—that the women take a room and the men take another. Everyone did not appear to be immediately taken by that idea, but they soon realized it was the most logical sleeping arrangement to be for the evening. No one was even going to attempt suggesting that Anu and Yuva sleep in the same room. They had taken up rooms and spent nights together numerous times before but as far as their parents were concerned, romantic relationships involved little more than holding hands between the couple. Whether this was actual ignorance or a pretence of ignorance, she was not sure.

Anu did not speak to Yuva alone for the rest of the evening; she decided to retire to bed early along with Janaki when he wanted to stay on until later and watch a movie. After getting on the creaking bed, which had a surprisingly comfortable mattress, she took her phone and dropped him a message that would stay with him through the night—at least that was what she had hoped would happen.

'Remember, this is not only about me impressing your parents. It's a two-way street. I also need to be comfortable with your home, your town, your parents, and your family. Stop acting like it is a one-way street.'

* * *

'What do your parents do?' Ratha asked, as Anu opened her eyes after a long contemplation at the quaint temple they found themselves in the next morning. All four of them had decided they would go out to a temple, then lunch, and then a visit to Sitiawan's nearby beaches over the course of the day, before the she and Yuva drove back to Kuala Lumpur in the evening.

'My mother is a teacher. Father is a banker,' she said.

'In Johor Bahru?' Ratha added. He was the only one making any effort to have a conversation with her—it seemed that Janaki had already made up her mind not to approve Anu as an additional member of the family, or her thoughts were completely dominated by other events unrelated to her visit.

'So, father is in Malacca, actually,' she smiled again. She knew what the next question was going to be.

'They are divorced. They have been divorced since I was a kid,' she said. Hearing about divorced couples was extremely rare in the Malaysian Indian community—especially among individuals who were still connected to their cultural and language identities at large. Ratha and Janaki came from a generation who were told to stick it out with their partners should anything go wrong—because the generation before that believed there was nothing that could not be fixed between two people. Couples who had been married for decades openly expressing their unhappiness or regrets with the marriage were not an uncommon sight. Anu knew her parents' divorce immediately made people look at her like she was a child from a broken family. But she also wondered if encouragement to stick it out in unhappy marriages was a good advertisement for the institution of marriage among the younger generation.

Anu gathered that Ratha and Janaki did not go out of the house much, not with each other anyway. They were more than happy to spend copious amounts of time at home together, albeit with ample private space for both, but hardly made the effort to go out and roam the town. The dissonance showed when they travelled, even if it was for a mini-trip around the town they had lived in for decades. They had arguments in the car while heading to the temple, even though Yuva was the one driving and he didn't need directions. They argued again at the temple about where lunch should be, even though Yuva already knew where to take them and Anu. Anu was beginning to get exhausted of these little squabbles by the time they reached the restaurant for lunch. It took them another few minutes to decide on the right table.

Shortly after, they had an animated argument that somehow started from a simple misunderstanding over an order. Yuva seemed to be used to the squabbling and the arguments, and he was largely indifferent to all of it.

'Should never come out with you!' both of them said to each other at a point, as Anu looked on uncomfortably. They did not acknowledge their fight with her, and continued as if nothing had happened. It was the first time she had seen Ratha showing any intense emotion. Yuva lifted his attention from his phone for a short while, looked at her, and acknowledged the awkwardness of that argument with a cheeky smile. He normalized the situation. For Anu, it was not normal; she had grown up with her mother, and spent weeks at a time with her father, and she would later gather that they opted not to be together because they would have such nasty arguments.

They went to the beach after that, and strolled quietly along the shores along the Malaysian west coast, looking at a seemingly endless horizon under the afternoon sun.

'What do you expect from a marriage?' she asked Yuva, interrupting a conversation they were both having about his parents and his general family, as his parents sat down in a shaded bench a short distance away.

'Commitment. Family. Kids?' he said with a smile. For Yuva, the answer was obvious. He thought this had already been discussed, and that there was no need to bring it up again. Problem was, it had never been discussed.

'What does commitment look like to you?' she asked him.

'I don't know. Living together. Taking care of the kids,' he said.

Images of her future started flashing before her eyes. She couldn't believe they had never had a proper conversation about this before.

She returned to the conversation half an hour later, as they were getting a bowl of cendol, a popular iced, sweet dessert, from a motorbike-attached cart parked under an intense afternoon sun. Yuva and his hometown friends had always sworn by this cendol stall, which was being operated by the same family for almost three decades now. Even if there were other cendol stalls that did a better job in serving one of the most ubiquitous desserts offered across Malaysia in the sunny hours between early afternoon to early evening, Yuva and his friends never admitted to it—such was their connection to the stall, and by extension, their hometown.

'You mentioned kids a couple of times. Are kids the most important thing about marriage?' she asked, just as they were finishing their dessert, sitting on a flimsy plastic stool, just about shaded from the scorching heat. Yuva's parents waited in the running car, as they preferred to enjoy a packed cendol at home instead. Anu was not big on desserts, and she hadn't had a lot of cendols in her life, but she had readily admitted not remembering tasting a better one than this.

'Aren't they? I mean—we are already together. If we get married, the primary motivation would be to live together and start a family, right?' he asked in return. Yuva had been in a visibly better mood today; Anu's strong message from the previous night probably did its trick. But neither of them acknowledged it in their conversations.

'It should be about us first, no? Sure, kids are a part of it. But shouldn't we talk about figuring out how we are going to be if we are going to live with each other?' she asked.

Yuva seemed surprised by the question. The question felt elementary, especially because they had been together for years and had known each other for years. Living together after knowing each other for so long should not represent a huge challenge.

'But we already know each other so well,' he said, adjusting his cap, and putting on his shades as the sun seemed to be getting stronger by the minute.

'Do we?' she asked.

'Do we have to do this now?' he asked.

'When else? You have been very moody of late, Yuva. I don't know what's going on with you, but I feel like I need to pick my moments to be able to have a conversation with you,' she said. He didn't reply. She stayed on, looking at him for a few more seconds, before standing up from the low stool, disposing of the paper bowl, and heading to the car. He followed behind her, but didn't appear interested in broaching the topic again, and she expected to resume the conversation in their own privacy on the drive back.

Once they got back home, Yuva and Anu started packing for their trip 'You think we don't know each other well enough?' he asked as they were getting ready while checking themselves in front of the same life-sized mirror in the master bedroom, standing close to each other. She thought about the question for what seemed like an eternity, standing in front of the mirror and adjusting her dress. She thought about long explainers to make sure that her answer did not offend him. And then she realized that getting married meant being fair to herself as well as to him. Putting his interests before her own views was a dangerous habit to cultivate if she was going to spend the rest of her life with him.

'No. Not as well as I previously thought,' she said curtly.

'Why? And what can we do to correct it?' he asked while also keeping up a conversation with his mother, who was in the kitchen packing up some food for the both of them. They were borderline shouting at each other between the room and the kitchen in Telugu.

'First, you need to pay full attention to me,' she turned around and looked at him dead in the eye. He was startled. He smiled, laughed it off, and kissed her forehead. He never responded for her demand for more attention.

Their drive back was uneventful—Yuva made everything seem and feel normal again. By now, Anu craved an honest conversation or an intense argument. Anything but a silence that seemed designed to pepper over the cracks.

As they drove back, they went up a single-lane, dangerous-looking bridge that connected Sitiawan and its neighbouring towns, villages and estates with Teluk Intan, just as the sun started setting in on the horizon. Anu looked at the Perak River slithering below their vehicle, with the vibrant colours of the sunset being reflected in the surface of the water. She had a clarity of thought that had not happened with her for a long time. She decided that she was no longer okay with normal.

'Are you not going to ask what my mom or dad said about you?' he asked.

'Are you not going to talk about all the concerns and questions I have been asking since just now?' she asked, and once again noticed his reluctance for a discussion, before moving swiftly to ask the one question that had been haunting her for over twenty-four hours.

'Okay, let's get to that. In what aspect do you feel that we do not know each other enough?' he asked. Anu was slightly surprised. At times, he made everything seem easy, but a lot of times, he seemed to make easy conversations feel difficult.

'I believe in personal liberties. I am a writer, and it is important for me. I believe in LGBT rights. I might have sounded sympathetic for that reason, but that's who I am. I probably didn't have a chance to realize how strongly I feel about it before,' she said. 'And, all these years, you didn't seem to know that about me. And I didn't know this about you— that you are not actually okay with people with different sexual orientations. Different preferences,' she added. 'I didn't know, until I heard you say it—that you believed in traditional gender roles. That men and women have their own unique roles in a relationship. How do we not know all of this? And how will we figure it out?' she asked.

Yuva stammered a little.

'Do you believe that your wife should do most of the housework, do most of the cooking, do most of the caring for the children? Would you ask your wife to stop working, regardless of what she is working as, if one parent has to stay at home for the children?' she asked.

He stammered and hesitated again, but didn't disagree. She decided to rip the band aid off.

'Yuva, these are serious things I need to think about. I love my job, I love my life as it is,' she said, sounding more serious.

'But it will be okay Anu. Yes, we have our differences, we have different opinions. But it doesn't change the fact that we like each other, right? As for events after marriage, I am doing well enough right now. I am not going to ask you to stop working. I will allow you to continue working as long as you can. Whether the family situation changes, we can have the discussion later on. But, of course, I will make sure I will provide,' he said.

'Allow?' she asked, looking a little taken aback. 'Fuck,' she muttered.

'You know what I mean . . .' he muttered, his hesitation seemingly matched by an uneven patch on the road they were going through, making their ride bumpy.

'No, I don't,' she said, clearing her throat.

'Yuva,' she said, reaching out and touching his arms as his hands were on the wheel. She seemed calm, but all of a sudden, tears started rolling down her eyes. 'I think I need a break.'

Chapter Ten

WALLFLOWER AND THE EASY ONE

2011. Wallflower.

Ashfaq picked up his tray of food, handing over what he felt was an exorbitant amount for a simple-looking meal, thanked the cashier, who barely appreciated the personal interaction. He turned around and scanned the open-air food court, hoping to see rows of empty tables and chairs where he could find a place to sit. Instead, all he saw was hundreds of people packed in the food court, with some strangers already sharing tables with each other. The way most, if not all Malaysians looked at him, with an air of caution and apprehension, he felt he was unwelcome at most tables. He walked the length of the food court, and negotiated past the badly arranged round tables and chairs, before he noticed a young man in a red shirt, looking just as lost and clueless as him in the food court—trying to finish his food gingerly. The young man looked at Ashfaq, and the latter wasted no time in gesturing, asking if he could join the table. The man smiled warmly and nodded. Ashfaq sat across him, and swiftly introduced himself in his broken English. The man, wearing an oversized red polo, introduced himself in return.

'Yuva,' he said. His hair was disheveled—he looked every bit like a foreigner to the environment they both found themselves in. He did not fit in.

'Bangladesh? Pakistan? India?' Ashfaq asked as he took a bite of what was an extremely poor imitation of a chicken biryani.

The man laughed awkwardly. 'No. Malaysia,' he said.

'But you look . . .' Ashfaq was surprised.

'I don't know. But I am Malaysian. Malaysian Indian,' he said.

'What blood do you have?' Ashfaq asked, looking perplexed. In his mind, he had been trained to believe that there was an easy way to distinguish the races in Malaysia—the dark-skinned ones are Indians, who are essentially descendant Tamils from India, the Asian-looking ones are Malaysian Chinese, who have been in Malaysia for several generations, and then there are the brown majority Malays, who are Muslim and indigenous to the country. But he had gotten most of his assumptions wrong since he had gotten here. He assumed a girl in his class was Chinese, but she turned out to be Kadazan, a major race in the state of Sabah in the island of Borneo, who are also considered indigenous. He spent the next hour after their class curiously asking questions to find out more about Borneo and other Malaysian states that are on the island.

'Telugu. Yuvaraj Rao,' Yuva said, clearly wanting to move on to another topic as soon as possible. He had picked up his eating pace considerably since Ashfaq had joined the table.

'You mean, Andhra?' Ashfaq asked.

'Yes. Great grandparents. Not me. I was born here,' Yuva said.

'Sorry, you look . . .' Ashfaq apologized, realizing how uncomfortable the conversation might have been for Yuva, but the former was busy discovering a new world. He had only travelled through Pakistan and north India, so anything outside of these zones and what was represented in Bollywood and Hollywood represented completely new discoveries for him.

Yuva shrugged his shoulder. He did not want to pronounce that the misunderstanding had been down to Ashfaq assuming all Malaysian Indians were supposed to be dark-skinned, and that was why he did not fit into the idea of how a Malaysian Indian would typically look like. Ashfaq was not the first person to assume Yuva wasn't Malaysian Indian, and he certainly won't be the last. Some people had chalked down the difference to his relatively fairer skin, when pitted against the skin tones of fellow South Indians. But he also knew that Telugus did not generally have fairer skin, so he could not pin down his different look to his ethnicity.

They segued to talking about their courses and classes, and before long, Ashfaq realized that Yuva took the same class and course as him.'How come I never saw you before?' he asked.

Yuva shrugged again. He was the perfect wallflower. He could be invisible in a room full of people. He was an expert in finding an empty table or chair at the far end of the class and just absorbing the lesson. He was an expert in showing up just in time and leaving right on time, preventing room for any socialization; not because he did not want it, but simply because he did not know how. For all intents and purposes, Yuva was a foreigner in the college. Although he was not from another country, Yuva's upbringing and social class made him feel very much like a foreigner, even when he was surrounded by people who spoke the same languages he did. The lifestyle of his fellow classmates did not register as normal to him—it was simply a different universe. They had regular meals outside, a number of them drove cars, they went to parties and consumed alcohol, and some of the jokes they made about each other were also a little too liberal for his understanding. Not all of them came from rich families, but some of them had liberties he could never imagine having. His roommate, another Malaysian Indian who spent more time with his Malay and Chinese friends as compared to other Indians in the college, appeared to come from an ordinary family; except that he could afford a new box of cigarettes every other day—which, in Yuva's universe, was the cost of two wholesome meals. Everything they did seemed to cost a lot of money; but Yuva was careful not to spend more than ten ringgits on a single meal. Fast food was a luxury that he rewarded himself to once a week, and there were days in the week where he survived on plain white bread. He thought what he was doing was normal because he had been told by his parents, cousins and relatives that this is how college life is supposed to be—making the most out of what was given to him. But all he saw around him were people who were making the most out of things in a completely different way. They lived like tomorrow was going to be snatched from their hands, and he lived for the promise of a tomorrow.

Yuva never sat with anyone else during lunches. Ashfaq was the first person to have sat on the same lunch table as him, but he was sure that would not be the case for long. Ashfaq was a good-looking man, with a fair complexion, and towering at over six feet.

Yuva's attention drifted away as Ashfaq was still talking to him, trained on a mixed group of young men and women giggling loudly as they walked past the food court back to their classes. Ashfaq noted the change of attention.

'You looking at someone in the group?' Ashfaq asked. Yuva merely nodded.

'Is it the fair, tall one in the front? She looks gorgeous,' he said, smiling, and now seemingly encouraged that he was able to bond with Yuva by talking about girls. The girl leading the group certainly hogged most, if not all, of the attention. But despite her height, Yuva never noticed her. His eyes were fixed on someone else from the same group—but he did not know her name.

'No, another one. The only Indian one, actually,' Yuva said. Ashfaq observed the group for a long time as they disappeared past the corridor.

'Not bad, that girl is beautiful,' he said.

Ashfaq and Yuva's friendship somehow lasted even though the former soon found enough friends of his own in the college and had his own group formed. Yuva was not really part of the group—he did not enjoy going out or smoking up as much as the others did—but he did accept an invitation to become Ashfaq's housemate when he and two other friends decided they wanted to rent a whole private apartment together.

Yuva slowly removed himself from the wall, and people started noticing his presence in class and during social events. He was known, in the very least, as Ashfaq's friend. Four months after they moved in, Yuva woke up in the middle of the night, when one of his promiscuous housemates was having one of his monthly romps in the room. He needed to use the washroom, which was a shared one that required him to take a short walk in the corridor of rooms, and struggled to go back to sleep, amidst the protests of his bladder and also the muffled moaning sounds traveling through the flimsy wall that separated his small bedroom from his housemate's. When the sounds subsided almost an hour later, Yuva put on pyjama shorts on top of his boxers, a T-shirt, and took a respectable walk to the washroom, only to find it occupied. Still clutching his bladder, he was about to turn around to walk back to his room when the bathroom door opened. A woman stepped out of the washroom, and upon seeing him, stopped in her tracks, and stared at him with guilt, shame and awkwardness. She looked awfully familiar under the bathroom light, but Yuva was barely awake and couldn't register a name to the image. Discarding it as a distraction, Yuva walked quickly to the washroom, his urge to pee overcoming any other necessity of the moment, mustering a faint smile as he passed her by the dark hallway, wanting her to feel comfortable. He saw her disappearing into his housemate's room before he closed the door. Just before he started emptying his bladder, a realization hit him. She didn't know who he was—but he knew her. He had been seeing her every day for the past half a year in the campus. He had been gathering information about her, little by little— she was a Mass Communications student, a great writer; she wrote articles for the university publication, helped promote the university at some events, and had a large social circle. She was generally very popular and constantly had suitors in the college. Up until two months ago, she had had a boyfriend—a local Indian with a ragged look and a beard that probably needed everyday grooming.

As he stood over the toilet bowl and finally started peeing, he felt like a weight was both being lifted and added at the same time. He felt the relief of emptying his bladder, but his heart felt suddenly heavier, like it was sinking to the floor. He had never had this feeling before; why was he feeling affected by the actions of a person he did not even know? He stayed in the washroom for an inordinate amount of time, and when he finally decided to get out, he took a peek to make sure he did not run into her again. He did not sleep that night.

He got up at his usual time in the morning—just as the sun showed, and found Ashfaq fixing himself a bowl of cereal in the kitchen. Still feeling the weight in his heart, or maybe his stomach—he could not figure out his body's anatomy at that point of time—he told Ashfaq about his weird early morning encounter.

Hours later, Yuva returned to the house after his morning class and could hear Ashfaq having an argument in Urdu with someone else. He walked in to the living room to see Ashfaq having an animated discussion with their housemate, Saif, who had had a special guest in his room the previous night. There was no rule against this, so Yuva was surprised that this was being brought up as an issue. When they noticed his presence, Saif immediately darted towards Yuva, clasped his hands, and asked for forgiveness.

'Sorry man, I did not know at all that this was the girl that you liked,' he said. Yuva was now reminded that he had told a fair amount of people, by his standards at least, that he was romantically interested in the girl he had been silently observing for months.

Yuva tried to brush it off. 'It's okay, it's not your . . .' Yuva mumbled in return.

'I don't think you should be serious about her, though. She fools around a lot. I know that for sure. I don't know a lot of things, but that, I know,' he added, as Yuva stood rooted to the spot. Again, he felt his heart sink a little. He hated this feeling. It felt like a bad heartburn, but this one hurt his head at the same time. Yuva merely nodded. Saif let go of his hands and turned around to face Ashfaq.

'She was just drinking at my friend's place and things just escalated and she wanted to come back with me,' he explained further, but by this time Yuva did not want the explanation. 'That's not the kind of girl you want to get committed to man,' he turned around to Yuva again. 'I don't even remember her name properly, to be honest. That's how little we knew each other.'

'Anuradha,' Yuva said after a small pause, his voice breaking as he said her name. That was the first time he understood a dream can be built and destroyed within the same person, without ever having the participation of another individual. He felt the meaning of a heartbreak before ever being in a relationship.

* * *

2013. Easy.

Dinesh woke up in a daze, accompanied by a pounding headache and an immediate realization that he will not have a fresh morning. He always craved for a fresh morning, yet inevitably ended up overdoing his night out when he went drinking—always waking up with a pulsating headache that made him feel miserable for a long time. He felt a weight next to him, and looked around to notice a woman—her bare back facing him, seemingly asleep. He then looked around to make sure he was still in his own room.

He was sure the woman wasn't dressed, and he instantly felt awkward about trying to wake her up. But just as he was staring at her bare back, she turned around, looked at him, and gave a courteous smile. She had no idea what to say either. She was still topless, and seemed comfortable staying that way. Dinesh hadn't had many one-night stands in his life, but all of his previous encounters involved women who would scramble to cover themselves up in the morning, if they hadn't done so already at some point during the night. That was why he hated one-night stands; they just didn't work for him; he needed a connection, and he got one for a few minutes, often while inebriated, but then the next morning they were back to being strangers with each other. It was like going through a break up, time and again, in a loop. The woman turned to lie down and face him instead.

She was a beautiful girl. Dinesh had been looking at her the whole night before, and convinced himself that he never stood a chance with someone like her. As the memories of their encounter returned, he met her gaze, telling himself he had been lucky to have her in bed with him. But he didn't feel like a lucky man. Not knowing what to do next, he went in for a kiss, his hand reaching for her bare breasts. She blocked his face with one hand, and gently pushed away his hand with the other, not showing any emotion. 'Good morning,' she said to him. Looking confused, he returned the greeting.

The woman got up from the bed, and stood naked, at the edge, casually walking and observing his room. 'Is there a towel you can give me? I would like to shower,' she said. He pointed to his flimsy plastic wardrobe and she helped herself to a towel and held it in her hands, standing with her bare back facing him. He continued observing the view. She knew what she was doing. She turned around, as he struggled to take his eyes off her, and smiled mischievously at him. 'I'll need a lift back home,' she said, entering the washroom and locking it behind her.

After a short shower, she got into the black shirt and black jeans she was wearing the night before. She maintained the smile she had been giving him. Both of them had worn black the night before—with their intended destination being a stadium in Kelana Jaya, in the suburb of Petaling Jaya, where all the urban, politically conscious Malaysians had gathered to protest against the general election results from the night before—the opposition party had won the popular vote but lost the election anyway, for a multitude of systemic reasons. The disproportionate design in the system only came into full view after the election had come and gone for many Malaysians. They thought their votes would make a difference. They carried that spirit over to the stadium, all clad in black and showing up by the thousands at the stadium. But people undertaking an act of civil disobedience have a tendency becoming their own enemies—the lines of cars parked and double parked illegally along the Damansara-Puchong highway, one of the main traffic arteries of the greater Klang Valley, prevented thousands more from joining the cause. Just like how they expected their first enthusiastic vote in years to yield immediate results, and a change, Malaysians expected to find parking in a moment's notice. They lacked the patience for the latter, and ended up getting in each other's way. Dinesh never managed to make it to the stadium, and his friend redirected them to a bar, where a friend invited a group of women college students who were on their way to the stadium, but met immovable traffic along the way as well. They decided that drinking as rebels, together, was not a bad alternative. The drinking led to other things.

Dinesh got dressed, picked up his essentials, walked to the front door of his apartment, and held the door for her. She walked gingerly towards him, smiled one more time, and proceeded to share a kiss, but broke it before he tried to let his hands roam her body. She smiled warmly, patted his chest, and said, 'let's go.'

On the way back to her hostel, they stopped for breakfast, both realizing they had pretty much been on a liquid diet the night before. Finally getting some food in their system, Dinesh and the woman sighed in relief, and fell back on their respective chairs, feeling relaxed.

'Do you want to do this again?' she asked him. He looked at her curiously. He did not know what she was asking about in the first place.

'What are you asking about? A drink, or what happened last night? Which part of it would you like to do again?' he asked. She seemed lost in her own thoughts for a while, struggling to find the right words to answer him.

'Look,' he said, realizing that he had not called her by name the whole morning. But he was not one of the assholes who would forget a woman's name after having their way, so he paused for a bit to allow his memory from the previous night return.

'Anu,' he said, restarting his sentence. 'I am not sure if this came up last night. But the whole reason why yesterday happened was because I recently broke up. I wasn't thinking straight. Don't get me wrong—I don't think it was bad— but one-night stands just fuck me up really bad. I'm not one of those guys; I am sorry. So, I don't think I should make hooking up a habit. Trust me, I've tried before, and it didn't do me any good, in here,' he said, holding his chest as though he was having a heartburn. 'Not good for this at all,' he said, his voice muffled by the end. He emptied a glass of water in front of him.

'Oh, no, I wasn't trying to suggest that. By the way, if you sleep repeatedly with the same person, I'm pretty sure that's not called a one-night stand. That's called being friends with benefits,' she said. With every word Anu uttered, Dinesh felt she was every bit an emotionally distant person.

'See, exactly why I can't do it. I don't know the terms. It's still the same for me. I just don't do well hooking up outside of a relationship,' he said.

'What I mean is maybe we can spend time again. Not a one-night stand, not a friends-with-benefits, maybe just a dinner, and then we see where it goes from there,' she said, 'I know, you are probably not used to seeing girls would be forthcoming about asking a guy out, especially among Indians, but I'm not like most girls.'

'I can see that,' he said. 'So are you asking me out?' he asked.

'I felt something different about last night. I won't lie, this wasn't my first rodeo, but I think I actually got along with you in a way that was more than about the sex or the drinking,' she said. He smiled. He was flattered.

'I was looking at you the whole night as well before we had a chance to talk. I thought I wouldn't have a chance, all the other guys were trying so hard,' he said.

'Yes, they were. But somehow, you grabbed my attention,' she said.

For the first time, he noticed her looking somewhat cheerful, even accompanied by a slight blush. He enjoyed looking at her reaction, and the knowledge that he might have flattered her after all. But his face changed soon after that, as he digested everything they had said to each other so far.

'You know, I think I could say that I do like you, at least from the little amount of time we spent with each other,' he said, hesitating to complete his sentence.

'I feel like there's a "but" coming . . .' she said.

He smiled ruefully to himself. 'I don't know how to say this. Yesterday night, in the midst of us doing it,' he said, raising his eyebrows, hoping she would recall something that would prevent the need of him verbally revisiting the details with her. But Anu merely nodded her head. 'You told me things. About your past. Not just general storyline. But details. Described some guys, described some acts, described some details,' he said.

Anu buried her face in her hands. 'Oh my fucking god.'

'I'm trying to say this in a way that you can understand. I am not saying I have problems dating someone who has been with other men. But, right now, after all that has happened, all I have in my mind are these images—because of how you told them to me—just images of you and other men. My last relationship ended because my partner, well, cheated on me.'

'So, you think I will cheat on you as well, and that is inevitable given my past,' she said. Dinesh thought his words came across wrong. He was not going to punish another woman for his ex-partner's indiscretions. He half-expected Anu to be angry, or worse, storm off, but she was surprisingly still calm and seated. She was objectively listening to what he had to say.

'It's not that. Whatever happened with you before us is none of my business. It is horrible of me to judge you based on that. It would be, because that is not how I am judging this situation. You see, I was with her . . . for several years. And since I know what she had done, these images keep coming back—questioning what was real and what was not. Questioning which part of the relationship were lies,' his voice started breaking. With a combination of a headache, the leftover alcohol in his system, and the memories he was revisiting, he was now on the verge of tears, though he fought them back, hard.

'Now I have these images as well. It's like we haven't even started and I'm already seeing these images of you with other men,' he said. 'Ideally, I should be giving us a chance—my ideology, the way I see relationships, even the way I see you tells me I should give us a chance. But, these images, they are painful to live with. I can't ignore that pain. Maybe it's just me. Maybe I'm not ready. Maybe I'm still hurting a little too much. I am not sure what or why or how. But that's the problem, I don't have that answer, that clarity, yet,' he said.

Anu remained rooted to the table and looked at him intently. Dinesh could sense disappointment in her reaction.

'What I'm trying to say is, I do wish I did not have to decline you, asking me out. I wish, I just wish, we hadn't met this way,' he said.

She put her hand out across the table. He wondered if she was offering to hold his hand. As he reached out, he realized she was passing him a tissue. He had lost the battle against his tears. But she wasn't doing much better either, tears had welled up in her eyes, and she quickly used her tissue. He wasn't sure why he was feeling such strong emotions about someone he had just met. It could be the alcohol still in his system, making him more emotional than usual. But he looked at her reaction and knew he wasn't alone. She had felt something too. He wasn't imagining it.

* * *

Wallflower and Easy. 2014.

'I'm going to ask you something, and I want you to answer me honestly,' Anu said, taking the first large sip of a pint of beer, sitting cross-legged on a cushioned wooden chair under the dizzying lights of the pub she was in, mixed with the lights of the surrounding shopping mall. She was having to speak louder than her usual volume and tone thanks to the deafening noise around them.

'Shit, I thought we came here because it would be quiet,' Anu said. Her friends shifted in their seat.

'You know, you used to like loud places,' one of them said.

'Yes, used to,' she sighed, looking at the surroundings.

'So, back to your question,' Wei Ling, who was sitting next to her, interrupted Anu's train of thoughts.

'Oh yeah, do you think I'm easy?' she asked.

Wei Ling looked blankly at her friend for half a minute. 'Why are you asking that question?' she asked.

'It's okay. Answer me. It's fine, be honest,' Anu said.

'Maybe, yes?' Wei Ling answered almost immediately after that. Anu pouted her lips, and nodded ever so slowly.

Both of them started entertaining other friends' collective chatter about their college memories, giggling and laughing out loud about not-so-funny stories that were made funny just because of the passion with which some of them were narrating it.

The chatter slowly died down, and they all went back to having conversation silos in pairs. 'But that was in college,' Wei Ling returned to the topic after the brief intermission.

'College wasn't that long ago,' Anu said.

'But it is still different. We graduated almost a year ago, so yes. One year is a long time. So, the question is, what is going on with you nowadays?' Wei Ling asked.

'I don't know. Work is work. I just started asking this question nowadays, you know—like how difficult am I supposed to make it for someone before I allow them to be embedded in my life? I just . . . think about it a lot,' Anu said.

'Tell me, how many people have you slept with since leaving college? At work maybe?'

Anu grimaced.

'Hell, no way. I don't eat where I shit, or whichever order you want to put it in. It's just dating sites, a couple of guys, and somehow it just isn't the same anymore nowadays. Now I am just extra conscious about not wanting to be seen as . . . easy,' she said.

Wei Ling sighed. She turned her attention completely towards Anu, ignoring the seven other women who were on the same table. 'Honey, it's not about easy or difficult. It's not about how you want people to see you. As long as I've known you, you fulfilled your needs, got what you wanted, and did not care what people thought of you. We never had this conversation before but you knew you made it easy for men to get in sexually with you, and you were okay with it. You were not oblivious.'

Anu paid all her attention to Wei Ling, shimmering her red dress, red pumps and red lipstick. She could not help but notice the roles being reversed.

In college, Wei Ling never stood out. She used to sit cross legged on a chair in a mamak, not drawing attention to herself, more than happy to be a part of a social gathering and just partaking in the gossip without trying to impress. Anu was always the girl who made sure she drew that extra attention to herself; she was the one who was dressed up for the most mundane outings that they had together.

'I think you have to continue to be selfish—the question rather is, have your wants and needs changed from what they were in college? Probably. I don't see you trying to impress anyone today. You didn't then, and you are not trying to, now. If you didn't start then, you shouldn't start now. Forget the sex; value, and protect your heart, and your emotions. Everything else you do, easy or difficult, will stand guided by how much you want to protect your feelings,' she said, putting her hands on Anu's chest. Anu was wearing a loose T-shirt, and Wei Ling's moment of profoundness was marred as her hand slipped to the top of Anu's breasts. 'Babe, that's protecting my boobs.' Both of them chuckled and laughed, loud enough to attract the attention of the seven others, who were disturbed from their little mini-conversations across the table.

'What are you two laughing about?' one of them asked.

'About the fact that she tried to give some sagely advice but ended up touching my boobs,' Anu said, laughing.

'There's always something going on with you two,' another friend said.

Wei Ling returned with an epilogue at the end of night, while both of them walked through the dimly lit parking lot, looking at pictures they took of their parking bays to make sure neither of them got lost looking for their cars.

'When we were young, Anu, some of us hurt deeply, but we moved quickly. Those of us who didn't hurt, just moved, going through the motions. But remember, this is adulthood now. Everything we do leaves a mark. Everything others do to us, leaves a mark. Wounds don't heal as fast. They don't just leave us with a memory to laugh at down the road, but they leave with visible scars. It will show on your face. We are no longer immune now. So, don't just ask about what you want now. Ask yourself what you want—five, ten, or twenty years from now. Because everything you do from now will help determine something for that future self.' By the time Wei Ling had finished sharing her profound wisdom, they had both spotted their cars that were parked not too far from each other. Anu reached out and hugged Wei Ling, who, probably for the first time in their friendship, drank more than Anu. Armed with an iced coffee, Anu got into her car, started the engine, and sighed calmly. She opened her Tinder account and lazily browsed through a couple of pictures, without really looking. She had her moods. There are no days and there are yes days. This felt like a yes kind of day—not to have someone over, but rather, to flirt from a safe distance, sleep early, and wake up fresh and set in the morning. Her phone pinged as she was about to put it down and start driving. She looked at the notifications; she had a match on Tinder.

She had matched with someone. She looked at his picture and stared at it for a long time. She felt like she knew him, but she could not figure out where she had seen him. She looked at his name—Yuva.

* * *

Anu's eyes were transfixed on the outline of the moon in the sky. It was a rare night—the skies were surprisingly clear in Kuala Lumpur. She saw stars littered all over the sky and she tried to feel the wind in her face. But it remained warm and humid, and she began to sweat under her simple T-shirt. She looked at Yuva, sitting next to her on the bench of an almost empty park, his eyes scanning a lot more things than the moon and the skies, fiddling his fingers. She felt his hand occupying the small gap between them on the bench a couple of times, but he didn't stay there for more than a few seconds.

She flipped her hair and looked at him—he was becoming increasingly uncomfortable. 'Why?' he blurted.

'I should ask that; you are looking at everywhere but at me. Is there something bothering you?' she asked.

'I was just finding a way to ask you if it would be okay to . . . hold hands,' he said, reaching out with his right hand, and keeping his palm open. She almost held his hand, but hesitated. Instead, she went for his disheveled hair, and combed it with her bare hands, with a warm chuckle.

'Before we go there, there's something we need to talk about,' she said, and she stopped caressing his hair and looked directly at him. His face changed.

'Are we never going to talk about the night we met for the first time? I feel it just lingering there,' she said. It was clear Yuva was not ready to have this conversation. But she was never going to start anything with him without having that conversation.

'It was the first time you saw me. It wasn't the first time I saw you,' he said. She knew he had strong feelings about that night.

'Come on, I was a different person back then. If you don't believe that, you shouldn't be wanting to hold my hands,' she said.

'I do, it is just difficult to forget sometimes. When I saw you, I was this innocent guy, really new to this city, and somehow, I thought we had a connection. That we would come to this moment. But that night was a very early shock to the system. It's like being wounded,' he said.

'But I didn't hurt you. I didn't know you. Maybe you should have come and spoken to me, in all those times you saw me and kept quiet.'

'Do you think things would have been different if I had done that? Maybe you wouldn't have been involved with so many guys,' he asked. She knew he was emotionally fragile. But beneath that layer of discomfort, he wanted to hold her hands. Unlike others, he was able to look beyond her past, and that was already saying a lot. Yuva had tried his luck in the months they had known each other—he went in for a kiss, sometimes more than a kiss, and she had pushed him away on numerous occasions, Dinesh's words haunting her in the back of her mind—she had to do it right with this man. She was afraid he would refer to her past promiscuity while protesting to her refusals. At times, it felt like he was thinking about it, he was asking that terrible question with his eyes, but the moment lingered and passed. He respected her dignity. The only alternative for him was to feel like he was her saviour. Telling him about her past was a heavy process—she wasn't about to tell him that she had slept around not looking for a cure for some depression, but instead, because she simply wanted it, and more importantly, because it felt like liberty.

What's important was how she felt now—knowing deep down she wasn't the same person. She no longer wanted that. She wanted that moment, when he held out his hands. She wanted to be important for someone else, and she wanted to care for a person other than herself. It felt like staring at a skeleton, and pulling a cover on it just as it was about to be ripped completely open.

'Yes, you would have saved me. And I wouldn't have had to go through all that. But you are here now, and it is not too late. If you are still okay, you can still offer your hands,' she said, leaning on his shoulders. She felt like she was lying to him. He offered his hand, and they held hands for the first time, after four months. Now, it felt right. Because she had waited, because he was worth it, because she had made herself worth it. She forgot about the lie.

Chapter Eleven

INTAN

November. 2018.

The sun was setting off in the horizon. Dark clouds gathered around it, not the kind that signalled impending darkness, but ones that signalled the distinct possibility of some night monsoon rain. With the wind starting to blow in her face, and the moisture of the impending rain starting to tickle her hands, Anu stood still, looking at an old Chinese man, in his motorbike cart, keeping the flame of his wok alive to fry a char kuey teow, stir fried rice cake strips. Her stomach churned, and she longed for a serving, but she quickly remembered the situation.

There was a short, rusted green bench near where she stood, and she helped herself to a seat. The car was several feet in front her and Yuva stood behind the car, pacing restlessly but never wanting to make eye contact with her. They had haphazardly stopped near a random shopping lot area at Teluk Intan the moment she told him that she wanted a break. She looked at the dimmed lights of the Teluk Intan leaning tower, often labelled Malaysia's own version of Pisa, before her attention turned to him again.

'Will you come and sit here?' she said loudly so that he could hear her.

He looked at her, shrugged, and shook his head in disagreement. Yuva could not decide if he wanted to persuade her or be outraged by her. He was oscillating between two very distinct moods, and he could not make an intellectual decision as to which mood he was going to stick with when he starts talking to her, inevitably.

'Please,' she said, tapping the small space next to her. He ceded to her requests. He sat on the edge of the bench.

'What are you thinking?' she asked, looking at him, trying to get him to look at her.

'Nothing is wrong with us. Is there someone else?' he asked, after seemingly hesitating to ask the question.

'No! You asked this in the car and I said no. And, I'm going to say it again. There isn't someone else. I've not cheated on you, if that makes you happy,' she said.

'Nothing makes me happy,' he said.

'That is the problem, isn't it? Nothing seems to make you happy anymore. I sure as hell can't make you happy anymore. You are always grumpy around me; you are constantly sulking with me. You want to marry me but somehow you manage to make me feel like you are doing me a favour,' she said.

'I am just going through a difficult time. All couples have problems, right? We work through them; we don't run at the first sight of trouble,' he sprang to life, standing on his feet, attracting the gaze of the negligible amount of people prowling the area.

'I have spent four years with you, Yuva. That is not bolting at the first sight of trouble. You think this is the first time I've felt like this in our relationship? You have no idea . . .' she said, realizing her voice was breaking with emotion. She retained her composure, not wanting to have an emotional argument with him in public.

'And, I'm asking for a break. I'm not seeing anyone else. I will not be seeing anyone else. I just need some time for myself. More importantly, I think you really need some time for yourself. Please find out what it is that makes you so unhappy with a lot of things in your life. You have this car, up until maybe yesterday, you had me. You have a sister you can turn to. You have parents who allowed you to bring your girlfriend into their home, however much they frowned upon it. You have a decent job. But none of that ever seemed to matter. I don't know what it is that you are chasing here.'

Yuva wanted to protest; he tried to say something, but right at the moment, the rain started pouring incessantly. Yuva stood rooted to the spot.

'What are you waiting for?' she asked, looking at the car.

'I am thinking if we should part ways here; you've been so unfair to me today,' he said, as both of them started trembling and shivering with the rain's increasing intensity.

'Yuva, if you leave me here, that's a break up. That's it. There's no coming back from that. So, I want you to think very carefully about what you are going to say next,' she said.

Yuva sighed.

'Get in the car.'

'You get in and wait for me. I want to get something,' she said, walking to the rear passenger door, and taking out the umbrella, before heading to the roadside hawker, who was assessing if he should close his business for the day due to the rain. Yuva got into the car and duly waited for her, groaning to himself in the process. He turned off the radio when a romantic song came on air that reminded him of better times he had had with Anu.

'Uncle, can you make one more?'

The man looked at her blankly for a moment, thinking if he had misheard her, before nodding in agreement.

She got in the car after several minutes, carrying a soggy polystyrene food container and a pair of slim chopsticks that were also made soggy by the rain. 'We do have food packed from home,' Yuva said, meekly. He seemed a little taken aback by her assertiveness earlier.

'I'm sorry, but I can't eat your mom's cooking. Not after you contemplated leaving me here. It's your mom's cooking, so you eat it,' she said, while slowly opening the packaging for the meal she had just bought. She took one long look at Yuva, knowing full well she was about to break one of his most beloved cardinal rules—no one should eat in his car, him included. But Anu was hungry, and these little details were no longer getting in the way.

'I will pay you for the entirety of this journey—fuel, toll and even something on top of it; I am hungry and I want to do this. This is happening, you have to accept it,' she said, keeping her eyes locked on him, as she helped herself to dinner.

'You know, this is what I am talking about. The person I got together with, all those years ago, was one of the most accepting persons in the world. And now, you are struggling to just accept. Accept people for who they are. Choices they make. For their own beliefs,' she said, taking a bite. After a few minutes, she extended her hand out carefully and held a chopstick worth of noodles near his mouth. Initially reluctant, he opened his mouth and took it in.

'Thanks,' he mumbled. The unmistakable smell of char kuey teow lingered in the car for the next hour, intensified by the air conditioning, until the rain subsided and Yuva was able to roll down his windows to let the air out.

* * *

'I will miss you,' Yuva said, sounding like a completely different person by the time they reached the outer limits of Kuala Lumpur. He did not elaborate. He wanted her to say it back.

'Hmm,' she said, barely nodding, with a faint acknowledgement.

'That's all?' he asked.

'I need time. I need space. If you still want me to say what you expect to hear, how are we going to work this out?' she raised her voice; almost pleading, begging him not to have another emotional outburst. He was still on the precipice, hanging by a thread. She wanted to make him feel better, but things had come to a point where any attempt to make him feel better would be at the expense of her own well-being.

'What am I going to tell my parents? What am I going to tell my sister?' he asked.

'You can tell your parents whatever you choose to tell them. Or not tell them at all, depending on how things are between us in the coming days. I will tell Geetha,' she said.

'What do you mean; are you going to tell my sister that you dumped me?' he asked, exasperated. He was feeling the injustice of it all. She does not get to cut ties with him and choose to retain some of his family members.

'She's your sister, yes. But she is also my friend. But I won't rob you of your pleasure, if you indeed want to tell her, you can tell her first. I will speak to her after,' she said.

'But she . . .'

'And I did not dump you, I asked for a break. There is a difference. If you insist on saying that I have dumped you, then you are closing the doors for any possible reconciliation,' she said.

'How am I supposed to react? You were all loving towards me until a couple of hours ago and now you sound like some stranger, putting on conditions. How long am I supposed to wait? Why do you assume I would want to reconcile?' he asked.

Anu stirred awake. She was so caught up in her own desire to stand up for herself that she was acting in complete contrast with how her behaviour with him had been for the past four years.

'I'm sorry. I am reacting badly. This is not me. I am struggling to process this too,' she said. 'I need to figure some things out about myself, too. I, too, have changed as a person in these past four years. So, I need to think about who I am and what I want, out of the marriage, and out of all of this.'

'Of course, you changed a lot. And you changed because of me, and now . . .' he was stretching his luck, seeing how much he could get away with. But the moment Yuva said it, and realized he could not take it back, he knew he had just damaged any chance of an amicable goodbye. She remained silent as the glittering lights of Kuala Lumpur skyscrapers came into view.

'That road leads to Sentral, right?' she said, her voice strained with a mix of anger and disappointment. He had never heard her that way before. She was referring to the city's main public transit hub. He nodded.

'Drop me there,' she said, some thirty kilometers before their journey was supposed to end.

'But, I was going to drop you off.'

'I can find my way back home. Thanks for driving up till this point. There are trains,' her tone was commanding. He felt like he had lost her before he had the chance to win her back. She did not look back when she got down from the car, and took her luggage. She took out cash from her purse placed in it in the dashboard compartment. He had never seen her this angry.

'Just remember something—I changed because I wanted to grow as a person, and you were such an accepting person. I didn't change so that you would accept me. But now it is clear—you weren't so accepting, after all. It's like I'm a sinner, and I repented, thanks to you. Thanks for making me feel that way.'

He wanted to retort, but realized he didn't have any points to argue with. 'Let me know when you are back home, at least?' he said. He wanted to get down from the car, but something told him she did not want him to be anywhere near her. She pretended as though she didn't hear his question, and walked off, dragging off her luggage clumsily. It was apparent that she had not originally planned to commute with her luggage in tow. She went through the doors of the station, went down the escalators, and instead found a resting bench, before rummaging through her bag for tissues. An auxiliary policeman walked to her and felt compelled to ask if she was okay—with tears running down her face, and the tissues barely doing anything to conceal her misery.

Her worst fears had come true—Yuva had never truly looked beyond her past. He claimed to have been able to look past the moment, but he had always harboured it. He was always going to use it against her just to hurt her, or to make her feel small. He managed to hold his tongue for four years, and for four years, she lived as his partner thinking she would never have to revisit the events of her youth again. One question had disintegrated a four-year journey.

Chapter Twelve

ENTROPY

December 2018.

Things were gradually disappearing from Geetha's home, but the reason was only a mystery for those who had periodically visited her home. She was not only getting rid of Prakash's possessions, but also things that she felt she no longer needed or wanted. Her shoe collection shrank drastically, half her wardrobe was donated, she sent multiple gifts of wine bottles to both her and Prakash's friends, clearing out her wine collection. Her 2,500 square feet of space was becoming increasingly empty and bare, making her feel like she was staying in an unnecessarily big space. With far fewer things in her possession and a far more simpler lifestyle, Geetha contemplated relieving Maria of her duties, but swatted away the idea as soon as it appeared; knowing full well that Maria would just end up at another house, not knowing what she might need to go through. Instead, Geetha kept her on and gave her fewer things to do. She watched more Netflix than Geetha did, she only spent a few hours a day in the kitchen, and the rest of her time was spent keeping Geetha company so that the latter would not be reminded of any emptiness in the house.

Anu stopped visiting, following her separation from Yuva, not wanting to make things awkward between her and her brother. Geetha didn't argue against it, but she wished Anu would stop being too considerate of the former's relationship with her brother, because Yuva never bothered to show up and check on her either. Her pro bono client was holed up in her house, jobless, and seemingly on the precipice of depression. Geetha was standing on a metaphorical cliff, and the only thing that kept her going was the court case, but that was nowhere near being heard in an open court. It seemed like everything was going wrong for everyone at the same time. Geetha longed for some attention, but everyone had their own demons to fight.

Geetha's mother-in-law, Devi, had showed up at her doorstep five months after her son's passing, just as she was done grieving her own loss. She wanted to visit and also spend some time in the house that her son had loved so much over the years. Geetha was happy to make space for another person in the house, given how empty it was becoming. But Devi's visit became so much more than that.

'I'm just here for a few days,' she had said, having showed up with one trolley bag, and with all the jewellery that she possessed. At times, Geetha squirmed looking at the number of bangles, necklaces and anklets Devi had—thinking about how heavy it must be to be wearing all of them at the same time. The days turned into weeks and Devi showed no signs of leaving. It became clear to Geetha that her mother-in-law had no intention of leaving the house anytime soon. She started teaching Maria how to make traditional South Indian and Telugu dishes, and both of them stocked up the fridge with a potpourri of meals every day, half of which Geetha never consumed.

'Ma, this is a waste of food,' Geetha said to her one month into her stay, as she collected several lunchboxes of old curries and dishes that she had to dispose. That did nothing to change the way Devi went about things—for her, excess was better than having someone in the family go hungry. She fed Geetha the way she would have fed her son, was he still alive and around and walking about the house. Both of them never made a single mention of his infidelity with each other. Geetha loathed him, but spoke kind words about him in front of his mother. But when the living arrangement veered towards becoming more permanent, she wasn't sure she could keep quiet much longer.

'Ma, do you not want to go back?' Geetha couldn't find a more subtle way of broaching the topic after dinner one day, as they sat on the dining table, drinking green tea. If she did not ask the question, she was sure she would end up having an outburst in the near future. It was a possibility she wanted to avoid at all costs.

Devi mumbled a series of circumstances that Geetha had become all too acquainted with by now. Devi was just finding excuses to prolong her stay.

'Ma,' she interrupted, putting her hands on top of Devi's ageing, trembling, wrinkled hands, inching a little closer. Devi moved her hands and her bangles clanked. 'It's been months since he went. Both of us need to move on from it. I'm sorry, but I think I can't keep having this arrangement if you want me to move on,' she said.

'You want to move on? Remarry, and stuff?' Devi asked.

'I don't know. I don't have the answers. But I need to live by myself,' she said. Geetha had never decided that before, but having Devi live in the same space gave her much needed clarity.

'Oh,' Devi said, seemingly surprised and confused. 'Actually, we were hoping to come here,' she added.

'Who's we?' Geetha asked.

'Both me and your father-in-law. If he's around we would have asked him and had a conversation with him about it.

But he's not, so I had no idea how to ask you,' she said, in a sympathetic tone.

'What happened?'

Devi reached out for her phone, which was at the centre of the dining table, and spent the next five minutes looking through the gallery of her iPhone with her trembling hands, looking for a picture.

'You should do something about the tremors,' Geetha said, as she handed Devi a glass of water. Devi, ignoring the glass of water, showed her the picture of a bank letter.

'That's how much we were paying for the house in Ipoh, every month. We haven't paid for it since . . .' she fell silent. 'And now there's a letter. We can't afford it. Business has not been good for several years now.'

'So Prakash had been paying for it?' Geetha asked, again being reminded of how little she knew the man she was married to for five years. Devi nodded.

'This is something that should be discussed, ma. Can the others chip in?' Geetha added, referring to Prakash's siblings, none of whom were as financially well off as him. 'No, it is too much for any of them.'

'You want to shift here as a result, but what happens to the house?' Devi sighed. 'Maybe we could rent it out and see we can cover the balance. Or have someone chip in.' Devi's face looked sullen, like she had lost much more than her son. Geetha felt sorry for her and her family, but yet again, no one was asking or thinking about what she wanted to do.

'We could stay there if you want the private space; I can understand. But we will need help paying for the house,' she said. Again, there was no question, just a suggestion. She had a cheating husband who took up a financial commitment without asking her and now she's being asked to take over that commitment. Devi was taking the long route in asking Geetha to pay for the house, and Geetha was adamant she was not going to fall for it. She would be paying through her nose for two houses with her individual income.

'Then we should have you both come over here,' she said.

'Are you sure?' Devi asked.

'Yes, ma, I am afraid we don't have an alternative. I will try to find a tenant for the house, and we will see what can be done for the shortfall,' she added.

The next evening, Geetha stopped by the side of the expressway while on her way back home, consumed by another anxiety attack. When she recovered, she broke down crying in the car, before wiping off her tears like nothing had happened, and rerouting her journey to a bar. For the first time in her life, she drank alone. She had always claimed that drinking alone was the first sign of alcoholism. She was sure she was not about to turn into an alcoholic, but she was also sure she had deeper psychological problems that needed addressing. She needed space. Instead, she was being suffocated.

She scrolled through social media mindlessly and came across a post by Sabitha—she was having a drink in another bar not too far from her. Geetha sent out a cry for help, against the protests of her brooding ego.

'Hey there,' she said in an Instagram message. 'I think you have to come rescue me.' Minutes later, Sabitha arrived, with a male friend in tow. She introduced him, but Geetha was too lost in the woods to be aware of his name.

'What's going on with you?' Sabitha asked.

'Long story,' Geetha said, curtly. The guy next to Sabitha was unbelievably quiet. He ordered his drink and tried hard to be absent from the conversation. Geetha shot him a couple of very strong looks, but he did not respond.

'What's your deal?' Geetha asked him, realizing she did not sound like herself at all. Drinking after an anxiety attack was probably a bad idea, she thought to herself, before taking a large sip from the glass of red wine in front her. Sabitha was sharing her wine bottle. Her friend was calmly powering through his beer.

'What do you mean?' he asked.

'You are extremely calm,' she said.

'He just didn't want to interfere in our conversation,' Sabitha said.

'Well, my name is Anand,' he said, seemingly formulating his reply for some time.

'Wow,' Geetha chuckled. Anand means 'calm' in Sanskrit.

As the night developed and disintegrated, Geetha realized why Anand was there. Sabitha was struggling to cope with work ever since she had come out to her family, wondering if her rather dramatic coming out spelled the end of her relationship with her parents. He was there to babysit Sabitha, and ended up babysitting Geetha as well.

Anand ensured both of them drank within the limits that allowed their limbs and trajectory to work accurately. He made sure both of them got back home safely. As Geetha opened the door to her unit, she found her father-in-law, waiting in the living room, watching a midnight news segment. It was the first time she was meeting him since he moved in to the house. She stumbled around, taking off her shoes, feeling the pressure and judgement of his watchful eyes.

'Hi, Nana,' she said, slurring, as she finally managed to stand up straight. She started addressing her in-laws as father and mother in Telugu, with the hopes that they will be as close to her as her own parents, when she married into the family. But that was the closest they ever got during Geetha's marriage.

'Hi, have you had your dinner?' he asked, making no mention of her state. She felt like she was fifteen, back to living with her parents, and caught coming home drunk.

'Yes,' she said, and darted off to her room—which was now her only private space. She ran a hot shower and refreshed herself. Some of the alcohol wore off, and some memories of the night returned. She realized she didn't drive home; Anand did. Anand drove Geetha's car, dropped Sabhi back to her apartment— where Anand also lived—and then drove Geetha home, parked her car at its bay, made sure she got into the lift, before he took an e-hailing cab back to the bar, where he collected his own car, and finally drove back home.

And then, she remembered the most important detail of the night—she had tried to kiss him on the drive back. Horrified, she closed her eyes, hoping the memory would go away in the morning. She woke up a few hours later with a splitting headache. She expected that. But the memory stayed. She had tried to kiss her cousin's classmate. She had tried to kiss a man who was almost a decade younger than her. And he had slithered expertly to avoid the kiss. She had made a fool of herself.

'I will never see him again,' she told herself.

* * *

Lakshmi was lying on a wooden bed frame, cushioned by a thin mattress, looking at the discolored ceiling and a wobbly ceiling fan that she was convinced would fall over her any time. But when she closed her eyes, she could see a sky of stars, interrupted by the clouds. This was a real image—stored somewhere far in her memories, and she couldn't remember where the memory was from. The chemicals in her system now were doing a phenomenal job in bringing out those memories for her again.

'Are you okay?' a voice next to her reminded her that she wasn't alone. Her absent mind returned to reality, and started deducting and recalling for a few seconds—who is the person next to her? Before she could finish thinking, the face loomed on top of her, blocking the ceiling view. She could smell the strong nicotine on his breath, which was now being overwhelmed by the smell of burnt grass in the air. She thought he was going to smother her, but instead, he stared into her eyes. 'Are you okay?' he asked again, in his broken Malay, throwing in a hand gesture for good measure.

She gestured that she was okay, and giggled for no reason. She could not reason anything with herself. She wished she could react to the world's chaos with such wanton abandonment when that not smoking a spliff.

'Do you want another drag?' still hovering over her, Bobby took a long drag and held out the remaining spliff.

She gestured that she was fine, her attention now shifting to the large dragon tattoo running from the top of Bobby's shoulder to his chest. He was wearing a white singlet, and a gold imitation chain hung from his neck. He had fantastic hair, which fell on his forehead, but he was the only one in his family who managed to grow a small, albeit visible, beard. Laskhmi never got around to pronouncing his full name, which began with Xiang. When she asked him what his name was, he told her it was Bobby. No one else called him Bobby. A number of Chinese people in Malaysia tended to have English names, or easy to pronounce monikers for the benefit of their non-Chinese friends, and at times, their fellow Chinese friends as well. But Bobby was something he had come up with because that the only 'Hindustani' film he had ever seen—a 1973 movie about adolescent romance. She would have never wagered on her ending up on the same bed with a man from another race, let alone a Malaysian Chinese. She only spoke Tamil and Malay; and she barely spoke any English. Apart from Mandarin and Cantonese, everything else Bobby spoke was in a broken, incoherent form. However, the moment he introduced himself and attempted to flirt with her with the little Tamil he had gathered over the years, she knew she had to give him a chance. He was, after all, her bike mechanic.

He slumped back on the bed beside her, closed his eyes, and seemed to let out a sigh of pleasure. He snuggled next to her, his head resting on her shoulders. She had been holding off sex from him—and he had taken that in his stride well, biding his time and finding many other ways to spend time with her. She had made him watch Tamil language movies featuring her favourite southern hero, Vijay Joseph. His movies were often filled with extreme chivalry, stunts that made little physical sense, extended monologues and nauseating camera movements. But she still loved to watch him on screen and she could not explain why.

When he finally came around to ask her to try something new, she thought the conversation was eventually going to lead to sex. Instead, he offered to smoke up together. Lakshmi never had alcohol in her life, but she was not against smoking up grass and figuring out its effects. She thought she would reward him after smoking up for not having pressured her into sex for almost half a year. But now, she was too lazy, hungry and giggly to get up and do something about it. With his eyes closed, she was sure he was feeling the same. The sex had to wait.

Her phone rang and woke both of them from their slumber. Still in her light blue factory shirt, Lakshmi groaned and shifted to her left, lifting her phone from the bedside table. Her sister was calling her. She was in no mood for a conversation, but Kasturi rarely ever called her. She picked up the phone, and the noise her sister made from the other end of the line seemed to flood her brain with so much information, that she could not process it.

'Shut up,' she raised her voice. 'And repeat everything calmly.'

Kasturi had a loud voice that could wake the entire neighbourhood. Her voice steered Bobby awake, and he looked at Lakshmi with concern, as the voice on the other end of the line seemed to convey something serious.

'Where are you? What time is it?' Kasturi asked.

'Can you stop being a mother?' Laskhmi asked back, her ego bruised at having her younger sister, whom she had cared for her whole life, displaying some motherly instincts with her.

'You should be back home by now,' Kasturi added. Lakshmi stayed quiet, rubbing her eyes and her face to become fully awake.

'Come back home immediately, there's something you need to see,' Kasturi continued. She probably realized how strong she had sounded on the phone throughout the conversation, so she mellowed again, and added in for good measure, 'Please, ka, it's urgent.'

Laskhmi was more concerned by the pleading in her sister's voice rather than the borderline yelling earlier. 'Coming,' she said, firmly, and ended the call.

'I need to go back,' she said to Bobby. He got up from the bed, went to the dressing table, and asked her to open her eyes wide. He applied eye drops to reduce the reddening of her eyes—she looked in the mirror within seconds and she looked as good as fresh. She grabbed her helmet from the bedside table, and walked slowly to her motorbike, parked outside his house, which was attached to the mechanic shed that he and his family had been running for over three decades. Bobby came outside just as she started her motorbike. 'Do you want me to drop you?' he asked.

'No, it's not time for my sister to see you yet,' she said sternly.

'Remember, don't think about rushing home. If you panic, you will not be riding home well. Just relax, and you will be home fine,' he said. She remembered his words well and she rode back home calmly for fifteen minutes and parked the bike soundly at the porch, without giving away any sign that she was stoned. The front door was open, as if waiting for her arrival. She walked in as fast as she could without losing her bearings, and saw Karthi slouched on the floor, leaning against the wall between the living room and the kitchen. Kasturi was sitting opposite her, keeping a watchful eye.

'What happened?' Lakshmi asked, becoming increasingly worried. She noticed a small pencil blade next to Kasturi on the floor. Kasturi stood up, leaned over Karthi, who looked exhausted, disheveled, and clearly had been in tears. Her forearm was covered by a blue, damp kitchen cloth. Kasturi removed the cloth. Still standing peering over, Laskhmi saw four cuts on the forearm, all done using the pencil blade. The cuts were not deep enough to cause persistent bleeding, but they were enough to leave scars. Karthi sniffled. Lakshmi watched in horror.

'We can't leave her alone,' Kasturi said, holding Karthi's arm, as if it was going to fall off if she wasn't holding it any firmer.

* * *

It had been a full three months since Sabitha had last spoken to her parents. Their relationship had been gradually declining, and neither she nor them were doing anything to arrest the decline. She put her phone on silent for long stretches of the day, hoping to pick it up much later and see a missed call from home. She repeated this act during any free time she had, it managed her own restlessness, and forced her to occupy herself with other things. She scoured dating sites, but never responded to a call for a date. Having read about the fate of a teacher who was loud and proud about her sexuality, she was afraid of being spotted or being called out for being gay by one of her colleagues. Anything that she did, needed to be very discreet. She couldn't afford to lose her colleagues after losing her family. Having been consumed by inhibited bravery when she came out to her family, she was now consumed by almost unreasonable levels of fear.

Her thoughts continued clouding her even when she attempted to watch a romantic movie with Anand one day at his house. Lying on his shoulders, she could only think about ways where she could mend herself to please her parents and her extended family.

'Initially, when we became friends after our break-up, did you still have feelings for me?' she asked Anand. He merely nodded, nonchalantly. She thought the question would make him pause the movie, but it didn't.

'Do you still?' she asked, with an almost childlike demand for attention. His eyes were fixed on the laptop screen in front of them. 'No,' he said.

A few minutes passed before she had another question, and this time she went for the jugular. 'Do you want to try kissing? See if we feel anything, still?' she asked. This time, he paused the film.

'What the fuck is wrong with you, man?' he went directly from being calm to being annoyed to no end. She realized the foolishness of her question even before she asked it. She wanted a reaction from him, and she got one.

'I don't know what's wrong with me,' she said, holding her head.

Anand sighed. 'I'm guessing we are not watching the movie tonight, then,' he said.

'What else do you suggest we do?' she asked.

'Anything that will make you stop asking such stupid questions. Or making insane suggestions. The movie is clearly not doing the job,' he said, exasperated. 'You should just call them instead of torturing yourself like this. And in case you didn't notice, you are torturing me as well,' he added.

Just as he uttered the words, Sabitha's phone rang. She looked at the screen and was startled to see Yuva's name as the caller. She showed it to Anand, who shrugged and asked her to answer it. 'Maybe that's the sign you have been waiting for from your family, albeit indirectly,' he said. He walked to the kitchen to make himself a cup of tea as she answered the call. He had a feeling it was going to be a long night. As he took the first sip of the hot tea, Sabitha appeared behind him, with a worried and confused look on her face.

'He's coming here,' she said. 'He said he needed to talk to me.'

'And what did you say?' he asked.

'Well, he is coming here. What do you think I said?' she retorted.

'I don't ever need to get married if I continue having you around, especially under the same roof,' he said.

She smirked. 'I can't fulfil all your other needs though,' she smiled mischievously. 'As if you guys give me any time for that,' he said, walking back into the room and resuming the film. He resolved to finish watching it that night, regardless of the interruptions the universe was going to throw in his direction.

'You guys?' she followed him and stood by the room door.

'Yes, either it's you, or your cousin sister, or now your cousin brother showing up at midnight. I don't have time to think about anything else, do I?' he said, laced with sarcasm.

Yuva showed up sooner than expected, with disheveled hair and reddened eyes. Anand stayed in the room as Sabitha attended to her cousin, fixing him a cup of tea and turning on the living room lights as he sat on the sofa.

'Is everything alright?' she asked, as she placed the cup of hot, steaming tea on the glass table in front of Yuva, before joining him on the sofa. He nodded almost by instinct, before realizing that his answer was practically a lie.

'Not actually,' he said, rubbing his head and his already messy hair further.

'Well, I don't see you much, so I would say nice to meet you—but I am not sure about the state that you are in,' she said.

'Thanks for allowing me to visit,' he said.

'No problem, I am happy to help however I can, but I hope it's not a family issue, because right now, I'm an outcast.'

'I wanted to talk to you about that,' he said. Her eyes widened, and she was jolted from her semi-sleepy state. She didn't want to be put through emotional phases at this time of the night, and wished he had visited in the morning instead, but clearly, he felt like he couldn't wait any longer. She merely nodded, waiting for him to start on the topic.

'Don't be offended, I'm just here to ask a few questions,' he said. She knew right then that he was going to ask a few offensive questions. Anyone who asks someone not to be offended invariably asks something offensive, especially when it comes to her sexuality.

'How sure are you about being lesbian?' he asked hesitantly, wary of her reaction to every word that he pronounced carefully. She didn't react to the question.

'As sure as I have been about anything,' she said, indifferent. She had faced such questions many times before, and she was already aware that he wasn't as accepting of her sexuality compared to his own sister.

'You never had any doubts?'

'Oh, I have had plenty of doubts, of course. I had to ask myself a lot of questions before deciding to come out.'

'So you are not 100 per cent sure,' he continued in his slow, hesitant tone. A reply came to Sabitha's mind but she immediately decided against pronouncing it as she did not want to escalate the situation. She sat silently but she could not find an alternative response to his question, and decided a confrontation was probably the best way to end this clearly unproductive conversation they were having. The conversation had something to do with his state of mind, and nothing with her sexuality.

'How sure are you that you are a man?' she asked, still wearing an indifferent tone.

'What the fuck?' he squirmed on the couch, almost letting out a shriek; his ego badly bruised by the nature of the question. She had anticipated the reaction.

'That's how I feel when you ask me if I am sure about my sexuality,' she said.

'Gender and sexuality are not the same,' he retorted.

'Yes, they are not, but my conviction about both is pretty defined,' she said. Yuva was taken aback. He thought that she would show him more respect and consideration given his age and seniority in the family, but he was shocked to discover she had no regard for convention and had no hesitation whatsoever in speaking her mind with him.

She stood up from the sofa. 'I think you should drink your tea before it gets cold,' she said. 'And get some sleep,' she added, ever-so-subtly kicking him out of the house. He paid no attention to the tea, and instead sprung to his feet, his tone demanding more respect.

'Is this how you speak to an older cousin? I was speaking to you nicely,' he raised his tone. She shot him a scathing look. Her sleep had flown out of the window.

'Oh, come on, where were you my whole life? Did you bother showing up for me, for anything at all? What do I owe you? I don't owe you any respect if you can't show any respect for my sexuality,' she said, raising her voice to match his.

Anand's attempts to watch his movie without any interruption were failing miserably. Acutely sensitive to any kind of noise pollution, especially in his home, he showed up at the hall unannounced, just as Yuva and Sabitha's conversation threatened to turn into a full-blown argument, if it wasn't one already.

'You live with him?' Yuva turned his attention towards Anand instead, pointing his hands at the latter. Sabitha shot Anand an apologetic look—as if she knew what was going to happen next. Anand stood near the dining table, his hands folded, without uttering a single word.

'What's your problem Yuva? Why are you here?' she tried to reduce the temperature of the conversation.

'I am here to ask you—why can't you be normal? Why can't you be like me, or us? We could all be alright, and we could all keep our parents and family happy. And the society would be happy too. Why do you have to make things difficult for yourself? And for us?' he asked.

Sabitha's hands were trembling—she was reliving the moment she had come out to her parents. She was being strong but was emotionally crumbling, once again realizing that she was falling into an abyss without family to hold her. She wanted to say a million things, but instead, just stared at him. And when she started blurting something out, she realized she was yelling, and she had never done that before in her life.

'My coming out doesn't have anything to do with you, or with anybody in the family. Stop making it about yourselves!' she bellowed.

Yuva was still trying to process the outburst when he felt a hand on his shoulders. He looked to his right and saw Anand, who was already slowly pushing him towards the door, without a warning. 'What the hell, man?' he said, trying to grab onto something to stop Anand's pushing.

'It's my house. And you should leave,' Anand said with a sense of authority. Yuva realized he was on the verge of being kicked out of a place by two people who were a good five years younger than him, and this was not something he was willing to accept. He pushed back.

Anand leaned forward, with a trembling deep voice that clearly showed he was trying not to let his emotions get the better of him, and whispered, 'I will hold your shirt and drag you out if you push back one more time. I repeat, this is my house, and you will not win this,' he said. By then, Anand was already holding Yuva's shirt and had started dragging him to the door. Yuva paused and signalled for a truce. He was going to leave the building of his own volition. But Anand was having none of that, so he escorted him down the lift, and past the guardhouse, up until the door of the car.

'I came here to talk to my cousin. This is becoming very disrespectful. And we are no longer in your house, so remember that,' Yuva said, as he unlocked his car. Anand had been shadowing him with an almost uncomfortable proximity the whole journey down. He realized he may have had overdone his own aggression towards Yuva.

'You talk to you cousin when it is not midnight, and when it is not in my house. Actually, going by that behaviour, you should probably do that in a crowded place because it doesn't sound like you should be attempting to meet her in a closed private space,' he said.

'What the hell are you insinuating? That I will do something to her?' Yuva retorted. Sabitha had followed the two of them down after calming herself, fearing renewed hostilities out on the streets. She wasn't wrong.

'Stop,' she exclaimed, as she came in behind Anand, and held his hands.

'He just said I was going to hit you. That is a flat out lie,' Yuva said, not making any eye contact with Anand.

'I think you should go before I hit you,' Anand added, clenching his fists. Sabitha noticed, and immediately held his clenched fists with her considerably smaller hands. She pleaded him to calm down.

'I'll talk to him,' she whispered to Anand, as he took a step behind, and she stepped forward, as Yuva finally looked like he was going to get into the car.

'Yuva, what just happened here tonight? What is the problem?' she asked.

'I've told you . . .' he started mumbling without any cohesion.

'No, you have not told me anything. How does me coming out have anything to do with you? Please tell me how it has affected you,' she said, clearly calmed down.

'You came out, and now my girlfriend won't stop referring to that, and goes and writes an article supporting you people. My sister supports you for it, and I express my opinion about it a couple of times and now suddenly I am the bad guy and she wants to leave me,' he said.

'Who's leaving? Geetha, or your girlfriend?' she asked.

'My girlfriend. In fact, she's left. All over a stupid fight over that article she wrote. I can't express my opinion apparently. If I do, I become a bad guy. She leaves me and now you kick me out of your house,' he said.

'I really don't think your problems will be solved by confronting me. Go and talk to her, no? Why the fuck do you want to drag me into this? Do I not have enough grief from my parents about this already?' she mildly raised her voice, as he got into the car, and shot her an apologetic look. Yuva pondered an apology, which he knew was the right thing to do, but his misdirected angst got the better of him and he drove away into the silent night. Anand and Sabitha stood outside their apartment, for a while, trying to digest everything that had happened in a whirlwind of a few minutes that completely disturbed what was supposed to be a calm evening.

'Your whole family is crazy, I tell you,' Anand said, and Sabitha looked at him with half a smile, realizing how much their argument resembled that of a married couple. She rubbed his shoulders in an attempt to calm his anger. Anand didn't go over the cliff very easily, but when he did, it was always difficult to calm him down. She knew he was not going to get any meaningful sleep in the night.

'Your sister tries to kiss me and now her brother comes to my house and almost starts a fist fight with me, and his grievances had nothing to do with me at all!' he said.

'What,' Sabitha stopped in her tracks as she started walking towards the guardhouse. She had decided to return to her own unit and leave Anand brooding for a while in the streets, but now she stood just before the guardhouse, demanding further explanation from him. Anand realized he misspoke.

'What did you just say,' she came close to him and yanked his arms with all her strength, making him face her. He tried to resist, but was surprised with her strength, and he almost tripped before steadying himself and facing her.

'It was just a drunken thing,' he said. 'I shouldn't have mentioned it.'

'No, you tell me everything. Why didn't you tell me this?' she asked, her eyebrows raised.

'Because she would feel awkward about it. It was just a drunken thing. I am sure she wants to forget it badly,' he repeated himself.

'Did you duck the kiss?'

'No, I just refused.'

'How?'

'I just said no . . .' he said, hesitant.

She nodded ever so slowly. A small smile appeared on her lips again as she processed the fact that her grieving cousin might finally be ready to go out and date other people. She tagged her resident's card past the guardhouse, and walked inside the building perimeter, a tall fence separating her and Anand, who was still on the street, calming himself down. 'She's hot, though,' he said, dropping an adjoining note with no context whatsoever. She stopped walking, and looked at him mischievously.

'Anand . . .' she said, in a manner a mother would call out a naughty child, before heading to the lift lobby. They both smiled to each other, as if they hadn't dealt with an angry confrontation less than an hour earlier. When a new possibility is lit up, it can overshadow the gloomiest day.

Chapter Thirteen

DRAMATURGY

January 2019.

Karthi stared at the blank, dull wall that was in front of her. Kasturi was napping, but her hand was firmly clenching Karthi's fists—making sure she didn't lose sight of the latter even when she wasn't awake. Karthi was wrecked with guilt for making both Lakshmi and Kasturi take turns in taking care of her, taking her to the hospital, and being a constant companion. It didn't help her already overwhelming sense that she was becoming a burden to the world around her. She kept her eyes on the wall, not wanting her wandering thoughts to turn her restless again, as they so often did. Her quasi-meditation wasn't doing the trick; the thoughts continued to stream in, and she was being swept away by the flood of her own thoughts. The last time she had allowed those cluttered, muddy, confusing thoughts sweep her away, she had blanked out and by the time she could come to, she had cut her own hands. She used her free left hand, and fidgeted through her light cotton bag for her phone and her headphones. She curated a playlist from the collection of ghazals and Indian classical compositions in her library, and put on her headphones. She didn't do well with songs that had lyrics—words brought memories, and memories invited thoughts that always took her too far. She had to stay in the moment, in the present. Just sounds did the trick.

She was startled by the sound of someone speaking very close to her. She looked around from her flimsy blue-colored waiting chair and saw a man in blue clinical overalls standing just in the periphery of her vision, trying to say something. He had a warm smile, and pointed at her ears. She took off the earphones.

'I have been asking them to put a wallpaper there for ages,' he said in a pleasant, professional voice. The writing on his chest indicated that he was the therapist she was waiting for.

'Are you Karthiga?,' he asked, reaching out his hand before noticing that her right hand was already occupied. She nodded, reaching out with her left hand, her phone in her grasp. He awkwardly shook her fists, never losing his warm, welcoming smile. 'Funny, my name is Karthik; just minus one syllable.' She reciprocated with a smile of her own.

She tapped her right hand and Kasturi stirred awake. 'The doctor is here. I am going to go,' Karthi said. Kasturi mumbled something unintelligible, half-asleep, and nodded in agreement.

'Oh, I am not a doctor, technically, just a clinical practitioner,' he said. He pointed to the name embroidered in the blue overalls, 'Look, there is no "doctor" here.'

'Oh, I am Indian, for us, anyone who works in a hospital is either a doctor or a nurse,' she said, following his lead into his consultation room. Unlike the waiting hall, his room was decked with visually pleasing artwork; every part of the room was curated with an aesthetic objective. She put her bag down and slumped into the comfortable sofa he had in his office. He took some time to settle down, and made sure she was comfortable as well. He offered her a glass of water and then asked if she wanted any hot drink. She politely declined. She looked around the room, and noticed how it seemed to have been designed to make people comfortable. The sofa was so comfortable she thought she might as well fall asleep on it. Karthik walked to the small pantry section he had in the room and made himself a cup of coffee. 'Sorry, many patients today,' he said, placing the coffee on a table that was between his chair and hers. He picked up his notebook and his pen which was on his chair, and held it on his hands, as he settled down comfortably. 'Shall we start? I am going to start with some screener questions,' he asked. She took a sip of the water, and nodded. With her consent, he recorded the session.

She hesitated to answer his questions initially, not wanting to be judged for who she was and what she was going through. Karthik dabbed his cheeks at some point, realizing the extent of her hesitation. He paused the session, and leaned forward.

'I am just going to go off record here, and say to you, if it is not obvious already, that I am not straight either,' he said in a calm, composed voice. 'Does that make a difference?' he asked with a smile.

'A lot,' she said, pausing her own train of thoughts. Karthi felt lighter. She felt like she no longer had to think through her answers. She no longer had to watch her choice of words; she didn't need to skirt around an issue with metaphors, hoping he would understand.

'Well, I hope someday we live in a world where a person sitting on *that* chair feels safe in a space like this, regardless of the beliefs and sexuality of the person on *this* chair,' he said, still smiling, 'or any chairs similar to these for that matter.'

She allowed herself to chuckle. She cleared her throat. But in that moment, she felt he understood everything about how she felt; anything else she could say would serve no substantial purpose apart from being extra details. With her permission, he resumed recording.

'What is the problem, you feel? Apart from all these circumstances which are obviously not ideal—what is at the core of what you are going through?' he asked, putting down the notes he was taking.

'The problem is—I feel like I've lost my identity.'

'What is your identity?'

She smiled, and looked at the far end of the room, towards the windows, trying to verbalize how she had felt, within, for most of her life.

'I never had good odds to begin with. The point is, I've come from rock bottom, and made something for myself, because I never once felt like I don't have enough strength for myself. I dealt with anything that was thrown my way,' she said. 'At one hand, there is this feeling of injustice. I have gone through enough hoops of fire . . . I don't think it is fair to add more in my path,' tears started welling up in her eyes.

'And then, there is this helplessness. This burden. This feeling that I am so heavy, emotionally, that I can't bring myself to overcome this. This is not as big as some of the rocks thrown my way. But it is one too many,' she said.

'So, you associate your identity with that of a fighter and you no longer feel like one.'

'No, I feel weak,' she said.

Karthik stood up. 'Don't worry, I just need to stretch,' he said, and started pacing the room, before deciding on a spot he could lean against the wall. Hand in his pocket, he looked at her, from across the room.

'Do you think you can be more than that?' he asked.

'More than a fighter?' she retorted, taken aback by the suggestion that there could be a personality that could be deemed stronger than that of a person who fights for her place in life and society every day.

'Yes, have you tried seeing life as more than a battle?' he asked.

'What else am I supposed to see it as?' she asked, baffled.

'A story' he said, casually, dialing down the intensity and seriousness of their conversation. But Karthik wasn't joking.

* * *

Orphanages and care homes have one type of gift that they are universally spoilt with—pre-loved clothes, and pre-loved books. As she grew older, Karthi's fondness for the pre-loved clothes that were being made available reduced drastically, she craved for more things that were her own, but one thing that she had never grown tired of were pre-loved books. She loved reading stories, from fiction to biographies—they all painted a universe of possibilities for her once it was time for her to leave the gates of the home.

She became aware of the acute realities of her life very early on, however, surrounded by benefactors and caretakers who spent much of their time trying to get her to go into the world with very, very low expectations. It's already great if she manages to find a professional working man to get married to—that would be an accomplishment. It would be great if she could land a job in a big company or a job with the civil service. She was reminded not to fly too high lest she fell and burned herself—she was climbing from rock bottom so she should be happy with whatever leverage life was able to give her. She was told to make lemonades her whole life, and it wouldn't give her anything more unless she was willing to be loud and fight for it. But Karthi always wanted more, mainly because she started with nothing—she should have the freedom to curate her world as she deemed fit.

The stories that visited her in these pre-loved books offered an escape to a world where things were more purposeful, where words allowed her to color her own imaginations—it was an act of independence that she didn't find in the stories and tales people were telling her, and the occasional movies that they so begrudgingly let her and her housemates watch. She never understood the obsession with not allowing the children to watch Indian movies growing up, as the elders were afraid that the children would be negatively influenced by the movies. Indian movies often contained larger-than-life characters and narratives that made most events seem illogical and improbable. Having been conditioned, their whole life, to take life with a pinch of salt, she never thought she or the other children were ever at risk at believing the plausibility of the stories in these Indian movies. But there were many girls who romanticized some of the songs to a point that it led to teenage pregnancy scares, and boys who worshipped some actors so much that they thought they were invincible from punches, beatings and in some case, cuts.

Books cut out the noise for her. She wished she was living in these universes that existed in the books, including the universes of *Harry Potter* and *The Lord of the Rings*. They also gave her something that would carve a career for her—the command over the English language.

'If you see your life as a story, how would you see it?' she snapped back into the room as Karthik asked.

'Am I the protagonist?' she asked.

'It's your story. Shouldn't you be the protagonist?'

'I feel like I am fighting to be the protagonist of my story,' she paused. They stared at each other and shared a subtle smile with each other.

'I have been watching society's narrative of me, and trying to change it,' she said.

'All of us, have limited energy,' Karthik said, as Karthi ran her hand over the wounds from the cuts—a reminder of her own limitations.

'It's great to fight. But we have to pick our battles. We can't fight all the time. We fight in order to be happy. But I'm sure there are things you can be happy with, today. That's one less battle.'

Karthi's smile returned to her face, after what seemed like a prolonged absence. As she left her consultation, she found Kasturi still sleeping on the waiting chair. Weight off her chest, she took in the sight with much more clarity than she had done before. She felt guilty for making Kasturi wait and having to accompany her to hospitals. The love she was looking for—the love that would probably come if her battles yielded greater acceptance among people—would never usurp this love, which had always been there for her since the beginning. She sat again on the creaking plastic chair in the waiting area next to Kasturi, again placed her right hand under hers, and tilted Kasturi's head to make her lie on Karthi's shoulders. Karthi put on her headphones again and resumed listening to the same music.

Karthik came out of his room, closed the door subtly behind him, realizing that Kasturi was still asleep right outside his consultation room. He smiled at Karthi, exchanged pleasantries, and walked along the seemingly endless corridor.

'Karthik!' Karthi was still watching him from a distance, headphones in her hand, when she heard someone yell out his name, which seemed to reverberate in the quiet corridor. The man who yelled was walking from the other end of the long corridor, and slowly came into view closer to Karthi, wearing a doctor's coat. Karthik stopped walking as well; instead, he turned around and walked back in the direction he had come from. The doctor called Karthik's name again, but this time in a more hushed tone as he glanced at Kasturi sleeping.

He darted forward to greet Karthik, with a female doctor walking right behind him. But she was not as interested in meeting Karthik, and walked past them in a much slower pace. Her attention was glued to her phone.

Karthi, who had paused the music, seemed to notice everything about this girl—from her dusky complexion to her eyebags that showed she had barely been getting any sleep. Karthi wondered if she would look equally weary if she were to stand in front of a mirror and introspect herself. The young woman seemed to notice a pair of eyes trailing her; she turned around and looked at Karthi curiously, and they both caught out each other's stare. Karthi broke her stare and tried to make out the letters on her name-tag. But she was far too ahead by now, and the woman turned forward and joined her friend and Karthik as they resumed walking in Karthik's original direction.

Karthi stopped craning her neck, afraid of waking up Kasturi, and returned to her upright posture, staring at the blank wall. She folded her legs on the chair, put away her headphones, and instead grabbed a copy of Charles Dickens' *Oliver Twist*, reading it until she saw a white coat appear close to her line of vision. 'Hi,' a gentle female voice greeted her as she looked up from the book and saw the same woman she had been noticing earlier stand above her, hands in her coat. There was something surreal about seeing this woman up close after that brief exchange of looks earlier. It was not meant to be any different than the countless encounters of fleeting attraction she had experienced before in her life—and she was sure some of those women were actually straight, and were probably mothers.

'Sorry to startle you,' she said. Karthi realized she must have reacted with a shock when the woman appeared in front of her. 'I noticed you just now, and I hope it is okay to ask, but are you the teacher who appeared in the newspaper recently?' she asked. By now, Kasturi had stirred fully awake. Karthi felt the weight lift off her shoulders, literally. Her attention returned to the young woman in front of her.

'Well, yes, I did appear in the paper some time ago, but I used to be a teacher. No longer am,' she said.

'Oh, wow, I just had to ask—I always wondered if I would have the chance to meet you,' she said.

'Why?'

The woman did not seem to have a well thought-out answer to that question. She shrugged her shoulders.

'Well, actually, I think my sister is your lawyer?' she stretched her question with slight uncertainty.

'Are you Geetha's sister?' Karthi straightened out her legs, put on her slip-ons and stood up.

'Well, cousin, actually,' she said. 'Sorry to interrupt like this; I couldn't recall your name from the article, so . . .' she said.

'It's Karthiga,' Karthi said, considering if she should offer a handshake. The woman's hands remained rooted in her pocket. 'It's nice to meet you. I have to go join my colleagues for lunch, they are waiting for me,' she said, and started shuffling her feet without introducing herself in return.

But this time, Karthi didn't miss the details; she had seen the woman's name tag. She sat in the seat again. 'Awake now? Had a good sleep?' she asked Kasturi, who was looking at her, bewildered.

'Why didn't you wake me up?' she asked.

'Because you are sleep deprived and you deserve to get some sleep. Plus, we are not in a rush,' Karthi said.

'Who was that?'

'A doctor. Her name is Sabitha,' she said.

'Now that's something different. A non-common Indian name,' Kasturi chuckled. 'What did she want?'

'She wanted to say hi,' Karthi said.

'That's all?' Kasturi asked. Karthi nodded and got up from her chair, urging Kasturi to do the same. The latter rubbed her eyes and a realization hit her. 'Do you think she could be . . .?'

'Could be what?'

'Could be . . . like you?'

'The word is "lesbian". You should say it more often.'

'Whatever. Maybe she's trying to get your attention because she's interested?' Kasturi pressed the matter further as they stood up to leave the healthcare facility.

'We don't know if she's lesbian,' Karthi said in a matter-of-fact manner, as they started walking back to their car. 'She could have a boyfriend. She could be married. She could be married to the doctor she was walking with. She could even have kids,' Karthi said.

'She's definitely not a mom and she's definitely not married. You might want to act oblivious, but I think she likes you,' Kasturi said. 'She's your lawyer's cousin, you will see her again.'

'Shut up,' Karthi retorted.

* * *

Geetha started spending increasingly prolonged hours in her office ever since her parents-in-law moved into her house in what could only be described as a form self-invitation. She made sure she returned home late enough to eat dinner by herself and go to bed, without having to spend much time with either of them. She craved for space to move on from her husband's death, but everything that was happening in her life provided her with very little space to deal with events, let alone her own emotions. Her upcoming battle with the government loomed large with her feeling unprepared, and her client Karthi suffering a psychological meltdown that would definitely be raised in the courts.

That day, Geetha was late even by her usual standards. It was 10.30 p.m. and she was in no mood to go back, even though only one light remained switched on in the office lobby and everyone had gone back. The sound of the air conditioning working overtime reverberated across the office, and she wrote draft arguments for her case, discarding some of them into the bin. The office was a mess; she was a mess. The office doorbell rang, startling her. She dropped her pen, and looked out at the office door to notice the silhouette of a man, which immediately enveloped her in fear. She thought that the ghost of Prakash had come to haunt her, to punish her for not missing him enough. But the silhouette stayed, and as she edged closer to the door, she could make out that there was a real person at her office door that late in the night. She opened the door, and saw Anand standing there, looking just as surprised as her.

'Wow, you really do work late. Sorry, I did not mean to show up unannounced. I was told you get off work around 9 p.m. and I was waiting downstairs and you never appeared, so I thought I'll just come up and check if everything is okay,' Anand decided he would be better off providing a lengthy explanation for his presence at her office doorstep late into the night.

'That doesn't answer why you are here, Anand,' she said, still without inviting him in. A storm was raging outside the building, and heavy raindrops started to shatter against the windowpanes, making conversation much more difficult between both of them.

'Is this a bad time? I just wanted to speak to you about something. We can always do this another time,' he said.

'I can't seem to find a good time, ever,' she sighed. She was tired of sounding tired. She wanted to sound anything but. She opened the door and allowed him to come inside. 'I am doing some work there. Is it okay if I multitask?' she asked. 'Sure,' he entered and stood dead in the center of the common area, unsure about where Geetha wanted him to be. She disappeared momentarily into her office, and returned with her documents and a couple of pens. She came to the common area sofa, and sat, belatedly gesturing him to sit across from her. She stayed quiet, trying to focus on work, while Anand waited patiently. Her brain had stopped working for the day—she couldn't focus. She was more curious about what Anand had come to say. But she did not let it show. She pretended to scribble something instead. Anand sat across from her.

'Is this personal or professional?' she asked.

'Actually, this is pretty personal,' he said. 'Um, Sabitha doesn't know I'm here,' he added quickly.

'I guessed so. It seems like she never leaves your side otherwise,' she chuckled. She regretted making that joke. She had a non-existent relationship with her parents, and the closest relative she could rely on—Geetha—was trying to deal with her own husband's death and the aftermath of it. She was glad

Anand always had Sabitha around, at all times. 'Sorry, should not have said that. I'm glad you are always there for her. How do you go on dates then? Do other girls not assume that you two are together if you are always seen together?' she asked.

Anand seemed surprised at the question. He did not reply and instead hesitated with a long pause, before clearing his throat.

'I am sorry, I am digressing,' she said. 'You wanted to talk about something, let's get to that.'

'Yes,' he cleared his throat again. 'About what happened the other night when I was going to drop you . . .' she dropped her pen and her note. He had her full attention. 'Oh, please, no, that's not your fault. None of it is. It was entirely my fault. I didn't make anything of it. I was just drunk and being an idiot,' she clarified.

'No, no, I don't want to discuss whose fault it was. I will not tell anyone about what happened. Sabitha knows, it came out accidentally, I can't avoid it because I sort of live with her, but that's not an issue. I just need to say something about things from my perspective that night,' he said.

'Okay, do go on,' she said, crossing her legs, and resting her chin on her hands.

He hesitated to start the topic for a while, looking flustered.

'You waited a very long time and came all the way up here to say something, you shouldn't hesitate now,' she said, smiling, hoping to put him at ease. But despite the million things that were going on in her head, none of them could prepare her for what he was about to say to her—it was one scenario she had never imagined in her head.

'Well, that day, I sort of ducked away from your kiss. And I realize how it might have seemed to you—that I didn't want the kiss. And I don't want you to think that,' he started. She started to sit upright.

'At some point, I think I wanted it, I welcomed it, but you were very drunk and that was not the moment for it,' he said. 'I wanted it to be . . . I can't seem to find a different word to use here . . . more meaningful,' he added.

Her jaw dropped.

'Please, don't think that I am asking for the kiss now. I am not. What I am saying is, the moment could have happened if one of us wasn't very drunk and too uninhibited. Because of that incident, can we not consider the whole possibility of another moment gone completely? Like, I would like to just put that on the table. From my perspective at least. The moment could still happen, I don't know when, but hopefully when both of us know what we are doing,' he said. 'Of course, that's only if you are even remotely interested in the idea. Right now, you look repulsed. But I wrestled with this thought for some time and I realized that if I want the possibility to be open, I should say it,' he said. 'Waiting is only going to make things awkward for both us and we would both probably never entertain the possibility ever again. And I don't want to look back and think of it as a missed opportunity,' he added.

His awkwardness and shyness in delivering his entire monologue, all the while shuffling nervously at the edge of the lounge sofa, as if he half anticipated her to yell at him and threaten to hit him at any point, amused her.

She had a million reactions and questions in her head— but his body language caught her attention the most. 'Are you intimidated by me?' she asked, a small smile escaping her face. He smiled awkwardly.

'Maybe,' he said, shrugging his shoulders.

'What for?'

'You are . . . intimidating.'

Her eyes opened wide. 'Yes . . . how so?'

'I don't know. It's just that—a feeling. You have such a big office; you are your own boss. You handle so many things on your own. You are all alone in your office at 10.30 p.m., without any fear. It could be any number of those things, or none of those.'

'Did you just suggest that you might want to try dating me? It feels like you said something very elaborate that basically meant asking for a date?' she asked, increasingly surprised at herself for not reacting more dramatically to Anand's nocturnal confession. In her mind, she imagined shrieking back at him, making dismissive sounds that would show how she would never end up with him, and how the idea of a romance between both of them was the most illogical thing on earth. But she did not do any of those.

'Yes, I'm too nervous to have asked properly. Not . . . enough training,' he said, adding in a brief smile.

'You asked for a date even though you are intimidated by me. Isn't that a mismatch?' she asked, standing up and walking to the pantry, realizing that their conversation was going to take time. She made herself a cup of coffee; her tired eyes were now getting restless. She already knew she was not going to get much sleep tonight after talking to Anand. Why should he have any effect on her?

She came back with two cups in her hands, she placed the cup of coffee on her side of the table, and handed him a cup of hot tea. 'I never asked you. I hope you like tea. I made it black,' she said, assertively.

He nodded subserviently. 'Yes, I'm fine with it,' he said, collecting the cup of tea from her hands and holding it in his palms. It was not too hot, so he started sipping it. 'Thanks,' he added. 'So,' he cleared his throat again. 'Why would it be a mismatch?' he asked.

'Because, correct me if I'm wrong, you seem to see me the stronger personality among both of us. Why would you date someone who intimidates you?' she asked.

'Why shouldn't I?' he asked again. She slowly felt the tables turn. She could feel that she was being drowned and trapped by the stereotypes that were contained in her own argument.

'Because, guys are normally the more assertive ones,' she couched her statement with diplomatic precision.

'I don't believe that is a universal rule. Do you?' he asked.

'I don't know,' she blurted. 'I haven't thought about that. But if you are asking me if I fundamentally believe in traditional gender roles, then I would say, no,' she added, sipping her coffee. She felt she was asking too many questions; she allowed silence to grow between them.

'I find you intimidating, but I don't find the prospect of dating you intimidating, if that demarcation makes sense,' he said after a while, his composure gradually increasing. 'I believe you are just like me—with similar amount of insecurities, with similar amount of fears. And being together with someone is about knowing all those and managing those together, right?' he said.

'Wow,' Geetha exclaimed. 'Anand, you do realize we are nine years apart. right? As in, I am almost a decade older than you. And I am married . . . sorry, was,' she sighed in frustration. 'I still need to get used to saying that. I am not sure you know what you are asking for,' she said.

'Of course, yes, I don't know. But I want to find out. That's the whole point,' he said.

'Wow,' she said for the second time during the night. He had succinct answers for everything she was throwing in his direction. He made the age factor seem negligible. She had to think about it repeatedly and magnify the number in her mind before she could acknowledge that it remained the biggest problem for her to be able to take his confession seriously.

'You are Sabitha's age. You are her best friend, in fact. It is just . . . weird. I watched her grow up. I saw her as a small kid while I was a teenager. And that thought is circling my mind even right now—you were also a kid like her when I was a teenager,' she said.

'And look at the three of us now, all adults; we can sit in a bar and have drinks as equals,' he said.

'You have an answer for everything, don't you?'

He shrugged his shoulders again.

'You surprise me. You seem so passive most of the time, yet you have the strength to come here, wait for me, come looking for me, and say all this,' she said.

'You surprise me as well,' he said.

'How so?'

'I expected you to have kicked me out midway through my really long speech,' he said, finishing up the last bit of tea, and placing the cup on the table.

'Trust me, I surprised myself on that account,' she added. 'But I really don't know what to say now,' she said.

He shrugged. 'I came here expecting nothing. This already feels like a bonus,' he said. He had a proud smile on his face. He stood up. 'On that note, I won't overstay my welcome. Unless you need someone to stand outside as a bodyguard,' he said as he approached the door, realizing that leaving a woman alone in an empty office was probably bad for his chivalry. She stood up as well and walked near him as he opened the door. She held it open from the inside, looking calm.

'We just spoke about traditional gender roles. Please don't do that. I'm leaving in five minutes, I promise. Just need to finish something and tidy up. Careful in the rain,' she said. He said goodbye and walked towards the lift lobby.

'Can I ask you another thing?' she stuck her neck out, just as he pressed the lift button. He nodded, under the faint flickering light of the lift lobby.

'How is it that you are capable of such romantic words, but you are not surrounded by more women—women you can date, I mean,' she asked.

The lift door opened, Anand stepped inside and held the lift doors from closing.

'Because, the woman who does surround me every day nowadays is the only woman I loved before. I guess my romance doesn't end at just words maybe?' he shrugged and disappeared into the lift. She closed the door after he left, before realizing— she was not only considering a date with her sister's best friend and classmate and housemate, she was also considering a date with her sister's ex.

'Fuck, give me easier choices,' she murmured to the rain, as if it was going to transport her message to the creator of all the opulent designs of the universe.

* * *

Anand's hands trembled as he knocked on the pale-colored door in front of him gently. He knew Sabitha would never hear him with such soft knocks. He knocked harder, and harder. Eventually, there was movement and she opened the door, bewildered by his unannounced visit. 'I was messaging you as well. And calling,' he said.

'I was watching something,' she said, with a smile. 'Cleansing. No phone near me. Nothing. I couldn't hear anything else and no one was going to disturb me. And then you did.'

'For good reason,' he helped himself past the door and into her room. His hands were still trembling. He could feel a faint pounding on his chest. He felt cold. It was raining outside, but he was feeling much colder than he was supposed to, in that weather. He could feel the adrenaline pumping through his body. He couldn't bring himself to sit down. He paced across the room.

'Okay, that is driving me crazy. You either tell me what's going on or you sit your ass down. I can't have you buzzing around my room like that without looping me in,' she said. She closed her room door behind her. He rarely entered her room because she lived in an all-girls apartment unit and the landlord had a strict policy about guys sleeping overnight in any of the girls' room. Each time she allowed Anand into her room, Sabitha risked being kicked out. But she was getting bolder with the rest every time, because there was always a fallback—Anand lived by himself in another unit in the same block, and he had rooms that she could occupy. In some ways, she was already occupying some room in his house.

'Okay, I did something stupid. I don't know, maybe it's not stupid. It felt like the right thing to do, and now I am afraid things won't be the same again,' he said.

'Don't speak to me in riddles, man,' she moaned, still standing, and unsure if she should return to sitting on her desk with him pacing around the room. 'Do you need me to hold you or something?' she asked.

'No. I am fine,' he said, stopping in one position. 'I went to see Geetha today,' he said. Her eyes widened.

'Geetha as in . . .'

'Yes, your sister,' he said.

'And?'

'And sort of asked her out,' he said.

'What?' she asked, surprised and somewhat amused at the same time. She didn't do very well at hiding her amusement.

'Why are you smiling like that?' he asked, bewildered.

'Like what?'

'You have a pretty stupid grin on your face right now,' he said. She closed her mouth with her hands, but the giggle and the grin were spilling through.

'Sorry, it's just, you . . . and my sister. I am imagining the two of you as a couple,' she said.

'And it doesn't look very good, does it?' he asked.

'It doesn't look very normal. But, hey,' she paced forward and held his arms, 'who wants to do normal nowadays?'

Sabitha was surprised at Anand's actions but she was not shocked by them. She saw something in his reaction when he recalled the moment he had previously had with Geetha—something she had not seen in him before. Anand had never done anything without telling Sabitha first, and that had been the case for years. She knew he needed a really good reason to break that habit independently—and Geetha was a strong enough reason for anyone to break from their habits.

'Let's not get excited, can we? If nothing works out, it means all I have done is make things awkward between both of you,' he said.

'She drove down and was there for me when I was coming out to my family, I am sure she will easily rise above this,' she said, her smile remaining. 'There's also this thought that I can't get out of my head—the two people who have been there the most for me in recent times, being there for each other.'

He smiled.

Sabitha felt a burden slowly lift off her back. She always had a question at the back of her mind that she avoided addressing—had Anand ever moved on from her? Regardless of his claims, she always knew she was selfishly holding him back—he was never going to be able to fully move past her if he spent almost every waking moment with her around. But no matter what life threw at them, Anand was all she seemed to have.

He was finally starting to pursue a relationship—and Sabitha could finally look back at the past and make her own peace with it.

Chapter Fourteen

LOVE IS A DREAM

2013.

Anand had never wanted to become a doctor. The problem was—he did not know what else he wanted to do if he was not going to become a doctor and follow in his father's footsteps. He had a clinic that he could take over upon graduation, and there was a succession plan that his father had already put in place for the takeover. It was literally what the doctor had ordered.

Anand only enjoyed one thing in life more than anything else—watching decidedly brown movies and listening to decidedly brown songs. His playlist stood out, compared to his peers—he did not have a single English song in his library. He predominantly listened to Indian music, but gravitated towards romantic melodies more than anything else; he wasn't listening to the same adrenaline pumping numbers his friends were listening to in their school days. Even as he observed school fights from up close, romantic melodies played in his head, in the background. He had the ability to romanticize any situation; the smallest of gestures was microscopically analysed. In a school where boys and girls hesitated to confess their romantic interests towards each other, he learned to pick up subtle cues that indicated interest. He built castles in his head and enjoyed the subtle flirting without ever making a concrete move.

'I am waiting for a special kind of connection before I do something like that,' he told his friends. Inspired and influenced by all the music, movies, and the eloquently crafted romance scenes, Anand was a master at thinking up one-liners and believing in the existence of the 'one true love.' He did not believe everything he saw in the films, but nothing was more real to him than romance and music. His story was going to be different, unique and successful. Being a doctor was already a given; being a great lover was his aspiration.

On the second day of his foundation orientation at one of the most reputable medical universities in the country, he was immediately distracted. The girl he had been stealing glances at, and who he was sure was stealing glances back at him, belonged to the same class as him.

'Excuse me,' he heard her voice a week later, as she asked if it was okay to sit beside him for a class. That's where she stayed for the rest of the semester—by his side. He was convinced that this was not a coincidence. This was all meant to happen. This entire journey was designed to bring her close to him. He dropped his quest to find love. Now, she became his purpose.

Anand started watching at her on every available opportunity. He was convinced she was the one but yet didn't try too hard. He observed, greeted her when they sat next to each other in classes, but otherwise benched himself as he saw the other guys in the class make a pass at her. Sabitha was an attractive woman by all means, and she attracted a fair bit of attention from men in the college. She entertained most of them, but kept everyone at arm's length. Sabitha was mysterious to most of the people in the class—but not to Anand. He was sure he knew her better than most people. In her eyes, he was mysterious. But Anand was not being mysterious. He was merely betting against the odds.

'Do you have to see your girlfriend?' Sabitha asked one day when Anand told her he was rushing somewhere after class. He stopped in his tracks and smiled to himself, away from her line of sight.

'I wish,' he said, curtly with a warm smile on his face. On that day, they exchanged numbers. One month later, they had started holding hands, the first time Anand had romantically held hands with anyone in his life. He felt proud to be walking next to her whenever they were seen in public, and not long after that, during a casual conversation with several classmates, she identified herself as his girlfriend.

'You are more than a boyfriend to me,' she told him when he brought up the topic with her in private. 'You mean a lot to me—that much I know. Calling you a boyfriend or a partner seems too simplistic,' she said. But there was a strain in her voice as she said it. She was being honest with him, but she was busy lying to herself. Three months after that declaration, and a couple of awkward kisses later, Sabitha uncharacteristically prolonged one of their regular nightly conversations into an all-nighter.

'I have to tell you something,' she typed in a text message, knowing well enough that he was not going to sleep until she had finished telling him what she was going to tell him. She wanted to talk to him in person, but she did not have that kind of courage within her. She was questioning her self-worth, and she was okay with being a bad person in his eyes, because she was sure she was going to be judged for he actions regardless of how softly she landed the blow on him. She started typing out long messages explaining an event that happened way before she had even met him. She had already lost her virginity before meeting him.

'I am sorry,' she said. 'I didn't know I would meet someone who would save so much of himself for me,' she added, referring to Anand's ideologies on romance. She was bursting the bubbles of perfection he had been floating around his head. Anand knew he should not be bothered by her confession—he was okay with anything as long as it meant she was with him, yet her little confession bothered him enough for him to ask for more details. She hesitated.

'That's the actual reason why I needed to talk to you about it,' she said. 'It wasn't a guy,' she added. Anand looked at that message for a very long time. He wanted to chalk it down to experimentation, as he knew some girls freely experimented with both genders in their teenage angst. Sabitha could have been one of them. He floated that thought out in a message to her, in a way, looking for reassurance for himself. 'Yes, maybe,' she said, without much enthusiasm.

Anand did not lend much weight to the matter, but Sabitha carried the guilt like a burden that she was refusing to let go. 'I am sorry,' she blurted out, out of the blue, after they had made out for the first time, two weeks later.

Over the next couple of months, he saw her shrivel to become a caricature of her former self, constantly troubled by thoughts in her head, and avoiding any difficult conversations about their future as a couple.

'You love a little too intensely. You need to give me some space,' she said, as they lied down on a blanket in a public park to watch the stars—exactly five months after they had gotten together. He had tried to pull her closer and take her hand, but she was more than happy to keep her backpack between both of them. Anand was taken aback by the demand for space. His whole premise of romance was set on the notion of being a man who never separates from his woman, but apparently that kind of love wasn't appealing to Sabitha. He had never entertained the possibility that the woman he would fall in love with would not want to love as absolutely and intensely as he did.

Sabitha's need for space only seemed to increase from that point onwards, and Anand was finding it difficult to be in denial about it. As they met at home for a movie date the following month, she insisted on sitting on a chair several feet away from him.

'What the fuck is wrong with you?' he asked, standing in his living room. 'Do you want to be here or not?' he asked again, as she remained unmoving from the chair. 'You know, being with someone was supposed to make me feel like I have someone to complete me. Right now, I feel even more alone than how I felt the entire time I was single. At least back then, I had some dreams. Now you've gone and shattered them as well,' he added.

Tears streamed down her eyes. She remained glued to her seat for ten more minutes, before she finally broke down and showed emotion for the first time in weeks.

'It was supposed to be a mistake,' she said, in between sobbing. His concern for her overpowering his own sense of injustice, Anand kneeled before her, trying to get her to pour out her emotions. But even before kneeling down, he knew his relationship with her was ending. He just didn't know why or how.

'What was supposed to be a mistake?' he whispered, as her crying got louder. He didn't want to attract the attention of his housemates.

'What happened with Cheryl was supposed to be a mistake. I am sorry,' she said again.

'You have apologized a million times now,' he said, exasperated, caressing her arms, unsure about his physical proximity to her.

'She was supposed to be a mistake and you were supposed to be the right one. You were the one who were supposed to make everything alright,' she said, her words increasingly garbled by her own sobbing.

'And I didn't?' he asked, his pride hurt at the suggestion or the thought that he wasn't the best boyfriend he could have possibly been.

She shook her head. 'It's not you,' she wiped her tears, realizing that the next few words were going to be very important. It was important to her that he understood what she was trying to say.

'It's the other way around. I think I made a mistake being with you,' she said. He frowned; his heart sank as he realized that he was being branded a 'mistake' as her partner. He was convinced they were the right one for each other, but he was apparently the wrong one for her.

'Whatever happened with Cheryl wasn't a random mistake,' she said, holding his hands. It began to dawn on him that she wasn't saying no to him because he was the wrong guy for her. She was saying no because he was the wrong gender.

'Cheryl?' he asked, never having met the woman before.

'No. It's not about her. Women. However I am with you, it's not the same as being with them. And I feel like I want to be with them. And I have just been dragging you along hoping this was all a phase and I can say the attraction towards women was a mistake. But actually, the only thing I feel odd about is being with you. Being with them feels natural,' she said.

She hugged him. 'Please understand. I love you, just not in that way,' she said. He smiled ruefully. Anand broke up with his first, and what was supposed to be his only, love that day. But he stayed in a relationship with her—as a friend, confidant, and eventually, a best friend. Over the years, each of them became the most important person in each other's life, while realizing they would have to grow out of each other's comfort, and stumble into individual relationships as adulthood knocked on their door. Adulthood came in a big way for Anand. He no longer believed that there was only one true love for him, but at the same time he remained a hopeless romantic. With Geetha, he took a step he had never taken with Sabitha—confessing his feelings before he had any indication of the woman's interest in him. He was against betting against the odds. With Sabitha, the odds were stacked against him by classmates. With Geetha, the odds were stacked against him by invisible forces—the forces that determined the accepted norms of society. He didn't know these forces, he couldn't put a face to them, and he had no idea how to fight them or how to overcome them. All he could do was take a leap of faith. Inspired by the prospect of finding his purpose in love again, he leapt.

'If you fall, I will catch you,' Sabitha said, her mouth full as they both chewed through street stall burgers at 2 a.m. in the morning. 'I know,' Anand said, feeling the midnight mist in the air, as the background of a Tamil romantic melody played in his head. He was dreaming again.

Chapter Fifteen

EQUALITY & CHIVALRY

February 2019.

A maroon Perodua Myvi pulled up at a mostly empty carpark in front of the Kuala Lumpur High Court, with the morning mist still in the air and the sun yet to come out. Anu yawned so loudly, she startled herself. She opened the door, grabbed her bag and walked across the empty car park as more cars started streaming into it. Her colleagues had told her tales of how the court car park got congested by the time most of the country had risen up to have their unhealthy nasi lemak breakfasts, and she was in no mood to be late or to be doing rounds in the car park for her very first court assignment—especially something that she had fought to get. She flashed her media tag at the security personnel as she reached the gate, before realizing that she was a little overzealous in wanting to flash her media tag to get access into a building. She had always showed up at lifestyle events where credentials were not given as much brevity as they were given the court complexes, the parliament building, political offices, and government buildings. She had not accessed any of those prior to this day, and she savoured the milestone.

She went up to the fourth floor of the court complex and set her things down on a long brown bench outside one of the courtrooms, and took a nap there while passing the time. She was woken up by a familiar voice.

'So,' Geetha said, decked in her full lawyer's attire, holding a heavy stack of files in her right hand, and a big lawyer's bag by her side, 'finally, someone shows up,' she said, as Anu slowly recalibrated from her nap.

Anu smiled. 'Do you expect me to say sorry?' she asked.

'No, I expect you to tell me how are you and what's been going on,' she said.

'I think that calls for a cheese and wine kind of date,' she said, smiling. Anu had barely processed her feelings ever since she had taken a break from Yuva. It did not feel like how she expected it to feel, either way. She was supposed to be cooped up in her room crying or figuring out if being away from him made her feel like she wanted to be with others. Yet, she spent more time by herself, asking herself questions that she had avoided for years. Yuva demanded answers—he called or messaged every week to make sure she did not erase him from her memory, and she took pains to explain to him that he was never going to be erased from her memory, regardless of whether they ended up together or not. Yuva refused to entertain the possibility of the latter. She ceded to his pressure and agreed to his requests to meet a couple of times, but the conversations had not gone anywhere meaningful. He wanted answers that she was still finding for herself.

Geetha tapped and gently caressed Anu's shoulders. 'I'm not choosing between you two,' she said, almost in a whisper, as she turned around and greeted a group of three lawyers—the government's lawyers.

'Eh,' the man leading the group, an elderly, senior deputy public prosecutor, interjected in his coarse voice. His glasses

were on the brink of falling off his nose, and his pace of walking
was decidedly slower than that of his two female colleagues who
flanked him on either side, one carrying his files and another
carrying his briefcase. He greeted Geetha, and took a moment,
as if recalling how familiar she had seemed to him.

'Rare day out of the office,' Geetha said, smiling. 'Should I
be intimidated?' she added.

Zulkifli's mind was somewhere else. He shuffled his feet
and looked at the two junior lawyers that surrounded him. 'I
must apologize,' he said to one of them. 'I forgot to have my
morning cigarette. It's in the bag,' he said, with a grin. He stood
over and waited patiently as his colleague put the bag on the
ground and kneeled down in order to rummage through the bag
before producing a pack on Dunhill reds. 'Did you happen to
find a lighter in there?,' he asked, as he felt through the pockets
of both his shirt and his pants, making sure he didn't have the
lighter on him. 'You can't give a man a cigarette, and not a
lighter, you know,' he said, handing the pack of cigarettes back
to the woman as he stood with the cigarette butt parked on
his right ear. She produced a lighter, looking relieved that she
did not have to kneel on her high heels anymore. He laughed
mischievously at his impressionable colleague, and started a slow
walk in the same direction he came in, before pausing in his
tracks. Bewildered at being greeted and having to play second
fiddle to the search for a cigarette, Geetha's attentions returned
to Anu.

'Geetha, right?' the man finally acknowledged her again.
'Geetha Rao. The Te-lugu lawyer,' he said, stressing and making
sure he had done his best to pronounce the word. She turned
around and smiled at him. 'You want to accompany this old
man down for a fag?' he asked.

She accepted his invitation, and then tapped Anu's shoulders. 'Go get a seat inside. After fixing yourself a little in the washroom,' she told Anu, before walking alongside the man. She realized she was walking much faster than him and slowed down to accommodate him.

'Sorry, I am getting old,' he said, as she got into the lift and held it for a good thirty seconds before he joined her.

'You are not that old,' she said.

He reached for the cigarette from his ear, in a lift filled with other lawyers, and put it on his lips. He turned around and looked at the other lawyers, most of them had clearly come to court to be called to the Bar—a process that allowed them to start practising as lawyers in Malaysia. They wondered, without uttering a single world, if he was going to light up a cigarette in the lift. The slow-moving lift seemed to take an excruciatingly long time to travel down four floors.

'I can't believe this shit. I was already past fifty when they built this thing,' he said, as both of them walked past the lobby to the front entrance of the building. 'And it already acts like it's older than me,' he added. He walked out a fair distance from the entrance of the courthouse before lighting up the cigarette.

'Bloody hell, I used to light these up right on that floor, just outside the courtrooms, and no one would have said anything. Bloody rules,' he said.

'Finding it hard to keep up with the times?' Geetha asked.

'I am seventy, and I have been doing this for over forty-five years, so forgive me if I'm a little weary. I feel like I've even lost that right now because we have the oldest prime minister in the world. He has diminished my right to moan and complain,' he said. Geetha continued to observe and listen to Zulkifli's antics.

'Nowadays very few of the young ones smoke. They use the vape,' he said, taking a long drag of his cigarette.

'I must have shaken some foundations to have you fall from the tree. I heard you haven't really been to a courtroom in some time,' she said.

He nodded, removing his glasses and folding them into his blazer pocket. 'Well, you did opt for a sensational case, in the very least,' he said, turning around and observing a group of photographers walking towards the entrance of the building. 'And my guess is at least some of them are here for our case,' he added.

'So my case is being seen as a threat by the people up high,' she said, swelling with pride.

'Anyone can start a battle; make sure you can win the war,' he said.

'Have you ever wondered why cases like these didn't happen when you were younger?' she asked, as he finished his cigarette and resumed his walk back to the court.

'Because in my time, people didn't walk to talk about it, and at the same time, the people didn't care so much about what the others did. For fuck's sake, we got called to the Bar, and then we went to the bar!' he chuckled, pausing and admiring his own joke. 'But man, fat chance of that happening today,' he added.

'You should say that in court,' she said.

He paused again as they were about to enter the lift. 'Before I forget, there was a reason why I asked you to follow me here. I know you wanted to put on a show. We want to avoid a show. So, a lot of this would not happen in an open court. A lot of this will happen in chambers. After all, it is a tort challenge. So, first, you will have to fight to even get it heard in open court,' he said, referring to the judge's chambers where the judge sometimes listens to arguments from both sides in a case. She sighed.

'Of course, I should have known,' she sighed. Geetha had been cautiously optimistic about her and Karthi's chances of winning the case, but deep down, she knew that the odds were stacked against them. She was never going to win a courtroom battle on discrimination in a country that actively practiced positive discrimination. But she expected activists and the media to sit in the gallery and listen to the arguments that the government was going to put forward. A lot of it was not going to be kind towards Karthi, but by this time the latter did not have much to lose. She wanted to hear what the government was going to say about sexual minorities in the country and the circumstances that they had to deal with in their daily lives.

Same-sex relationships were outlawed in Malaysia, but the country still did guarantee civil liberties and basic human rights for all its citizens under its constitution. Many of the court battles in Malaysia with regards to civil liberties were an extensive negotiation between elements of the law that were seemingly at odds with each other—provisions that say everyone should be treated the same, and then provisions that ask for one group of people to be treated differently compared to others.

'Thanks for tempering my expectations,' Geetha said, as they stood in the lift. Zulkifli merely nodded.

'It's your first rodeo in the human rights arena, right? You will get used to it the more cases you do,' he said, as the lift reached the fourth floor.

Zulkifli's walk was laboured, just like his breathing. She could hear the effort it was taking him to simply breathe with every step he was taking. In deference, she stayed a couple of steps behind him, allowing the tall, hunched man with barely any hair left to tower in front of her. It was befitting of his ego, and his sense of pride. Geetha admired lawyers and solicitors who constantly negotiated the grey area of civil liberties in courts, and at the same time had to negotiate their own personal views and stands on a matter. This was probably why lawyers gravitate so easily towards politics, and are known to make a name for themselves in pursuing public office positions—because they are so used to making this negotiation a part of their daily life.

Karthi was already outside the court, with a bandage around her arm, her head dropped low at the sight of Geetha. Geetha stayed back at the corridor as Zulkifli entered the court, and rubbed Karthi's shoulders, before holding her by the wrists, and dragging her into the court.

'I am sorry,' Karthi whispered. Geetha smiled. 'I almost gave up.'

Geetha merely smiled, as a million things raced through her head. She had made Karthi's fight her own. 'But you didn't. That's all that matters,' she said, before both of them entered the courtroom.

Karthi proceeded to take a seat on one of the long brown benches in the gallery, while Geetha directly headed to the lawyers' bench. Geetha settled down in her seat before she turned around and took a long look at the rows of benches behind her—Karthi, Lakshmi, Kasturi, and Anu sat in a row on the same bench, animatedly talking to each other. Karthi, however, looked lost. Her face had lost all the zeal and vibrancy that she had possessed when Geetha had met her for the first time. Karthi was the only one who caught Geetha's gaze, as she looked like she needed help, like a drowning person looking for a tether. Geetha nodded at her, warmly, but Karthi continued looking nervous. Geetha shifted her attention back to the duty at hand.

The court officer entered the room shortly after, prompting everyone in the court to stand up. Instead, the officer approached the lawyers' bench and immediately whispered to Zulkifli and his team. He looked at Geetha with a regretful smile. 'Told you,' he cleared his throat, putting on his glasses again. Geetha understood what he meant—what he had prophesied in the lift earlier had come true on the very first day of court. She carried her bags, and walked into the judge's chambers, this time leaving Zulkifli behind. This was going to be a long, drawn out battle.

Karthi mindlessly scrolled through her phone as the three women next to her spoke in whispers. She kept looking ahead, hoping that Geetha and the other lawyers would emerge from the chambers, but they stayed there for quite some time. She looked at the digital clock up ahead and realized they had been in the chambers for more than thirty minutes. The court police officer was sitting on his little blue chair, scrolling through his phone, and he was distracted by the conversations and looked in their direction. Karthi was sure he had read the case docket and knew what this case was about. He was a young officer who looked like he was already bored with his job. He stood up, and walked towards her, she half expected him to ask if she was the plaintiff in the civil case that she had brought against the government. She noticed his name—Imran, stitched into his dark blue uniform. He approached her, and in his northern dialect Malay, asked her, 'Does your hand hurt?'

Everything about that question took her by surprise—him not probing the reason she was there, him not probing if she was the plaintiff, and also him choosing not to ask what happened with her hand.

'A bit. But it's fine,' she said, looking at her hand and realizing that her hands were trembling due to the air conditioning in the courtroom coupled with the fact that there were hardly any people in the gallery.

'I won't expect much from today. I think they will have a hearing another day, they will postpone the case. The judge has to be somewhere at ten,' he said, turning around and looking at the time. 'So, you won't miss anything if you step out if it's really cold in here,' he said.

She smiled at him as he returned to his seat with a courteous nod. Just as he returned to his seat, Geetha came out of the judge's chambers, with Zulkifli trailing behind her, looking a little taken aback. Geetha had a small smile on her face, and looked at the four women sitting on the benches, especially Karthi. Karthi saw the smile and was confused. Geetha looked like she had won the case. The lawyers from both the sides packed their bags, and Geetha nodded at Karthi, indicating that they were done in court for the day.

Karthi whispered into Lakshmi's ears and all of them walked out of the courtroom, one at a time. As the mid-morning tropical heat reintroduced itself to Karthi, she stopped in her tracks as a familiar face greeted her outside the courtroom. Sabitha was leaning against the white marble pillars of the corridor, standing next to a man who looked vaguely familiar. She had a wide grin on her face.

'Akka, she's chasing after you,' Kasturi whispered in her ears. Karthi stuck out her hand behind her and pinched the first skin that came into her grasp.

'What the fuck are you pinching me for?' Lakshmi exclaimed, pulling her hands up. Sabitha waved her hands at Karthi, and mouthed an inaudible hello. Karthi returned the smile with courtesy, and merely nodded with a brief hand gesture. She was contemplating staying where she was, but Kasturi nudged her from behind, and this time, she felt compelled to go forward and approach Sabitha.

'Hi, I am Anand,' the man standing next to her stepped forward and introduced himself with a handshake. Karthi's movement was still very laboured and hesitant.

'We thought we would come and show some support,' Sabitha said, grinning. Karthi nodded indifferently, but she was smiling inside. It didn't feel like the right place to feel excited about anything. It didn't feel like it was the right juncture in her life to feel happy or excited about anything.

'Thank you for coming,' she said with a warm smile, not wanting to be seen as rude. She turned around and gestured the other women to come closer, and introduced all of them to each other.

'Ah, yes, I might have heard about you,' Sabitha said as she shook hands with Anu.

'I might have heard about you as well,' Anu replied sheepishly.

'We were told there would not be any hearing in the courtroom today. Instead, whatever is happening, is happening in the chambers,' she said. The chatter at the corridor grew as the women became acquainted with one another, with Anand standing slightly removed from the rest, looking on like a keen observer.

Geetha stepped out of the courtroom shortly after. She approached Karthi to brief her about the case, before pausing her explanation. She took a step back, and had a look at all the people who had surrounded Karthi in a small huddle right outside the courtroom.

'Wow, now this has turned into a party,' she said, noticing nearly all the women in her life right now getting to know each other. But beyond that crowd of women, she noticed Anand, peering over them, waiting to see if she would notice him.

. 'He insisted on coming along,' Sabitha said, a mischievous smile on her face.

'I am sure he did,' Geetha said, and turned away, restoring her attention in the direction of her client.

'I am sorry, I brought everyone here for no reason,' she said. Sabitha was already hovering really close to both of them, and again interrupted the conversation.

'It doesn't have to be for no reason,' she said. 'Maybe Karthiga can meet new people. She can have some coffee. Or tea,' she said, looking at Karthi. Geetha and Karthi's face erupted with a wide grin. Geetha looked at Sabitha while Karthi tried to look everywhere except at Sabitha.

'Oh my God, I am actually present and witnessing my gay cousin hitting on another woman,' she said.

Sabitha held Geetha's arms and pulled her closer, to a whispering distance. 'Hey, right now, my ex-boyfriend is going after you. So, on the scale of weird, uncomfortable scenarios involving both of us, this is nothing,' she said.

Geetha turned around again and noticed Anand sitting on the pillars of the fourth floor balcony, looking blankly out into the horizon.

'Yeah, that is weird,' Geetha said.

'But not weird enough for you to say no,' Sabitha said, with a mischievous grin on her face.

Geetha seemed to snap out of the chatter as she noticed a couple of journalists, including Anu, waiting at her wings. She tapped Karthi's arms, and faced the journalists, who put up recorders near her mouth. This was happening to her for the first time ever. Her smile returned. Karthi, still, did not know what had happened inside the chambers. The accompanying group, along with Anand, quietened down, not to disturb Geetha's press briefing.

'Today, we have had a change in the legal provision we had been using for this suit. This legal challenge was initially an attempt to introduce privacy and sexual orientation discrimination tort into Malaysian law when Karthiga was transferred due to her sexuality,' Geetha said, and she shot Karthi a glance.

'But, as some of you may have known, Karthiga had her employment terminated on the grounds that she had affected the Education Ministry's reputation due to a media interview she gave in November. So, another avenue had opened up for my client. The judge called us into the chambers today to discuss the merits of a tort challenge, which is when I brought to the judge's attention that we have filed to have the legal provision changed. We are now suing for discrimination that goes against Article 8 (1) of the federal constitution, which guarantees equality before the law. The judge has taken it into consideration, and new dates will be given for the hearing to commence. We expect our case to be stronger now that we are arguing on the basis of a constitutional provision, and thus a court should deliberate a constitutional question,' she added, and the press briefing concluded soon after, with the journalists turning their attention towards Zulkifli. A small smile escaped Karthi's lips.

As the motley group of women along with Anand left the courtroom that morning, they were beaming as though they had won the court case. Zulkifli stood back and watched in silence, his junior lawyers restlessly fidgeting with their phones, waiting for their boss to make a move. Zulkifli waited for the coast to clear.

'I am glad I finally came out of hiding for this,' he said, sighing and taking baby steps as the group disappeared past the lift lobby. 'Yes sir, I hope we win,' one of his juniors was clearly trying to make an impression. She was clenching her fists, pumping the air at her chest level, with a motivational grin on her face. He turned towards her and looked her up and down. 'One day, you will realize it's not so much about winning cases anymore,' he said. 'But you need this enthusiasm at this age. Keep it up,' he said.

As the lift door opened, the group split up differently than the way they had arrived at the court. Karthi invited Sabitha to join her and her housemates for a meal in the city, but Kasturi and Lakshmi took themselves out of the equation. Karthi and Sabitha ended up in the same car. Anu offered to drive Kasturi and Lakshmi back to their home, nodding at Geetha in the process—she wasn't going to do cheese and wine with Geetha today. As everyone went their own ways, Geetha dragged her heavy briefcase through the road leading to the car park, and Anand walked beside her, clearing his throat a couple of times. She stopped, shielding her eyes from the rays of the sun. She was wearing heels, and was a good few inches taller than him. 'You have my attention,' she said.

'You . . . are tall,' he said, with a smile on his face.

'Is that a problem?' she asked back.

'I am twenty-three. You are thirty-two. Yet, I am still here. How shallow do I look?' he retorted. A small smile appeared on her face.

'Okay, you're getting lunch,' she said, walking matter-of-factly to the car. They walked side-by-side through the packed car park, and Geetha turned to her right, unlocking her BMW. Anand stood in his tracks, watching.

'Nice,' that was all he could muster. Geetha opened the boot of her car and was about to move her luggage into the space, and he immediately offered to help.

'Who do you think was carrying my bags all these years? Not even my husband did that,' she said, managing to lift the briefcase after a momentary struggle. She closed the boot and tapped the body of her white BMW twice. 'It looks like you didn't expect this to be my ride,' she said. Anand smiled cautiously.

'Overwhelmed?' she asked.

'Maybe. But I'm not quitting,' he said, taking a couple of steps to head to his car.

'Where are you going?' she asked.

'To get my car,' he said.

'Jump in this car, we will go together. I'll drop you back here later,' she said. He hesitated.

'I should be the one driving you,' he said.

'This is how it is going to be if you want to do this,' she said. Anand tried to contain his smile. She was warning him about taming his male ego and traditional gender roles in the relationship, but beyond that, she was giving him a clear indication that she was willing to consider something more serious with him. He knew he had a shot. He sheepishly got into the car, and sat next to her, and couldn't help but admire its interiors.

He pulled out his phone from his pocket and started to do a Google search to identify the nearest restaurants.

'So, there is—'

'You can turn your search off, I know where we are going. All you have to do is sit, and enjoy the ride,' she said, again with a mischievous smile that indicated she was consciously trying to flip dating gender roles. Shortly after that she started cursing and mumbling obscenities at faceless strangers who had parked their cars on the shoulder of the parking lanes, partially blocking the room she needed to turn her car out of the parking zone.

'Happens every bleeding time,' she said, still grumbling as she finally got out of the car park. Anand nodded quietly, listening to her rant. Seconds later, she was back to her pleasant self, and pretended like he wasn't present in the car for her mini-outburst.

* * *

'I like the color,' Sabitha said, admiring the car in front of her, as Karthi rummaged through her bag to find a bottle of lotion, which she duly applied on herself. She offered some to Sabitha. 'It's a really hot day,' she said, realizing that sweat was tricking down her neck towards her chest—the only time she detested living in a tropical country. Sabitha dabbed a little bit of lotion, her eyes still fixed on Karthi's car, now parked asymmetrically and without permission in an affluent housing area at Bangsar.

'And I liked your color as well, during the interview,' she said. 'Just like the car. I see the symmetry there,' she added.

Karthi smiled ruefully. 'I know, I look like shit,' Karthi said.

'No, you look like you've lost a bit of color. It's fine; that can be retrieved any time,' Sabitha said, subtly brushing her fingers over Karthi's bandage. 'Does it hurt?' she asked.

'No, right now, it doesn't,' Karthi said, and they walked closely to each other, their shoulders brushing off each other, before reaching a row of plastic tables and chairs that looked like they had been randomly strewn along an uneven brown sidewalk, under a large tree that shed its leaves all over the sitting area. Next to the substantial seating area, a middle-aged man with a coarse voice shouted orders at his workers, as they quickly threw together plates of nasi kandar, a dish popular in northern Malaysia, to move along a file of customers that stretched to the road under the hot sun.

'Wow,' Sabitha said, never having come to this establishment before. Karthi smiled at her, as they joined the queue and got themselves a hot plate of rice and fish curry and squid, and dipped into a meal that was surely going to make the heat feel much worse after.

'My hands will smell like fish after this,' Sabitha said, as she decided to give up using cutlery, and opted to go in with her hands. Karthi never bothered to pick up cutlery in the first place.

'Why are you here?' Karthi asked, halfway through her meal, as the quantity of the food began placating her hunger.

'What do you mean?' Sabitha asked.

'I mean what are you doing here with me? I'm a bit of a mess,' she said.

Her mouth full, Sabitha held out her hands and asked Karthi to wait for answer. Ten minutes later, her plate half-clean and her hands washed, Sabitha returned to the question.

'Sorry, my mom taught me not to talk while eating. It was a big thing in our house,' she said. 'What about . . .,' she wanted to add a question, but immediately trailed off. 'Sorry, forget about it,' she added. Karthi merely nodded with a subtle smile.

'Anyway, I haven't spoken to my parents in months. I came out to them, and ever since then they haven't spoken to me, and I haven't gone back, and they haven't visited,' Sabitha said. 'So, I'm not any less of a mess right now.'

'But you don't look like a mess,' Karthi said, a barely noticeable grin on the side of her lips.

'Was that your attempt at a pick up?' Sabitha asked, chuckling into her glass of water.

'If it worked, yes. If it didn't, then, no,' Karthi said, her eyes trained on Sabitha and partially on the latter's plate.

'Why are you staring at my plate with such disapproval?' Sabitha asked.

'Your mom didn't insist on clean eating as well? Your plate makes me uncomfortable,' Karthi said. Sabitha smiled.

'I am sorry. Is that some deal breaker? I guess you might have to deal with that discomfort, because I am a messy eater,' she said.

'Not really. I might just help finish a messy plate like that,' Karthi said.

'Oh, wow, you want to?' Sabitha asked, her eyebrows raised.

'No, we are not there yet,' Karthi held back. But Sabitha was beaming. It was the first verbal admission by Karthi that they might consider a long-term commitment to each other. Now, she knew she had a chance.

* * *

Geetha drove Anand to a mall near the courtroom, with the afternoon heat becoming more and more unforgiving as time went by. As the trees around the courthouse continued to disappear to make way for further construction in an area that was already perched on a small hill, the heat seemed to get worse every year. Both of them were comfortably protected from the heat in the car, but as they stepped out of the car into the mall's parking lot, they couldn't help but react to the amount of heat that was trapped and circulating in that space.

She walked in front of him— she walked much faster than he did—and she seemed to know the place she was bringing him to in a heartbeat. They ended up in a restaurant with courtyard seating that faced a small water fountain. They were safe from the heat, yet it gave them the feel of being approximate with nature and not being completely boxed indoors.

Anand browsed the extensive menu card with the items printed on really small fonts, and struggled to make a choice, most of the time looking at the price of things. Geetha observed him for a couple of minutes, before reaching out, and blanking out the price with her hands.

'Now, make your choice. Don't look at this column. At all,' she said.

Anand struggled to design a retort. He picked something at random, and backtracked when Geetha pointed that the dish had beef. Minutes later, Geetha was served with a beef dish herself, and his eyes lit up in curiosity.

'I asked if you knew that you were ordering a beef dish. I didn't say I have anything against it. I knew what I was ordering,' she said, picking up her cutleries mid-air, before haphazardly putting them down again.

'Go ahead,' he said, with a smile. 'You must be hungry,' he added for good measure.

'Are you not?' she asked, while gesturing that she was going to wait for his food to arrive. Her phone chimed. She reached for it, and instead of picking it up, flipped it over—the screen was facing the tablecloth and was no longer a distraction.

'I was. And then my hunger went away,' he said with a cheesy smile. Geetha looked at him, her eyes wide open.

'You just reminded me of your age. That is so cheesy and so yesterday,' she said.

'Doesn't make it any less true,' he said, shaking his legs nervously but exuding unrivalled calmness in his upper body. Geetha stretched out her legs and tapped his feet.

'It's distracting,' she said, just as his meal arrived. He had the smile of a guilty child as he stopped shaking his legs and consciously tried to keep it still. 'Dig in,' she said.

The afternoon was longer than Geetha had intended it to be. She ended up having a couple of drinks after the meal as their conversation seemed to flow effortlessly. Geetha was convinced that most of Anand's attraction towards her was superficial—it was not substantial enough to hold water during a boring lunch conversation. But the conversation was anything but boring, and she found it increasingly difficult to leave the conversation as the time went on. Anand seemed happy to simply be in her company and found excuses to extend their stay in the restaurant. Geetha moved around all of her pending work and appointments to prolong her time with him. But the fear of the Kuala Lumpur traffic eventually got the better of her, and they decided to leave the place after spending four hours with each other. Unlike her expectations, Anand did not make any mention about going for more dates, or trying to discuss future scenarios between both of them. He acted like a good friend, and simply offered companion unconditionally for four hours. By the time their date was over, the clouds quickly morphed from white to dark, and the sweltering afternoon heat gave way to heavy evening rain that was evidently going to wreak havoc on the traffic. Geetha looked at the rain quietly for a while.

'Are you thinking about something?' Anand asked her. She had her bag in her hands, all ready to leave, but the rain seemed to have distracted her.

'The last time I watched it rain,' she said, her voice melancholic and in stark contrast to how casual and cheerful she had sounded for the past four hours, 'my husband passed away.'

'Oh,' Anand let out an instinctive reaction, not being able to come up with a more substantial response. 'Damn.'

She turned her head around to face him, with a warm, endearing smile. 'And you almost made me forget about all that, all about home, for four hours. Thanks for that,' she said.

Anand was getting excited. He had millions of things to say in response. He had hundreds of questions that he wanted to ask to further probe the level of seriousness and interest that she was developing for him. But he held his tongue. Geetha was loudly wondering if she made a mistake getting married so soon after meeting her late husband—and he knew she was not going to rush any relationship she was getting into next.

The bill came to the table, and Anand quickly sprung on his feet to grab the bill holder from the centre of their table. Without looking at the numbers on the bill, he wedged his card in the pad, and held it in his palms, quickly calling the waiter to collect it from him.

'No way,' Geetha's voice was now a pitch higher. 'I brought you here,' she added. She was reaching across the table, but she knew she would have no opportunity to pry the bill away from him. Anand was back in his seat, and was keeping the bill close to his person.

'Let's split it at least. Go dutch,' she said, taking her seat again.

'Why? Give me a good reason why we need to split and I can't get this bill?' he asked, handing over the bill holder to the waiter who had showed up at their table.

'Because,' she stuttered. Anand felt the power dynamic between both of them was momentarily changing. He stopped feeling inferior to her. And it had nothing to do with him paying the bill. He knew how this conversation was going to go and he had the perfect response to it. 'Because, equality,' she said.

'Geetha,' he said out her name loud for the first time in the evening. 'Equality doesn't have to come at the expense of chivalry,' he said, and stood up from his seat. Her jaw dropped. Realizing he couldn't top that line, he started walking out of the restaurant. She stood up, her bag on her shoulders, and followed his lead. 'Now, that was a really good line,' she said.

* * *

Yuva was halfway through typing an important report that was due on the same day, when he felt his brain switch off momentarily. He opened another tab and almost instinctively opened his Facebook. He read a couple of news articles, and started feeling inspired again. But before he returned to his report, he took a few minutes to write a few comments on Facebook news articles, mostly trolling or deriding comments made by some politicians. He yawned instantly as he returned to his report, and picked up his iced coffee and took a long sip.

The report writing task was not holding his attention for long. Before he knew it, he was looking at his phone, and scrolling through his messages with Anu. He was trying to find a reason to communicate with her today, but so far, he could not find a strong reason to do so. He had met Anu a couple of times, but the conversation didn't seem to be going anywhere. She was stubborn, set in her ways, and was not seeing things from his perspective. He made sure she remembered his existence by constantly sending her text messages, mostly links to articles or music videos which had particular significance to both of them. As he was looking through his chat window with Anu, she messaged him.

'Have thirty minutes over lunch?' she asked in a text message.

He beamed, looking at his phone. It was a sign that things were returning to normal for both of them. This nightmare will soon be over. He cleared his throat and replied calmly. 'Yes, I do,' he typed, hiding his enthusiasm.

'Cool, I'll come over,' she replied back, sounding more like a good friend rather than a girlfriend or even an ex-girlfriend.

Energized, he continued working on his report, wearing an ever-present smile, before discarding his iced coffee and going down twenty floors in his office building, and finding a cute little table for two at the cafe where he had met her for lunch numerous times over the years. He ordered another cup of iced coffee, a pastry, and a cup of hot tea. When the drinks arrived, he placed the cup of hot tea neatly on the opposite end of the table. She arrived barely seconds later.

'You drink was here before you,' he said. She looked at the drink.

'Wow, not bad,' she said, with an impressed smile.

'Thanks for finally calling. Or texting,' he said, pushing the plate of pastry to the centre of the small table. 'You can share this if you want,' he said, pointing to the fact that he already had two small spoons on the plate. She politely declined, but the plate stayed in the centre, Yuva carving out small pieces from his half and consuming them.

'So, what brings you here?' he asked. She let a huge sigh, almost a look of dread, before it turned into a smile. He didn't like her reaction. His face started to change.

'Well, I wanted to speak to you, basically. I think I am finally ready to have a conversation, and make a decision,' she said.

'What is that?' he dropped his spoon back on the side of the plate, and looked right at her. In an instant, his pleasantries seemed to have gone flying with the strong gush of wind that seemed to indicate impending rain. She smiled again, but did not say anything. She sipped the hot tea cautiously, not wanting to burn her tongue.

'Did you come from work yourself?' he asked, realizing he needed to make her comfortable and not be openly hostile.

'Yes. Just came from court,' she said. She could have stopped there; he did not ask a follow-up question, but she felt like she wanted to egg him on a little further. She wanted to make him uncomfortable, and wanted to see his reaction. 'It's the case I wrote about, by the way. The lesbian teacher, Karthiga? I'm sure you remember. Your sister is the lawyer, after all,' she added. 'And I saw Sabitha there too. She had come to give moral support. It was nice to see so many known people there,' she said.

Anu knew there was a good chance Yuva would not react well to this comprehensive piece of information. 'It seems like everyone was there,' he said. 'And I was the only one who missed out,' he added, his tone bordering on sulking.

'Well, would you have come even if you knew about it? Or even if you were invited? Last I remember, you didn't sound particularly enamoured by this story, or what Karthiga is trying to do,' Anu said.

He sighed, and did not reply. Anu might have betrayed her inner troll; a small smile appeared on her face as she kept egging him on to answer her questions.

'Are you enjoying pissing me off?' he asked.

'You don't have to be pissed off, that's my point. The whole story has nothing or very little to do with you. I don't know why it should elicit a reaction from you,' she said, her tone now normalized and serious.

'Like, am I not entitled to have an opinion of my own?' he asked, raising his voice.

Anu closed her eyes for a brief moment, and started a sentence before holding herself back. And then she realized she didn't have to hold herself back.

'What is that opinion?' she asked.

'I disagree with it all, that's all,' he said.

'Disagree with what? The court case?'

'Lesbians, gays, people of such orientation. I have nothing against them. I won't stop them from living their lives. But I disagree with them. And I believe I should be allowed to disagree with them,' he said.

'Did you disagree with my lifestyle choices, too, then, when you first met me?' she asked.

'What has that got to do . . .'

'It has something to do with everything. Do answer,' she said.

'Yes,' he said, curtly.

Anu shook her head. 'Yuva, right now, I think of you as an asshole.'

'What the hell?' he said the moment he heard her direct profanities at him.

'You disagree with a lot of things that have nothing or very little to do with you. You sound judgemental, ill-tempered, and hostile towards personal choices some of us make. You don't only have an issue with them, the point is, by extension, you have an issue with me. You actually have an issue with anyone who does not subscribe to the same values of relationships that you have. Unfortunately, acceptance isn't one of the values. So, yes, you are an asshole,' she said.

'Anu, I would like some respect,' he tried to interrupt, but she wasn't done.

'I am breaking up with you. It's over. That's what I came here to say. The decision was made before this conversation, by the way. But I must thank you for making it so much more easier for me to say it,' she said. 'I was so afraid about how much I would hurt you when I said it out to you, but right now even that does not concern you,' she added.

'Hey, I am treating you well enough, right? You watch your language with me,' his voice was now fully raised, and his finger was pointed at her face, just inches away from her nose. She had to tilt her head back to avoid the discomfort of having his finger pointed at her. A couple of neighbouring tables at the cafe began noticing Yuva and Anu's table. Anu raised her hands, and squatted away his fingers.

And don't you fucking point your fingers at me,' she said. She had said what she had come to say, and found no reason to stay given the direction their conversation was going in. She stood up and walked away from the table, without as much as a goodbye. But he was like a dog with a bone. Yuva stood up almost immediately after she did, and followed her through the building lobby. Wary of his colleagues being in the same lobby, he waited till both of them were outside of the building before he called out to her.

'That's it? You came to break up and you don't even bother saying goodbye. Not even a simple wish for the future, after the years we spent together?' he was trying to get her attention.

'You know, at the end of the day, you are no different than so many assholes out there that you always talk about. You can't even give an ex-partner the respect he deserves,' he added. She stopped. He knew he had touched a nerve. 'I still treated you well, you know,' he added, knowing he had her attention now. He approached her, and stood uncomfortably close, facing her.

'You still think you never treated me badly?' she asked, looking directly at him. 'You set a very low bar to define treating someone well,' she said.

'Don't simply accuse me of things,' his voice was now at an all-time high, and she had dropped her head low. The noise was distracting, and was clobbering her into submission. She wanted to apologize. She thought about saying sorry just to end the unproductive and clearly toxic conversation they were having. She wanted to promise to meet him again under better circumstances, although she knew those circumstances would never occur. And just as she was about to pronounce all the things that she was considering in her head, she felt a nudge on her shoulders. It wasn't Yuva. When she heard the voice, a feeling of relief washed over her. She never knew she needed help until she got it from the unlikeliest of sources—Kasturi.

'Hey, do you speak Tamil?' she asked Yuva abruptly, without introducing herself.

'What, why? Who are you?'

'I am trying to figure if I have to scold you in Tamil, Malay or English. I understand you are Telugu but I can't speak that language, unfortunately,' she said.

'Who are you?' he asked, exasperated. Lakshmi was standing a short distance behind Kasturi. But she knew Kasturi didn't need her help. She folded her hands and watched in amusement at her sister's antics. And she wasn't the only one watching.

'I'm her sister,' Kasturi said. 'Not by birth, but a sister nevertheless,' she added. Anu cupped her mouth to hide her grin.

'Why are you raising voice against her in a public place, and standing so close to her, as if you own her?' she asked. Kasturi naturally had high-pitched voice, and she was attracting more attention than Yuva did with his earlier tantrum.

'That's between me and her,' he retorted, but in a rather muted manner. He needed a stronger response, but the shock in his system meant that he was unable to come up with one.

'And you want to ask her to tell you if you ever treated her badly? What the hell was that then, raising your voice over her, pointing your finger to her face, shouting close to her face? The male superiority you feel within is coming out, huh,' her already loud voice was getting louder. Yuva was sure someone had taken out their phones to record the interaction in case it turned into a full-scale fight.

'If you can be loud, I can be louder than you,' she said. 'And if you can make a scene, I can make more than one scene. At least I think you are concerned when people notice you being loud and being an asshole. But do you think I am concerned? I don't give an ass even about that. I won't be seeing these people's faces anymore. You, on the other hand,' she said, actively involving the bystanders and onlookers by now.

Yuva looked flustered and his face had tuned borderline red. He sighed, and slowly and walked up the small flight of stairs. But he needed some final say. 'I can't engage with people like you,' he said loudly, just before he entered the building.

'You better watch your back if you come to Rawang. You might not know what hit you,' she said, and immediately, Lakshmi reached over and covered her sister's mouth.

'Everything up until now was fantastic, but I am pretty sure that was a criminal threat. He does look like someone who is capable of making a police report about something like this,' she said, slowly guiding her sister away from the place.

Anu was beaming with happiness. 'I am so glad you guys came along. You are such a riot,' she said, as the three of them walked towards Anu's car. Lakshmi smiled at her, and with her mouth still covered by the hands of her much wiser sister, Kasturi's eyes drifted towards Anu, and she raised both her hands and gave her a thumbs-up sign.

Chapter Sixteen

DAY OF THE UNIVERSE

April 2019.

Geetha stirred awake at 7 a.m. on a weekend, with legal files and documents strewn to the right of her bed—the space where her ex-husband had supposedly slept before he passed away. She had a good sleep after a long time, and smiled as she opened the blinds and let the sunlight stream into her room. Her stomach grumbled, and she walked towards her room door, before opting against opening the door. She did not want to face her in-laws so early in the morning. The sound of chatter and plates being moved around the kitchen was audible—she was sure her mother-in-law was already awake and was making the house help prepare some Indian breakfast for all three of them—which, more often than not, would be consumed by just her and her husband. Geetha did all she could to avoid spending a lot of time with them.

Holding her grumbling stomach, Geetha returned to the bed, reached for her iPod and put on some music. All of her playlist was from the late 1990s to the late 2000s—before life had happened to her. She listened to music not for the beauty of the composition alone, instead, she related and mused about every memory that came along with those songs—the crushes, the small or significant memories, and also the dreams that she used to have as a teenager and a young adult.

She didn't have very big dreams for herself—but like many Indian girls who were brought up to believe that marriage would be the single most important decision they made in their lives, she dreamed of having a happy, functional marriage, a couple of kids, and a comfortable life with her husband. When she finally got married, she thought her life was 'settled', and that 'rest of her life' was going to begin. No one told her marriage was going to feel like a pretend role-play where everyone acted like nothing was wrong even when the problem was staring at them in the face. Her in-laws still were not willing to discuss the infidelities of their son, and continued to rue and miss him. She wished someone had asked her if she had thought of their son in the same away. Does death wash away all the hurt caused by someone?

She ramped up the volume, lied back down on her bed, and closed her eyes, listening to music while being half asleep for what seemed like a very long time. Her hunger went away, her heart felt lighter, when all of a sudden, she was jolted by a loud, urgent knock on her door. She darted to the door and saw her mother-in-law, before taking a cursory look at the wall clock in the house.

'It's so late, ma,' her mother-in-law said, looking at her from top to bottom. Geetha was sure she looked like a mess. Her mother-in-law peeked past her and looked at the documents strewn on the bed.

'Maria,' her mother-in-law bellowed. Geetha grimaced. She was never loud in the house, especially in calling her maid. 'Please clean Geetha madam's room later,' she said in her broken Malay.

Her attention returned to Geetha. 'You have a visitor. Your brother is here to see you,' she said, with her cooking spatula still in her hands. Her mother-in-law smelled like spices, sweat and oil. Geetha immediately felt her stomach, which was otherwise quiet up until then, grumbling. Indian spices always managed to create hunger in her even when there was none.

She nodded, and walked to the hall and found Yuva, bearded and sullen, on her couch. 'Hey,' she said.

'Hey,' he said with a forced smile. He looked like he had not had any sleep at all.

'I'll be back,' she said, before taking a shower, and putting on the biggest loose shirt she could find to keep herself comfortable and heading back to the living room to sit beside Yuva.

'Hey brother,' she said. He merely nodded.

'I need to talk to you,' he said, and both of them looked straight ahead towards the kitchen and surrounding areas. Geetha's mother-in-law, who was coming in and out of the kitchen, was occasionally looking at them. Her father-in-law did the same, who was sitting at the dining table, did the same. It was too many eyes for both their liking.

'Let's go to my room,' she said, leading him to her room, which had significantly lesser sunlight than the living area. But that was all the personal space she had to offer in her house now, a stark contrast to the abundance of space she seemed to have when she had a husband who was alive. She got him a glass of water, before closing the door behind her.

'Isn't it ironic, I used to have so much more space in this house when my husband was still alive. Now, I barely have any, and I don't even have a husband or kids.' The faint beats of 90s melody filled up the room—thanks to her earphones still playing songs in full volume. Sans the noise interruption from the living area, the music filled up the room, like a background score to their conversation.

'So, a brother finally visits his sister. But I am guessing the visit is not to ask how I am doing?' she asked, taking a seat on the bed next to him, after clearing her documents and reading materials and stacking them on a chair.

'How have you been?' he asked, although she knew he was merely fulfilling his courtesy as a visitor.

'How do you think I have been?' she asked in return.

'Hopefully better than me, at least,' he said. Their relationship had always been difficult to describe, and one of the greater challenges in Geetha's life. They used to be very close to each other in their years growing up together and well into their teenage years. But adulthood seemed to change the dynamic completely. Geetha was in her mid-twenties when she got married, and was not present for Yuva when he went through his challenges figuring out his life and his career as he graduated and entered the working world. Prakash never made Yuva feel welcome whenever he came to visit, and after a point, Yuva stopped visiting. For their parents, the daughter belonged to another family once she was married off, and they thought their job with her was done the moment her wedding was done. They focused on Yuva, and as a result, their relationship with Yuva remained much stronger over the years, while Geetha felt her parents' absence in her life.

By the time they tried to get to know each other better as adults, they came to realize that they were distinctly different people, and Geetha was not particularly keen on a lot of the choices that Yuva was making about his life—or at least the motivations, ideologies and judgements that were informing those decisions.

The only glue that held together their fragile, complicated bond was Yuva's girlfriend Anu, whom he had introduced to her and Prakash during a double date dinner at a fancy restaurant. The two women hit it off instantly; at times, Geetha found herself rooting for Anu more than her own brother, and saw them as something of a mismatch, although she never professed her opinions out loud.

'Tell me what's going on with you. How has it been since the break up? Doesn't look like you are having much success picking yourself up,' she said, rubbing his thighs. His head was hung low and she had never seen her own brother as emotional as she was seeing him right now. Out of the blue, he started sniffing, before starting to cry and sob as though he had just attended a funeral. Taken aback, Geetha hugged her brother for the first time in close to a decade, and caressed his hair, kissing his forehead.

'Please talk to her,' he said, in between his sobbing and crying.

'What . . .'

'Please talk to her, ka,' he said. She did not need to ask him whom he was referring to. 'Please,' he pleaded. Yuva had never asked much from her in their lives up until this point, and Geetha was wary of his request.

'I know you guys are close,' he said. 'She won't talk to me. I need your help,' he added.

His face was buried in her arms now, and she shushed him, not wanting his crying to attract the attention of her in-laws. She did not want to be explaining and discussing her brother's personal life to them.

'Can you wipe your tears and calm down for a bit? I don't want them to see you like this. Let's go somewhere more private—step out for a bit. I think you need fresh air,' she said. It took Yuva five minutes before he could put himself together, and they walked out of the room together.

'We are going out for a bit. I'll be back,' Geetha told her parents-in-law, her stomach still grumbling with hunger. She made sure they exited quickly, but Yuva's disheveled face had betrayed the fact that he was emotional or had cried. Geetha was sure she was going to inevitably face questions when she returned home.

'I am sorry,' he said, as they waited for the lift to arrive. 'I know you are probably going through shit of your own, but I really want another chance, and only you can help me get that,' he said. Geetha wanted to disagree—the only person who could give him another chance was Anu. But she did not say it out, and instead continued listening to him earnestly. Geetha had made it a point not to overtly discuss their relationship, so that she could remain neutral towards both of them. Now, she was no longer a neutral party and had turned into some sort of a mediator. She was duty-bound to be one.

It was early morning on a Sunday, and she knew that her neighbours and fellow residents at this posh condominium would not be populating the common facilities until much later in the day. The artificial garden would be empty, and so would the swimming pool.

As the lift arrived and its doors opened, Geetha's phone rang. It was Anand. She asked her brother to hold the lift door open while she answered the call.

'Can you either tell me your unit number or step out of your building for a bit?' Anand asked. Her eyes opened wide at the realization that Anand had showed up at the condominium. She looked at her brother, waiting and holding the lift door, which had started to make a beeping sound. She gave Anand her unit number, almost in a whisper. 'But I'll be downstairs, in the common area. Come there,' she said, before ending the call and stepping into the lift.

Geetha and Yuva got out of the lift, and stepped into the artificial garden space. She immediately noticed Anand sitting on a bench, waiting for her. He immediately stood up and walked towards her, but he seemed surprised by Yuva's presence, as much as the latter was surprised by his.

'Dude, what are you doing here?' Yuva asked, pretending like they did not almost get into a fist fight the first time they met each other. Still bewildered, Anand pointed his fingers at Geetha.

'You know him,' Yuva said, looking at his sister, and then back at Anand. He wasn't asking a question. He could feel the tension in the air.

'We need to talk,' Anand said, looking straight at Geetha, ignoring Yuva's presence in the same place.

'He needs to talk too. To me, I mean,' she said, pointing her fingers at Yuva, before adding, 'He is my brother, by the way,' realizing that Anand might interpret their relationship differently.

'Oh, we have met,' Anand rolled his eyes.

'Oh, I have so many questions,' she said, and looking at Anand and Yuva, who were now standing almost next to each other. There was only one thought that was crossing her mind—her younger brother was older than the man who had been trying very hard to date her.

* * *

Karthi carefully followed the instructions on the navigation on her phone as the aggressive sound of her red car reverberated through the quiet road she was travelling on. 'I have offered to hold it many times now,' Sabitha said, holding her hand out for the umpteenth time in their journey.

'No, I need to see it to be able to understand it,' Karthi replied. The car swerved to the left and right as Karthi was wary of not missing the road, given she had hardly been in an upmarket neighbourhood. As the road swerved, she doubted if they were on the right road towards their destination, but relief washed over as she saw a guardhouse appear in sight. She was still driving slowly, intimidated by the security gates in front of her.

'I have no idea what they will ask of me,' Karthi said, cautiously parking the car in the single parking slot that was drawn just outside the big guardhouse. She scrambled in the car to make sure she had all the documents with her as Sabitha watched on, slightly amused. Karthi was decked in the red saree, with a red sticker pottu on her forehead, and a subtle red-colored streak on her hair. She was already beginning to sweat. Sabitha helped wipe some sweat off her forehead, as Karthi was satisfied that she had all the documents in order. She finally got down from the car, and headed to the guardhouse; she informed them of the purpose of her visit and collected a visitor pass. Karthi put the documents on her lap and drove into the building compound.

'What was the need to bring all those documents with you?' Sabitha asked. She grabbed the documents from Karthi's lap and held them carefully as the latter found a suitable parking spot in the expansive-looking campus.

'Do you think it would be okay to park here?' she asked, still looking perpetually lost. 'I am going to look so out of place in a place like this,' she added.

'Yes, you will look out of place in any place, in fact. Because everyone's attention will be on you, in a good way,' Sabitha said, getting down from the car. The two of them walked in close proximity with each other, their hands brushing with each other's, down a small garden path that led to the campus' main door. Karthi reached and held Sabitha's hand for a short moment, but let go of it the moment she saw someone crossing paths with them. Sabitha merely tried to hide her own amusement. They entered the building, and Karthi and Sabhi separated briefly, as the former approached the reception, stating the purpose of her visit. Sabhi stood a short distance behind her, observing the environment inside the campus building. Karthi returned a few seconds later.

'Okay, they said that I need to go up to the third floor,' she said, with a sigh. 'Where will you be?' she asked Sabitha.

'I'll be fine,' Sabitha said, reaching out and drubbing off the sweat from Karthi's forehead again. A nervy Karthi looked around to see if anyone was noticing their subtle intimacy. 'You go first,' Sabitha said. Karthi nodded, before heading towards the lift lobby, which was behind the reception desk.

'Hey, so you needed this at the guardhouse but not here?' Sabitha asked just as Karthi was about to press the button on the lift, waving the folder of documents that she was holding with her left hand. Karthi smiled and smacked her forehead, before collecting the document.

'Thanks for coming along,' Karthi whispered to Sabitha. The latter nodded. 'You better go before the receptionist jumps on you. Cause that is how he has been looking at you,' Sabitha said. Karthi got into the lift, and Sabitha, who was awaiting the commencement of a crucial semester, later found a cozy spot to sit in in the lobby, accompanied by a novel that she had been slowly trying to finish for months now. A residual smile lingered on in her face; she was infused by some positivity that she could not quite make sense of.

Despite the apparent issues that they were both facing individually, Karthi and Sabitha didn't really struggle in developing their relationship to a point where they accompanied each other for even simple chores or appointments, even if one of them had nothing more to do other than being a sidekick— as Sabitha was doing today. The first date quickly resulted in countless other dates, spanning at least once a week. When they realized they couldn't keep meeting for external dates, they quickly domesticated their relationship—visiting each other, Karthi accompanying Sabitha when the latter was busy studying, or Sabitha helping Karthi sift through job applications. Before they knew it, they were spending nights with each other, and Anand had started complaining about Sabitha not showing up at his house as often as she used to.

Karthi waited impatiently and nervously in a small meeting room surrounded by flipcharts, with the document folder placed firmly at the centre of the table. Her bladder was full, and she resisted the urge to step out to look for a washroom. After several minutes, a middle-aged Chinese woman showed up and greeted her warmly.

'Wow, look at you today,' she said, her eyes opening up wide as she took in Karthi's dress and overall appearance.

'I hope you mean it in a good way,' Karthi said, sheepishly.

'Are you kidding me? You look awesome,' she said. Karthi smiled and relaxed. She forgot about her nervousness and her full bladder. The rest of the interview seemed elementary.

She walked out of the room an hour later with a smile that was difficult to erase from her face. She got into the lift, got to the ground floor, and saw Sabitha lost in her book, having made herself comfortable in a cozy corner in the campus lobby.

'Hey there,' Karthi said, approaching Sabitha. Sabitha was sitting cross-legged on the couch with her slippers removed. Sabitha snapped out of the comfort of reading, and smiled warmly. 'So, how did it go?' Sabitha asked.

'Let's go,' Karthi said, and Sabitha duly packed her book and stood up from the chair. She hounded Karthi for an answer as they walked out of the lobby. Karthi maintained her composure the entire time, even finding time to wave a teasing goodbye to the receptionist on her way out. Once on the garden path again that led to her car, Karthi held Sabitha's hand again, and this time, for good measure, planted a kiss on her cheeks. This time, Sabitha didn't need Karthi spelling out what had happened during the interview. She knew what happened.

'Goddamit, you got it!' she shrieked, and jumped on Karthi and hugged her. She stopped short of a kiss, wary of them being in a public place.

'No one can wipe this smile from my face for the rest of the day,' Karthi said. They got into the car, and Karthi rummaged through the bag and picked up the lunch that she had cooked and packed for Sabitha.

'Okay, now I have to ask you something,' Karthi said. Sabitha nodded curiously. The car engine started and the air conditioning was on full blast. This conversation might take some time.

'Remember the thing we sort of promised together in case I got the job?' Karthi asked, hoping that Sabitha did not have to be reminded about it.

'Yes, I do,' Sabitha said, and the smile reappeared on her face.

'Were you serious when you mentioned it?' Karthi asked.

'Yes, I actually was,' Sabitha said.

'So, this is happening.'

'I hope so. It will happen if we make it happen,' Sabitha said, holding Karthi's hands.

'In that case, I want us to have lunch elsewhere,' Karthi said. 'What are you going to do with that, then?' Sabitha asked.

Karthi drove the car to the guardhouse, and as she returned the visitor pass at the guard house, she handed over the lunch meal to the security guard. 'I am starting next Monday, so I will see you then,' she said to the bewildered man. The guard, who seemed to have had an uninspired morning up until that point, suddenly seemed rejuvenated.

* * *

Anand looked up at the clouds as he sat by the children's swimming pool, with two children splashing about, and occasionally getting him damp in the process. Dark clouds gathered and he wondered if it was going to be another rainy day. His attention returned to the news articles he was reading on his phone. He had walked around the courtyard wishing he would live in a place like this with his own partner, and he needed to quieten his mind from thinking too far ahead. He looked to his right, and saw Geetha rubbing Yuva's back—he looked like he had taken the emotional beating of his life and desperately needed his sister to heal him. He smiled at the sight, and again buried his face in his phone. He was tempted to text her and demand her attention, but opted against it. Merely moments later, he felt her hand on his shoulders.

'Let's sit somewhere else,' she said, and led him to an indoor seating area.

'Where's your brother?' he asked, as they settled down in a concrete sitting area.

'He will wait now. I heard what happened between the both of you,' she said.

'I hope he told you a version where I didn't look like a villain,' he said.

'He tried to, but I think I can paint an accurate picture of what actually happened,' she said.

She rested her chin on her hands and looked at him enquiringly. 'So, what brings you here?' she asked.

'You,' he answered curtly. She smiled.

'Man, you and your lines,' she said, clearly flattered.

'But they do nothing to you, right?' he asked.

'Lines aren't everything. I do enjoy them, but that's where it stops,' she said. 'Anything important?' she added.

'Yes, this. Us. The lines. I want to know my place,' he said. He didn't seem to have much time to beat around the bush, as he normally did during conversations with her.

'What do you mean?' she asked.

'We had a couple of dates, and we haven't moved much beyond that. So, is that it? Will there be more? Is there hope or have you declared it over?' he asked.

'I did not declare anything over.'

'But you are not letting anything start. I am knocking, and knocking. You have to let me in. You don't reply to me most of the time. You don't plan to meet with me. I make all the plans. I make all the calls. I send all the messages,' he said. 'It's exhausting.'

'But I was just . . . busy. It was not malicious.'

'If you are interested, you will make time. I don't think time will just happen. I thought you would know that better than anyone else,' he said. Geetha smiled ruefully. There was nothing to argue against his statement. He was absolutely right.

'You know, because I have a lot of hindsight does not mean I am equipped with foresight right now. That's a very rare gift,' she said. He smiled.

'I came here because I simply wanted to know if you are still interested. Should I interpret your lack of engagement as a lack of interest? I don't want to interpret things. I would rather that you told me straightaway,' he said.

She touched his wrists for the first time ever. He felt something he had never felt before as she did that.

'I might not have a lot of foresight, and for that I must apologize. But what I do have is an ability to be honest. If I was not interested at all, I would have told you very early on in this conversation, or even before you had to make this trip,' she said.

'But at the same time, what I can tell you is that while it is not a no from me, it is not a yes either. This isn't binary. You have to take as it is—I am not saying no, that is where we stand at the moment, that is where I stand at the moment. I realize that is making you wait or go slower than your own expectations, but I come with warning signs. Big ones,' she said. 'In case you don't fully get what I am saying, let me illustrate. I live with the parents of my dead husband. I still treat them as my parents-in-law, though my late husband has been dead for months now. I can't even invite you for a cup of tea or coffee for the same reason. And it is my house. I haven't spoken to my parents or visited my hometown in months because I blame them for nudging me to get into this marriage even when I had very deep uncertainties about taking the plunge. My brother is apparently a homophobic and chauvinistic person who is in denial about his own characteristics. My cousin came out to my whole extended family, and having seen all their reactions, I can't help but to feel they are all homophobic, including my own parents,' she said. Anand was quietly digesting every sentence she was uttering.

'And,' she started again, clearing her throat. 'My husband was cheating on me. In fact, he was with someone when he died. That person died with him. Not me, the wife; it's him and the lover—whatever label you want to put on it—who went up, together,' she said. 'It's a big deal that I still believe after all this—to even think that this,' she pointed at both of them, 'was still possible.'

'This is me. I am going to be very slow. And it will test your patience. It clearly is already doing that. That is something for you to figure out,' she added.

'Wow,' Anand said, rubbing his face. 'I am not asking anything of you that you can't give yet. My only question is, and you don't have to answer me right now, is that are you putting the 100 per cent that you have into this? Your best doesn't have to be measured against my best; it's not the same. But are you doing the best you possibly can?' Anand added.

'And, I've got nothing to say about the cheating bit. Thanks for telling me. Helps me understand a little more,' he said. He stood up. 'Tend to him; he looks like a mess,' he said, and she stood up and almost instantly gave him a hug that he never expected. He had a million questions about the meaning of the hug—but he knew he would not get an answer no matter how much he probed. The hug lasted longer than he expected, and he watched on as Yuva noticed what was happening and immediately stood up, shooting a disapproving look in their direction. But Geetha was lost in the hug, until her phone jolted her with a notification. She saw her phone screen and noticed a message from Sabitha with a picture. She opened the picture and looked at it for a long time. Anand, who was shorter than her, did not have a great view of what was on the phone screen, so he tried to read Geetha's face to determine if she had received good news or bad news. He was hoping there was no more bad news after everything she had gone through in recent months. And then he checked his phone and realized he had gotten a similar message.

Yuva, who had never stopped looking in their direction since they started hugging each other, walked behind Geetha, close to her, and tried to take a peek into her phone screen, but by that time, she had put her phone away, and was rubbing her face.

'Wow, this is some day indeed,' she said, and a small smile appeared on her face.

She looked at Yuva, who was demanding answers from her. 'My client,' she smiled in the direction of Anand, 'is moving in with our cousin,' her hands pointed towards Yuva.

All the early morning arguments and emotional outbursts suddenly appeared trivial. There were more questions than answers on everyone's mind. But the questions didn't matter. Only one fact mattered.

'They are moving in,' Geetha said again, as if reiterating the fact before anyone professed any doubts about what's happening. 'And it took them only three months to decide upon that,' she added. She took a deep breath, and leaned against the wall as the strong wind from the darkening clouds blew on her face. She looked at Anand. 'I'm sorry,' she said, in a moment of madness and honesty that she had never felt capable of. 'It seems elementary, all these little fears, all the things that are stopping me. Karthi should have more fears than mine; more insecurities, yet she was able to commit to someone and see it through,' she said. Anand smiled.

'Don't pre-judge based on any of your past experiences, that is all I am asking,' he said. 'Consider me for me, and you. Not because of anything that has happened before,' he added.

'That's easier said than done,' she said, smiling. The exchange happened in Yuva's presence, and by now he had a clear idea what was going on between his sister and Anand.

'What the hell? Him?' he pointed out with a grimace and a sign of disapproval. Both of them smiled at him.

'How old are you?' he asked Anand. Anand answered by holding up his fingers. 'Nine years!' Yuva said loudly. 'Has everyone in this family forgotten how to make normal choices?'

'I think we are beginning to make choices based on what we want, not based on someone else's idea of our lives,' she said, stepped forward and held her brother's hand. 'Let's get some food,' she said to Yuva. She turned around and shot a flirtatious glance towards Anand. 'Mind joining us for lunch?' she asked Anand. With a wide grin, he nodded.

As Yuva stood between both of them in the lift, he wished this was a temporary nightmare and nothing would come out of it. He imagined how his entire family would react to these relationships, and dreaded being the person facing their wrath, as much as he dreaded how they would digest these developments. The odds were stacked against Sabitha and Karthi—primarily because same sex relationships were not even recognized in Malaysia.

And then he checked himself; he was scoffing at his own sister's romance—he was unable to feel happy for them. Yuva had met people like this during family functions numerous times—those who arrive at celebrations stripped of any celebratory spirit; those whose sole purpose at these events seem to centre around espousing Murphy's law—everything that can go wrong, will go wrong. And when it did go wrong, they found great pleasure in saying, 'I told you so.'

He always hated such people, and he had never envisaged becoming one of them. He was slowly realizing that he was turning into one such person, if he hadn't already. Yuva realized individuals could easily turn into the very people they despised, and not realize it happening at all. He hadn't realized. He didn't need a mirror to show him what he had become—unhappy with himself, and as a result, being unhappy with others.

Life had turned him into being one of those men—the one who mansplains, the one who finds the nearest woman to blame for all the problems he is facing in his life. As the lift doors opened, Yuva held the doors and noticed how inspired his sister was; Karthi and Sabitha's decision was fueling her own little rebellion. 'Let's introduce Anand as my friend,' he said, letting the two of them step out into the lift lobby.

'No, why should I continue hiding and lying?' she asked, her voice slightly raised.

'Do you want the unnecessary drama in the house now?' Yuva asked. 'Are you guys getting married tomorrow?' he asked.

Geetha and Anand looked at each other, slightly perplexed. Yuva understood the look. 'Yes, so, one battle at a time. Court first . . .' he said, encouraging them along the corridor to the house.

'Aww, probably the wisest thing I've heard you say in a while,' Geetha said.

Chapter Seventeen

HETERODOXY

May 2019.

Battles against the state were not won often; not in Malaysia, at least. The state's influence ran deep, and the odds were often stacked against those who attempted an audacious bid to bring the state apparatus to its knees, even if for a brief moment. Karthiga did not know her father's original name, and over the years, she had learned that she would have been declared stateless if she was not fortunate enough to have a birth certificate. If she was stateless, she would not be a registered citizen, could not be employed in the civil service, and more importantly, couldn't have taken this battle to the government. There were layers to this battle, it wasn't so much a battle about sexuality as it was a battle of the minorities going up against majority. She looked at Lakshmi and Kasturi, huddled close to each other in the back bench of the court—they did not know what it took to hire a lawyer and mount a legal challenge less than a year ago, but they had now stuck with Karthi every step of the way—and at times had acted like pro bono legal assistants to Geetha. The three of them were not supposed to have this much limelight in society. Society was happy to accommodate them as long as they operated in the peripheries. But Karthi had come into this world with nothing, and she had never shied away from asking for more. In fact, that was the only way she knew how to live. She was used to rejections.

Geetha wasn't. Hands on the sleek, black table with brown skirtings, she looked up at the elevated judge's chair, and wondered how it must be from up there—to come in for brief moments and pass the judgments that make and break many lives, and to live with that. She was part of that same system, but she had never quite contemplated the consequences of her actions as much as she was doing right now. Her files were closed and folded in front of her, and all she could hear was her own deep breathing. She turned around and looked at the viewing gallery. There was a steady stream of people there. Anu, leaning opposite one of the entrances and making small talk with the court officer, looked at Geetha and nodded subtly. Geetha noticed several activists and some other lawyers coming into the gallery. The calls and messages in the past few days indicated that she was now considered to be a part of the 'activist' community—a motley group of lawyers and self-learned experts of the constitution whose only goal in life seemed to be to annoy the establishment, at the cost of their own safety and sanity. Geetha had read the names some people had called her in the comment section of articles featuring her legal battles. They called Karthi names. They did the same to Anu for writing the article. Geetha looked to her right, and Zulkifli looked half-asleep, his glasses on his nose yet again. He was now using a walking stick. She had wondered if he was going to be found napping if the judge were to abruptly step in. When she did, Geetha immediately sprang to her feet, as did the rest of the courtroom. She looked next to her and saw Zulkifli holding on to his walking stick, and standing upright, facing the judge. This is why he had done this for four decades, she told herself.

After clearing out the mentions of a couple of other cases, the judge came to the all-important docket that was holding all the media attention. The judge looked at the gallery and immediately realized the amount of attention this case was going to attract. Zaleha had wanted to chide the Education Ministry officials who made the decision to sack Karthi, but she had to maintain her composure as a judge. This docket initially came to her filed as an attempt to introduce a privacy and discrimination tort, which she felt would lead to a largely academic trial, and as such, could have ruled on its merits in chambers. But the sacking helped the plaintiff's case—it had now become a suit about unlawful termination prompted by discrimination that allegedly breached the federal constitution, and Zaleha now had no choice but to give the spirited Geetha the courtroom trial that she had been pushing for. This was not a matter for the chambers anymore.

Zulkifli seemed disinterested most of the time, but when the trial started, Zaleha's eyes twinkled as she watched a highly regarded public prosecutor and a highly regarded civil lawyer battle their wits out in her somewhat modest court. Headline generating cases rarely came her way, and she was wary of editorializing her judgement, knowing that the issue of sexual minorities often divided Malaysians. Both the lawyers had made valid points—Geetha had argued that sexual minorities deserved protection under the federal constitution's broad tenets, but Zulkifli brought together provisions under different laws to make his case that any interpretation of the constitution must be 'qualified'. He pointed out the criminalization of same-sex relations under the country's Islamic laws, and the criminalization of sodomy and unnatural sex under the Penal Code. A person who might be falling foul of other existing laws in Malaysia due to his or her sexual orientation cannot be afforded the same treatment as law abiding citizens, he argued.

In a subtle and refined way, he had called Karthi a 'lesser' citizen because of who she was. It wasn't very flattering, but Geetha expected this line of argumentation to come up.

The day for a decision had come and Zaleha was sitting higher than everyone else for that very reason. Zaleha cleared her throat, and started reading out her judgement, as couple of 'shushes' reverberated throughout the court. From the second page onwards, it was clear to the lawyers the direction she was heading towards.

'. . . end of the day, the matter before this court is to rule whether discrimination has happened in such a way that it violates the Federal Constitution. This is by no means an indication or a judgement that justifies the manner in which the Education Department, the Ministry of Education, and other defendants have acted in terminating the employment of the plaintiff. Whether this is a lawful, proper termination, is something for the Industrial Court to rule on. This court finds that in the course of arguments and evidence presented, there might be enough merit for the plaintiff to pursue an unlawful termination case at the industrial court and seek damages from the defendant. But, as the question put before this court is one that involves the Constitution, it is in the court's opinion that the Federal Constitution's provisions should always be qualified by being read together with other elements of Malaysian law, failing which, the interpretation of such liberties become too broad. As such, the court dismisses the plaintiff's application, with no damages ordered.'

Geetha had a rueful smile on her face. Zaleha's eyes briefly met Karthi's, and she had a very similar smile on her face. The junior prosecutors started flashing a grin—this was a victory for them. Zulkifli was indifferent. Zaleha, after giving Geetha and Karthi their day in court, had chosen to dismiss the lawsuit. But her judgement was also scathing towards the government, and she refused to order Karthi to pay any damages to be paid to the government, an indication that Zaleha thought there was valid grounds to the case. There were groans and murmurs in the court.

Outside, Sabitha was sitting on a bench with a bouquet of flowers that she felt would be suited for any eventuality. A lone skinny man passed through the court, chanting against the LGBT community, and like a playground bully, quickly jogged to the lift lobby, his point being made. Sabitha didn't understand the point of the heckling.

Zaleha stood up and dismissed the court right after reading her judgement, and the whole room spilled out, with journalists cramming the entrance to wait to speak to Geetha. Some activists lined up behind the journalists, wanting to acquaint themselves with Geetha. Some state-backed media organizations formed a small group, and lined up at the other door, waiting for Zulkifli. Kasturi and Lakshmi's euphoria had died down, they looked heartbroken and disappointed. But Karthi still had that smile on her face. She was being strong for everyone else who had joined her journey so far. Geetha knew the decision was inevitable and yet, she seemed unable to stand up from her chair; her assistants waiting for her after having packed their briefcases. Zulkifli stood up and reluctantly accepted the congratulations that were being directed at him by the junior prosecutors. He gave them cursory attention, before turning around and facing Geetha.

'Hey, lady,' he said. Geetha mumbled a congratulations, with a look of defeat on her face. She extended a handshake.

'Don't want to get up?' he asked.

'Still feels weird. I don't take defeat very well,' she said.

'Because you are not used to it,' he added.

She nodded.

'That's what happens with these cases; you don't tend to win them. Not in here, at least,' he said. 'So, if you want to keep doing this, start celebrating your victories outside, not your defeats inside here,' he added.

'What do you mean?' she asked.

'When we walk out of here, those lining up to interview us will treat you like the winner, and me the loser. Out there, you win, a little bit. In here, you don't stand a chance against me,' he said, tapping his walking stick against her legs. 'Remember, I have been doing this since before you were born. Now, get up,' he added. Geetha adjusted her hair and packed her briefcase, before stepping outside of the court, following Zulkifli's footsteps. As they stepped outside, Zulkifli observed the larger group of journalists huddled together and instinctively knew they weren't waiting for him. He stepped aside, and gestured towards Geetha to head in their direction. He headed to a smaller group of journalists gathered down the corridor. Geetha took the media storm, while Karthi opted to keep quiet. With the cameras focused on Geetha, she stepped away from her lawyer and approached Sabitha, who was still sitting on the bench outside the court.

'I thought those were for me,' she said.

'Yes, but I was not sure if you would still want it,' Sabitha said.

'I want it,' Karthi said, smiling. Sabitha's worries flew away in an instant. She picked up the bunch of flowers and passed them to Sabitha. 'Thank you, roommate,' she whispered in a hushed tone.

'So, we lost,' Sabitha said.

'No, we fought. That's the whole point,' she said.

As the media crowd returned to their normal lives, and all the attention around her cleared, Geetha looked around and saw all the people who were left. Sabitha, Karthi, Kasturi and Lakshmi sat on the same bench, as if waiting for her to join them.

'We were thinking about a nice, hearty lunch,' they said. Geetha smiled, but she declined their offer. Leaving them behind, she walked back to her car, and the feeling of goodness within her soon evaporated along with the early afternoon heat. She had just lost a case, she reminded herself, and there was no reason to celebrate. Out of her own desire to help someone free of charge, she got Karthi fired from her job, and dragged through a very public trial where she had been essentially 'outed' by the media. The lesbian teacher—everyone will now know her for it. She feared the repercussions of her actions; she was afraid Karthi would lose the lifeline she currently has—her new job at a private international school. Geetha can't have that on her conscience.

Geetha returned to her office and locked herself in it. Armed with only coffee and some liquor she had hidden in her office cabinet, she powered through the rest of the day looking at the files of the other cases that would actually bring money to her coffers—all of them private civil disputes and divorce cases. It wasn't until the evening that she opened up her tablet and Googled her name; it was the first time she had received substantial media attention for her case. She read the reports and also the comments in social media; she indulged in the flattery and outright hatred directed at her and Karthi. She handled the comments that were directed at her, but the thought of Karthi's name being dragged through the mud unsettled her. She wanted to give up being an activist–lawyer after just one case. How can anyone be an activist in a country that seems to take innate pleasure in hating someone simply for being themselves? She looked at the city below her and only felt resentment inside her, all the events from the morning felt like distant memories by now.

Her office work cleared up by evening, and Geetha found herself being the last person in the office once again, reluctant to go back home and face her parents-in-law. They might have read the news; they might have not. They might raise the matter with her, or they might be subtle about it. None of that mattered; she would still be disturbed and tensed while wondering what they were thinking or wanting to say to her. It was too much of a mental exercise. She wanted to run away from the situation. Then, she broke character and called Anand. 'Fancy paying me a visit at the office yet again?' she asked him. He showed up in under an hour, with a brimming smile and a packet of food for her, knowing that she had not eaten since breakfast.

She opened the door for him—literally and figuratively. It was the first time she had actively sought companionship or help from anyone since Prakash's death. It was her learning to fall again, and learning to trust someone else to catch her when she fell. Anand was eager to show that he would be the person who would allow her to be vulnerable, and he jumped at the chance.

She allowed herself to come out of her mulling shell, and had a hearty meal, before sitting on the same sofa next to him. She took her laptop to work, but he shot her a disapproving look. 'The idea is to take a break from work,' he said. She sighed and smiled a little. Her mind raced with multiple thoughts, chief among those being the age difference between both of them. She played a television show instead, and over the course of the next hour, found her head slowly inching towards his shoulder. Her thoughts clouded her inhibitions yet again, and she yanked her head back, sitting up straight, tired and yawning.

'What are you thinking?' Anand asked. Geetha merely shook her head.

'What is stopping you?' he changed the question.

'From?'

'From leaning against me. You came close but you stopped. I'm not blind,' he said.

'Nothing, just thoughts.'

'Like?' he was demanding a conversation when she was not prepared to have one.

She paused her show. 'Just generic things about us, like the age difference. You are my cousin's best friend. This should be some brotherly thing, or something along those lines. You are younger than my brother!'

Anand looked exhausted. 'We can only move forward if you can look past that, you will only give us a fair chance if you manage to do that. Otherwise, you will always be stuck at some halfway point,' he said, giving a glimpse to another side to his usually calm and smiling exterior. She grimaced, somewhat playfully. She was sure she would be able to get over it someday, but she did not know how. She had mulled about it for weeks and months, but they had been stuck in some dating loop, largely due to the wall she had built around herself.

'Kiss me,' she said, out of the blue, again breaking her character. Anand looked at her, wide-eyed. 'Did you not hear me?' she asked again, looking at him in the eyes, unwavering, after waiting for ten seconds. 'I think many guys would have jumped by now,' she added another line, as Anand continued to look immobilized by the entire situation. 'What's wrong with you?' she finally asked, after being convinced he was never going to take to the invitation.

'You can't pressure me like that. That's not how you create a moment. Like, I wasn't ready for that. It should be organic, not instructed,' he countered, his breath trembling. Despite his hesitation and trepidation, she could see the effect she was having on him, and she enjoyed it.

'Why, do you wait for a perfect moment?' she asked him.

'Yes, it has to happen . . .' she didn't give him a chance to finish the sentence. She jumped on him, and kissed him right on the lips. He took some time to reciprocate, but as he started experiencing the kiss, she broke the kiss, and sat back on the couch. He looked at her blankly, questioning his own ability, and unsure if he should continue. She smiled.

'Okay, I think I know how I might finally start to see things beyond the age factor,' she said, musing loudly. Again, without warning, she sprung on him, and kissed him a little harder. He reciprocated immediately, and whispered in between, 'Come back with me.' She paused and broke the kiss again.

'Woah, slow down, man,' she said. He had a guilty look on his face.

'I just don't want to continue kissing in your office, and on this sofa, that's all. And we can't go back to your place obviously, because you know, of the people there, and all. It will be awkward . . .'

She smiled and laughed, knowing that she had him in her grasps now. 'Chill, I know, I understand, calm down. How is this going to work if you are so intimidated by me all the time?' she asked.

'What's wrong with that? You are not my enemy. I am intimidated by you because you are confident and do such big things by yourself, like owning the firm,' he said. 'I am not there yet. I am still, technically, a student. There's that fear, that I won't be able to match up to your level of achievements,' he added.

She smiled. 'I started this law firm thanks to some money fronted by my late husband. It was not some slog. I would say life very much felt like it was on cruise control mode until he died,' she said. 'So, I am just figuring things out. If you want me to look past the age, you have to stop putting me on a pedestal. We both have our issues that we need to overcome,' she said. She sat upright on the sofa again and tidied up, putting her clothes in proper order again.

'All that said and done, I have an issue at home that I simply can't deal with today, so I don't want to go back. At the same time, I'm not going to your place either. I am going to do what an exhausted working woman likes to do, some self-pampering. I am going to book and stay in a nice hotel room tonight,' she said, putting on her shoes, before leaning close to him.

'But, I do have room for a partner,' she said. Anand smiled.

She dropped a message to her mother-in-law and her father-in-law simultaneously, not knowing which one of them will check their phones faster, telling them that she would not be coming home and that she is spending the night at a friend's place. Her mother-in-law was the first to read and reply; she asked, 'Who?' Geetha groaned. 'Where do they draw the line with their questions?' she asked to a bewildered Anand. 'Tell you tomorrow,' she delayed the problem with her reply.

* * *

A small gap in the blinds allowed sunlight to enter the vast, luxurious hotel room, stirring Geetha awake. She took some time to process her surroundings, and looked at the hand that wrapped her by the shoulder and neck. She hadn't felt intimacy for years. She looked to her left and Anand was soundly asleep. She smiled to herself, and gently removed his hand. She noticed her clothes strewn all over the floor, and got up from the bed to pick them up, realizing she had to wear the same set of clothes again without a new pair to change into. The sounds she was making woke Anand up. By the time his eyes were wide open, she had showered, dressed and prepared to leave.

'You can check out a bit later,' she said.

'What about breakfast? What about spending some time until check-out?' he asked.

'Sorry, I have to leave now,' she said curtly, and he instantly wondered if he had done something wrong over the course of the night.

'Wow, feels like you walking out on me after a night together. I feel used,' he said. She smiled, realizing how the whole sequence of events might have looked like from his perspective. She darted to his side, and leaned over him for a kiss on the forehead.

'I would have kissed you on the lips, but you haven't brushed,' she said. 'I am not walking out. I just need to do something very important. I'll tell you later. And I want to do this right,' she said, pointing at both of them. 'Everything I've done since Prakash's death was a reaction to how the universe treated me or made me feel at certain points of time, including last night,' she said. 'But not anymore. I want to be more than that. I want to be more than my circumstances,' she said, putting on her shoes. 'I am starting today,' she added, darted out of the room. Anand looked lost and clueless, but nevertheless he basked in the kiss that she had just given him. He wasn't being dumped after just one night—that was all he needed to know.

Geetha drove straight back home, but spent some time in the car after parking, just to make sure she still looked presentable in spite of the night she had had. When she was satisfied with what she saw in the car mirror, she headed up to her unit, and gingerly opened the door. She immediately noticed her parents-in-law sitting together in the living room, and they looked at her questioningly, non-verbally demanding answers. She acknowledged what they were looking for. 'Wait, nana,' she said to her father-in-law.

She headed straight for her room, where she took a second shower for good measure and changed into a new pair of home clothes. She stepped out of her room soon after, and headed straight for the living room, and joined them at the sofa, sitting across from them. She put her phone away to her side. She crossed her feet and took a deep breath, knowing there wasn't an easy way to say what she was about to say.

'I am going to tell you something, I hope you don't take it the wrong way,' she said. 'But this is something I have to do because what has happened, has happened, and we all have to move on from it, including me,' she enunciated her sentences clearly in Telugu so that nothing would get lost in translation.

'I don't think it is ideal for us to stay together. He's gone, he is not going to come back, and I have to move on,' she added.

'Are you making plans to remarry?' her mother-in-law asked immediately.

'Maybe, it could happen,' she quickly interjected. 'And I am not kicking you out, I know that might be the next question. Please, listen to what I am trying to say. This is not easy for me,' she said.

'This was bound to end someday, this arrangement that we have here, and I think it is better if it ends sooner rather than later. But that doesn't mean anyone has to move out. I understand the situation you guys are in and I feel partly responsible for it because Prakash fronted the money for me to start my law firm all those years ago. So, in a way, some of the money made there should be used to help whatever difficulty you guys have,' she said.

'But, you are doing free cases now,' her mother-in-law was piling on the questions now. Geetha lost all the patience to get to her point.

'I am selling this house. It has too much of him, too much of memories, and it is too much of a burden for me. This house fetches a good price,' she said, raising her hand to stop her mother-in-law from asking any further questions. 'All the profits from the sale will be directed to you. I am not taking a single cent from it.

'I will find my own place after this, and I am sure, with that money, you can get the house in Ipoh again. If that is what you want. I will help, financially or otherwise, for you to find a new place. But what I won't be doing is living with you,' she added with such a sense of finality she felt a burden lift off her shoulders.

'But until then, we can continue being here. There's nothing that needs to change instantly, just that I will spend more time with my family, my brother who needs me to be there with him, my cousin who is getting married, and my partner,' she was surprised she had casually mentioned the latter—referring to Anand. There was silence, and she did not want to hang around to break the awkward silence. She knew they needed time to digest what had been said, so she stood up and excused herself for brunch, deciding to get a meal at a shop outside the building despite food being available in her own house.

'Ma, there is food here,' her father-in-law said. Regardless of the tension, all the elders in her entire family knew one surefire way to mend ties—discuss, or serve food. 'No, I will eat out this time. You guys take time and discuss as well. Sorry if I sounded rude. I am just trying to say this in the best way possible,' she said, leaving the house. Maria stood bewildered, not understanding what was being discussed but understanding the tension that was in the house. She wanted to resume cooking but she knew she would end up making a mess of the dish she was making without the aunt's guidance.

'That was abrupt. After all our son did for her,' Geetha's mother-in-law said after a short pause. 'Including cheating on her,' her husband reminded her. She shot him a strong, venomous look, and immediately mellowed down. She looked at the mantel in the middle of the house, and stared at his portrait. She wanted to remember him for all the right reasons. She did not have the strength to acknowledge Prakash's infidelity and various imperfections to her daughter-in-law. We are taking care of her like our own daughter,' she said.

Her husband stood up, and put his arms around her shoulder, a rare show of physical affection. She hadn't felt that affection for years. 'No, we are not. If we were treating her like our own daughter, we wouldn't have been hesitating to acknowledge that she was wronged by her ex-husband, and stopping her from moving on from what was clearly a less than happy marriage,' he said. 'Treating her like our own daughter means acknowledging that our son was far from perfect. In fact, he might have been a bit of ass. And that's a failure we have to share,' he added. His wife started sobbing. 'But he was so young and brilliant,' she said.

'Then, choose your son, and let's leave her alone,' he said, rubbing her shoulders.

Chapter Eighteen

HOME

October 2019.

Sabitha was stirred awake from her deep sleep by the smell of fried eggs wafting through her sleeping space. She was not ready to wake up, but at the same time, the smell of the eggs and the general cooking aroma was unsettling her. She opened her eyes, and looked to the left of her bed at the studio apartment. She saw the sofa merely a few feet away, a television cabinet, a supposed dining table, and then saw her partner moving about at the cramped kitchen space—in her shorts, busily cooking. The curtains were still closed. Sabitha reached for the bedside table and picked up her phone. It was past 9 a.m. 'What are you making?' she said, half mumbling. But there was only ten feet of distance separating her and Karthi—she heard her clear and well.

'Sausages and eggs,' Karthi said, holding a cooking utensil with a certain pride. She took a couple of steps back to see Sabitha slowly getting out of bed.

'Aww,' Sabitha said. Sabitha felt something on her legs, and immediately noticed there were clothes on the bed—Karthi's clothes from the night. Her mood immediately transformed. 'How many times have I told you, babe. Please don't strew around your clothes like this. Not on the bed, at least,' she said, grumbling. In a slightly hushed tone, Sabitha continued mumbling about the little idiosyncrasies of their living arrangement.

'Don't start sounding like an old lady on a Sunday morning, please,' Karthi said assertively, as she emptied a pan of scrambled eggs into two different plates. She picked up defrosted sausages and started cooking them, when the house suddenly brightened up. Sabitha drew open the curtains and went to the kitchen, still groggy.

'It's not about sounding like an old lady. It's about me saying the same thing again and again and you not listening, she said, standing beside Karthi and scanning the kitchen top for something to do.

'There's nothing for you to do here. And I've said many times, that you should not start doing anything in the house until you have at least brushed your teeth,' Karthi put the sausages in the steamer pot, and looked at Sabitha, hands on her hips.

'Living with you is difficult, I tell you. And this space is so small,' Sabitha continued to grumble. She sounded every bit like the older person in the relationships even though the opposite was true. She picked up a towel from the dining table chair, and disappeared into the washroom. Karthi smiled at Sabitha's tantrums, but she then turned around and looked at her sausages, wondering how much truth there was in Sabitha's complaints. They lived in a 400 square feet space. They couldn't afford a bigger condominium or apartment unit, and they didn't want to share a room and deal with other housemates who might be curious about the nature of their relationship with each other. The space was decidedly small for both of them. They had everything—a bed, a TV, a sofa, a kitchen. Problem was that all the amenities were merely a few feet away from each other. They lived in a space where both of them couldn't have online meetings at the same time. And as much as Karthi had been independent in her life, she had never led a household in her entire adult working life. And she was beginning to believe Sabitha's words—she might not be so easy to live with. She picked up her phone and impulsively messaged Lakshmi.

'Was I difficult to live with?' Karthi asked Lakshmi in a text message.

'No, darling. You were so easy to take care of,' Lakshmi replied in Malay, with a smiling emoticon. She wasn't particularly good in typing messages in English.

Karthi sighed—that was the whole point. She was taken care of. Now, she was supposed to be the one taking care of another person. But the problem was that Sabitha seemed to be the one taking care of Karthi, and the former, on most days, was just an exhausted, slightly irritable final year medical student.

'How were the eggs and sausages this morning? You didn't tell me,' Karthi asked that evening, as both of them were looking at the sausages from the deep freeze section of a hypermarket that evening.

'Yeah, they were nice,' Sabitha said, yawning, slightly disinterested.

Karthi changed the topic drastically. 'Am I exhausting you?' Karthi asked. Sabitha was taken aback by the question.

'Exhausting? Why are you using such words? Did I ever say that?' Sabitha asked back, eyebrows and voice, both raised.

'It's a yes or no question, really,' Karthi said, as she continued walking towards the dry foods aisle.

'Where is this coming from? No, you don't exhaust me. Why are we having this conversation here, by the way?' Sabitha asked. Karthi brushed Sabitha's hands. 'True, not the place for it,' she said. She realized that their frequency in holding hands had also reduced significantly in recent times.

Karthi waited until dinner was over before she ordered a beer at the restaurant they were at, and calmly brought the topic up again, waiting till Sabitha had also taken a sip of her own drink. 'Maybe we should talk now?' she said.

'So, you are serious about this conversation . . .'

'Yes,' Karthi said. 'Because I feel like I'm a bad partner, at least in a domestic sense. And I don't how you are taking it,' she added.

Sabitha chuckled and smiled.

'You appear irritable, you are cranky a lot of times, you have a long list of complaints about little things,' Karthi continued. Sabitha extended her arms across the table and tapped on Karthi's arms. Karthi paused.

'This is me. Just me. It has nothing to do with you. Anand dealt with me for years, and this is what he had to put up with,' she said, half-smiling. 'What are you afraid of, Karthi?' she asked further.

'I'm afraid this won't be enough at some point,' Karthi said.

'I'm not going anywhere,' Sabitha said, reaching out and holding her hands in a restaurant filled to the brim. It was the first time they had shown affection in front of a crowd in months. Karthi smiled, almost in relief. 'This is home,' Sabitha said.

* * *

The following day, Karthi went to work at the private school where she worked and taught the relatively well-off children about modern history and English, received a hug from at least five of them at the end of the school day, and then drove to the hospital for her sixth appointment with Karthik. She waited in the same corridor, went inside when called, politely refused his offer of a hot drink, saw him make one for himself, and settled down in the comfortable chair.

'I don't know why you come here anymore,' Karthik smiled. 'I can look at your face and tell you that you are so much better now,' he said, sipping his coffee, and making himself comfortable in his chair.

'I like talking to you,' she said.

'You know you can meet me outside of the hospital, right? As a friend?' he asked.

She smiled.

'What's niggling you?' he asked, after a momentary silence.

'Future. My relationship is good, but I can't stop thinking about the future.'

'What's with the future?'

'Like, what's next?' she asked. 'Unfortunately, we don't have that option here in Malaysia—so I have a lot of thoughts. I want to have a future. I am hard-wired inside, wired to be ambitious, to want everything that "normal" people get. But I know I won't get the same here,' she said.

Karthik sighed, and seemed to be mulling what to say. 'You mean you are entertaining thoughts about leaving the country?' he asked.

'Yes, but I don't want to. But I also know I will always feel like I am missing or being denied something because of the system. I'm afraid of what it might do to me. What it might do to my relationship,' she said.

Karthik nodded. He understood what she meant. Heterosexuals could always dream about events to celebrate their relationships—an engagement, a wedding, a celebration with family and friends, starting a family of their own, watching the children grow up. But for sexual minorities, not being explicitly recognized by the legal system meant that all these options were not available. He had had many friends from the community who had left Malaysia to live elsewhere, where they enjoyed more rights. Even he had been planning to leave for the United States for the past five years, and had been meticulously carving his clinical career path with a goal in mind. But Karthi did not have the same urge. She did not have a country in mind; she was feeling rejected in the country she wanted to belong to.

'So, you are not particularly keen on leaving. You want to stay. Have you thought about what is making you stay here?' Karthik asked.

'Family. I have family. I have something I've looked for my whole life, I have it all here. I love the weather, the food, even the people. I am okay,' she said. 'But I want a little more.'

Karthik took a big sip of his coffee. 'You feel like the system is not working in your favour, right?' he said, before seeing the irony of his statement. The system wasn't designed to work for people like him and her. 'Well, for me too.' Karthi nodded.

'You tried changing the rules of the system, and you were unable to,' Karthik expanded. Karthi nodded again.

'Why not make your own rules then? If the system doesn't recognize you, it is not making the rules for your life. You are,' he said.

Karthi smiled, content.

'Try. You can think about leaving again if you tried making your own rules, and are still unhappy,' Karthik said, standing up and pacing the room a little, before leaning against a wall. It was another habit of his during sessions.

'Did you try?' she asked him, knowing full well about his ambitions to go abroad.

'Not as hard. Because I don't feel like I belong. But, in your own words, you don't want to leave. A part of you belongs. So, I know you will try harder than I ever will,' he said.

* * *

The following weekend, Karthi accompanied Sabitha to a famous temple hidden in the heart of the city centre. Despite her affinity for sarees and traditional accessories, Karthi was not very religious, at least not as much as Sabitha. But the temple was the perfect excuse to bring out the red saree, which Karthi had not worn for many months now.

Sabitha often found a certain sense of calm by going to temples, and it was a practice that she had always maintained, especially now that she was in the final stretch of medical studies, faced with a series of exams that would surely send her spinning to the deep end.

Karthi followed Sabitha's lead as the two women prayed, circled the temple's main altar three times, lit up a small earthen lamp, before sitting cross-legged near one of the ballasts of the temple, leaning back against it. It was considered bad practice to leave a temple right after prayers, and devotees were often encouraged, through some unwritten rule, to spend some time quietly sitting around the temple before leaving. Sabitha didn't necessarily follow such conventions, but she had always liked the calm of being in a temple, so sitting in its ambience was definitely the highlight of her visits to a temple.

They heard a chatter from the chief priest's room, which was located just behind the spot where they were sitting.

Sabitha turned around and noticed a young couple discussing dates to have a wedding organized in the temple. Karthi had also turned around, momentarily eavesdropping on the couple's conversation with the priest. Their attentions returned to the temple, and to each other. Sabitha looked at Karthi.

'I always wanted a temple wedding, you know,' she said. 'I hated weddings that happen inside halls. I like the intimacy of temple weddings. A couple in the centre and people just moving around them in close proximity—it feels . . . personal,' Sabitha said, reflecting at the structure of the temple. 'I should encourage others in the family to have a temple wedding so I can be involved in one,' she laughed to herself.

'I don't get your enthusiasm about temples and temple weddings,' Karthi asked. 'I just can't reconcile those two things. Temples and religion forbid people like us from being us and getting married. How do you still get excited about them when you know it's not accepting of you?' Karthi asked, in her own reflective state.

'No, that's where you are wrong. The people in these places forbid us from being us, from getting married. Not the temple or the religion. For what it's worth, Hinduism does not explicitly forbid same-sex relationships,' Sabitha said.

Despite the adverse reactions she had faced for her sexual orientation, Sabitha never stopped going to temples because she knew the existence of various ancient texts that acknowledged, if not validated, same-sex relationships. Homosexual acts are depicted in some temple carvings, while same-sex relationships are also referenced to in the ancient Indian text on sexuality—the *Kamasutra*.

Sabitha tapped Karthi's hands. 'So contrary to what you think, we do belong here. We just have to miss out on the

temple wedding part,' Sabitha said. Karthi nodded quietly, lost
in her own thoughts. Inside her mind, a thousand thoughts
raced together—because she just had a moment of clarity that
had eluded her in recent months. She knew what she needed to
do next.

* * *

Sabitha waited by the red Mitsubishi at a mall parking lot that
night, fiddling her thumbs and checking her watch. Karthi, who
had excused herself to the washroom, had now been gone for
close to twenty minutes. Sabitha grew irritated. Why couldn't
Karthi go to the washroom when they were still in the mall?
Why did she have to go when they had already come down to
pay for the parking and drive the car out? She thought about
messaging Karthi a couple of times, but decided against it—
presuming that Karthi was probably having stomach troubles.
And then she thought about the saree Karthi has been wearing
that evening since their temple trip and how difficult it would
be to go the washroom and getting the saree right after. She
calmed down.

Five minutes later, Sabitha saw Karthi coming down the
escalator, shopping bags in her hands. Karthi paid for parking
and approached the car.

'You could have left the bags in the car before you ran
upstairs again,' Sabitha said. Karthi merely smiled. 'Rushing,'
she said, before putting the bags in the trunk, and getting into
the driver's seat. Sabitha sat in the passenger's seat, and Karthi
indicated that she did not want to go directly back home. She
kept the destination a mystery, though largely heading in the
direction of their apartment, until turning a junction earlier to

enter a sprawling public park that was located a short walking distance from their apartment.

'You want to be in a park at this hour?' Sabitha asked.

'No, I just want to be somewhere with you, somewhere that is not home,' Karthi said. She took off her seat belt, shuffled her saree as she opened the door. Sabitha opened her passenger side door, and stepped down from the car, looking on perplexed as Karthi went to the trunk of the car, and rummaged through their shopping bags from earlier in the night.

The wind blew in her face, and there was barely anyone in the park. Sabitha loved the wind but was not keen on taking a walk at this hour as the park near their house was unusually big and she was not keen on getting lost at night. Karthi closed the trunk and seemed to be holding something in her hands, which she quickly hid at her back, before gingerly walking towards Sabitha, with a smile that was all too radiant, aided by the floodlight, which was shining directly on Karthi.

'What are we doing here? What are you doing? What are you holding?' Sabitha asked. She could have easily asked a few more questions, but stopped herself.

'First, I sort of have a question to ask,' Karthi said. 'I didn't plan this all too meticulously, so I hope this is fine,' she added, bringing out a small black box. Sabitha's jaw dropped, as Karthi flipped open the small box, and displayed a ring that was shining under the shadow of the floodlights. Sabitha realized that Karthi never went to the washroom as she initially claimed. She thought of the ring as a gift, until she started reaching out for the box, and she realized where Karthi was headed.

'Wait . . .'

'Sabitha, I listened to you talking about nudging someone else to have a temple wedding to fulfil that small desire you have.

But I don't think you need nudge anyone else to have a temple wedding. Because I think you deserve, and you should, have one for yourself, no matter the scale. No matter the location. I will be there, right next to you, signing up for that same temple wedding,' Karthi said.

'That is, of course, if you say yes,' she added. 'Sorry, with what I am wearing it's difficult to get on my knees.'

Sabitha remained stoic and speechless. She held both of Karthi's hands, and pulled her closer. She put her palms on top of the box and gently closed the lid, but kept her hands on top of the box. She didn't push it away. But she did not take the box either.

'Karthi, why are you doing this?' Sabitha asked.

'I just told you . . .'

'No, you are talking about getting married. This has to be much, much more than that. I'm not saying no, but I want to know what made you come to this decision'

'It just felt right. I happened to be wearing this dress again,' Karthi said, chuckling. 'It has been a good day. And when you talked about the temple wedding, I just imagined us doing it. Why can't we? We deserve to experience these things too,' she added. But her face had changed. She expected Sabitha to immediately accept the gift, and was surprised that the latter wasn't quick to say yes.

'No, Karthi. It looks to me like you are motivated by your need to make a statement. It's not about others versus us. It's not about what they have versus what we have. A marriage has to be about us, and us alone. It's about where I want a wedding, it's not about the dress you wore today. I don't read into these signs as much as you do. For me, only one thing matters— whether you are ready to spend the rest of your life with me.

And whether I am ready. Whether we are good for each other. Whether we are willing to figure each other out, and willing to put up with these other parts. I'm not as intensely romantic as you are, as tonight clearly shows. A part of me did jump in joy, but this is me. I am practical, logical. And I can't make such a huge decision on such a whim,' she said, holding Karthi's hands in fervent hope that it didn't sound like a rejection.

Karthi merely nodded, and sniffled a little. She kept her emotions at bay, and instead told Sabitha she was ready to go back home. The couple returned home, still awkwardly quiet around one another as they showered and got ready for bed.

'Do you want to talk?' Sabitha asked, as she put on body lotion while sitting on a chair near the bedside. Karthi looked sullen, lying down on the bed and staring blankly at the ceiling. 'I don't know. What is there to talk about? I will just wait until you are ready to make a decision,' she said. All her fears and insecurities were boiling over, but she didn't know how to verbalize them coherently.

'It's not about me alone, babe,' Sabitha said. 'I am saying, ask for the right reasons.'

Karthi seemed suddenly incensed. She could no longer contain the litany of her thoughts. 'What the fuck?' she said. 'Are you telling me all the reasons I have now are not the right reasons?' she said, sitting up on the bed.

'Not for me. It looks like another statement. People can get married in temples, why can't we? It's valid, Karthi. And I love that drive about you. I love that you take these small battles on. I love that you are trying to make little rules for you, and for us as well. It's one of the things that I love the most about you. But don't forget how we met. I saw you with cuts on your hands. I saw a vulnerable woman, a woman like me, before I met this fighter. And I love both sides of you. I want you to be vulnerable with me and fight your battles with the world,' she said, getting on the bed, sitting cross-legged, across from Karthi, and holding her hands, facing her. 'But I am not a battle you need to fight. We,' she pointed her fingers at both of them, 'are not a battle you need to fight. There is no statement that needs to be made here. I will happily live with you, temple wedding or not. You know what's more important than a temple wedding, it's being with you.'

Karthi pondered for a moment. 'I want a direction for this relationship. I want an evolution. I want to be more than a roommate. I am not sure how much of that is influenced by my need to fight battles. But this is truly what I want. I want to be with you, and I want us to be more than what we are now,' she said. 'I keep thinking about leaving the country, to someplace where we enjoy more rights.'

'Wow,' Sabitha seemed to be taken back. 'I didn't know you were thinking this. Karthi, I have no intention of leaving. I have not thought about living abroad at all. Question is, do you want to leave?' Sabitha asked, dreading the answer. In her mind, a dream was disintegrating. 'Karthi, did you propose to sort of lock us down, so you have a reason to stay?' Sabitha asked further.

Karthi, who was looking sullen, suddenly seemed to slightly cheer up. She shook her head vigorously. 'You've got it all wrong,' she said. 'I have been thinking about leaving, like there's a logical part telling me to leave, but my heart,' she said, 'says stay. And you know I listen to my heart more, right?,' Karthi said.

Sabitha nodded warmly. 'Why does your heart say stay?,' Sabitha asked, raising her eyebrows.

'Because, this is home. I mean this,' Karthi pointed her fingers towards both of them, 'is home.'

Sabitha grinned from ear to ear. 'You should have led with that.'

'Led what?'

'The proposal,' Sabitha said, nodding subtly.

Karthi shrieked mildly.

'But ask yourself if you can live with this. You stay back because of your heart. I am staying largely for logical reasons. I don't do all of this again, and uproot myself somewhere else. My little world is here, I am okay with it. This is the difference between us,' Sabitha said.

'Well, that's why we call it family. So that we can accept the different ways we both are. And that's what we will be to each other—family.'

Chapter Nineteen

MUHIBAH

November 2019

Yuva pulled his car cautiously by the side of a narrow housing estate road in Sitiawan. His brand-new car glistened under one of the few sporadic street lights on the road he was in. He turned off the ignition, and got down from the car, closing the door and allowing the late night wind to blow in his face. He had finally shaved his beard after spending months trying to look the part of a heartbroken man—although he still regularly oscillated between being cranky and extremely pleasant as a human being. Geetha got down from the passenger's seat, came around to stand next to him, leaning against the driver's door.

'There's a bag in the boot. Open the pocket zip and get the thing that is in there,' she said, and he duly followed her instructions. When he felt what was inside the bag, his expression changed drastically. He picked the contents out and saw a box of cigarettes with a lighter.

'What the—' he raised his voice, before controlling it immediately, realizing it was probably past bed time for most of the people who lived in the neighbourhood. He heard her chuckle and laugh at his reaction. He handed the box over to her. 'When did this start?' he asked.

'You know something, I have been doing this for years, but not regularly. Maybe it's one a day at the most. Nothing more,' she said, and lit up a stick, and playfully offered one to him. Yuva took an inordinately long time to say no.

'Oh my god, you are that depressed that you are considering starting smoking at this age,' she said, taking a deep drag and releasing into the night wind. She saw the wind carry her smoke. 'You should stop being so stuck up about how you think the world should be. First, be easy on yourself. Go, get drunk, vent, make a fool of yourself. Let it go. And then figure out how you want to be, who you want to be,' she said.

'What do you mean? I do know who I am; I haven't lost my mind,' he said.

'Do you, though? I am not talking about work or even family. Who are you—how are you as a person?' she said. 'Do you know what "Muhibah" means?' she asked, pointing to the big sign board that was in front of them that read, 'Taman Aman Muhibah'.

'Harmony,' he said.

'But have you felt it?' she asked.

'In this country, fat chance. It's all lip service,' he lamented. Muhibah was the word they had heard since their childhood, and it was used to define interracial relations in Malaysia. There was always a picture of an Indian, Chinese and a Malay, in drastically different attires, with the word Muhibah strewn over the image. Occasionally, the people making these advertisements and slogans would become more inclusive and incorporated the images of the indigenous people of Sabah and Sarawak.

'Of course, we all know how everything is designed by race,' she said, taking another long drag. 'But have you ever felt that here?' she asked, pointing at her own heart.

'I think I already answered your question previously,' he said. She shook her head, and threw the cigarette butt to the floor, squashing it with her feet. 'The tenet of harmony is coexistence. And for coexistence to happen, first there must be acceptance,' she said. 'You are tolerating, not accepting. Start accepting people who are around you first, and then you can take that angst to the society,' she said.

'Is that why you pointlessly made me stop just a few hundred meters away from the house?' he asked. She smiled. 'No, I just wanted a smoke. Mom and dad still think I am a good girl,' she added and got into the car. Geetha needed the smoke because it was the first time she was returning home after almost a year. So much had happened in a year that she did not know where to start once she met her mother. But the problem was, there was a very clear objective why she had come to see her mother and father—she was practicing the advice that she had just given her brother. She had to start accepting her parents for who they were, and that included their belief systems, regardless of how outdated she thought they were. As they pulled up to the house, the gate was already open and the front porch light had been turned on. Ratha was awake, wearing a sarong and singlet watching old 1960s Tamil songs on the television. He sprung to his feet as Yuva drove the car into the porch. Ratha immediately came to the porch to greet his children. It was the first time he was seeing both his children travel back together from Kuala Lumpur. Geetha got down from the car, and her father walked to her, rubbed her shoulders, asking if she had had her dinner, before going to the back of the car to pick up Geetha's bag and walk into the house. Yuva was left to pick up his own bag.

'Wow, it's like you are some new guest; he completely forgot about his heartbroken son,' he said, with a smile.

Geetha inhaled the crisp sea breeze smell that lingered in the air, and took a long look at her front porch, and the entrance of her house; the place she grew up in. She had only been away for a year, but she felt like she was a completely new person entering the house again.

* * *

Earlier that evening, Sabitha drove in, almost hesitantly, on the rocky road that accommodated a single car at the best of times, and stopped it right in front of her house, which she had not visited in a year. Dread filled her up. She had not spoken to her mother in ages, and now she was going to break to her some news that was probably going to further damage their already fragile relationship. Her father was a religious person who was known to have a temper for things he did not approve of. She knew none of this would go down well with either of them, and she was ready for the consequences.

Her father stepped out of the house, a set of keys in his hands, headed to the makeshift garage next to their house, and unlocked the two wooden frames that were flimsily attached to each other. He pried open the self-made wooden gates, and guided Sabitha to park inside the garage. Parking in front of the house always meant obstructing the path for anyone else who was passing through the same road. Having parked, she got down from her car, walked to the porch, and her mother stepped out of the house, holding sweets in her hands.

'Welcome back,' she said, caressing her daughter's forehead for a short while until a smile appeared on Sabitha's face. She offered the sweets. 'I went to the temple and did a prayer in your name when you told us you are coming back today,' she said, opening her palms. Sabitha gracefully accepted the sweets, and her mom placed sacred ash on her forehead.

'Stop keeping her outside, she must be tired after the long drive, let her keep her bags inside and get some rest,' her father said, standing by the door of the house. She entered, knowing full well she was going to unleash hell in the household tomorrow.

* * *

Sabitha woke up early, helped out with breakfast preparation, all the time making small talk, sat down and had a hearty, big breakfast—idlis. As she smothered the cakes in the hot lentil broth, as she always loved doing, she wondered if this would be the last time she enjoyed this dish at home. She took a good look around the house she grew up in, the old wooden structure, the creaking floorboards on the first floor, the rusting swing on the front porch, and the sound of chirping birds and roosters cowing. This was the cradle of civilization for the Malaysian journey of her people, but she was increasingly finding it difficult to reconcile her lifestyle and her desires with these stories of her genetic history, which came with cultural and traditional baggage and expectations which she simply could not fulfil. How much cultural identity should be defined by the generic acceptance of the larger community?

The heavy breakfast and musings now over, she visited her room and made sure that her bag and her car keys were all in order in case she had to leave the house immediately. Having made sure she had packed her things, she went to the living room and turned on the television. Her parents joined her soon after.

'Is it okay to speak now or do you want to speak later?' she asked after reducing the volume on the television, not wanting to put too much pressure on the need to have a conversation. Her parents were already expecting her to discuss her sexuality— the white elephant in the house. Her father took a deep breath, partially threw his glasses on the living room table, and laid back on his chair, nodding his head. 'Sure, go ahead,' he said. Her mother looked worried. She did not say anything, she merely followed her husband's cue. Sabitha looked at her car parked in the small makeshift garage next to the house and mentally prepared to be kicked out of her own house.

* * *

'When are we going to broach the topic with them? I feel like I am walking on a minefield,' Geetha whispered, nudging her brother as she held a bowl of marinated chicken in her hands in the kitchen.

Yuva had a mischievous smile on his face. 'Hey,' he said, clearing his throat and rubbing his eyes as he put down the knife that he was using to cut onions at the dining table. 'I was not the one supporting a gay marriage here,' he added.

If a look could kill, Yuva would have died that instant. She picked up the knife and held it inches away from his face. 'If you don't help, I won't even pay heed to the fact that you are my brother. I will kill you, or you will get a tight slap,' she said. 'Should have slapped you a long time ago; you would have grown up to be a better man,' she added, and walked away from the dining table, leaving the knife behind. Yuva smiled to himself. Yuva had had a better relationship with his parents, mainly because he was the son and he had lesser restrictions in the house compared to Geetha. Geetha's decisions, choices and path in life had been dictated with absolute detail by their parents, but

Yuva got to do whatever he wanted to as long as he was able to fulfil the generic expectations they had of him—become a moderately successful, well-earning engineer. His only act of rebellion was dating a non-Telugu, but even then, he was given enough leeway to bring her to their home and introduce her to them. Geetha was never likely to get such privileges, at least not in her twenties. He could understand why she stayed away for so long—she was reclaiming her own space and at the same time was sending out a message—whether her parents wanted control of their children's life or they wanted to be included in their children's life. It was always going to be a tall order to convey these dynamics to their parents.

Janaki came to the kitchen and monitored Geetha deep frying the chicken and boiling potatoes on a pan and a pot on the stove. She nodded her head in approval, and came and sat beside her son on the kitchen table. 'Oh my god, you seem to be struggling,' she said, looking at the uneven onion pieces that were on the chopping board, and Yuva's generally laboured pace in getting through the onions without rubbing his eyes at every opportunity. He had a better relationship with his mom compared to his dad, and he decided that he was going to broach the subject like it was not something that demands serious attention.

'Mom, I want to tell you something,' he said, sniffling, his eyes increasingly red, moments after he staved off her attempts to hijack chopping duties from him. 'It's serious, and I want you to listen to me,' he added. Janaki, meanwhile, had taken over onion cutting duties from her son.

Geetha was standing over the large wok with the oil occasionally sprinkling outside of the wok, with some sweat trickling down her forehead. She closed her eyes, surprised that her brother had chosen such an odd time to broach the subject. But there was never going to be a good time to say what he wanted to say.

'Nana,' she called out before her brother could continue. She was scheming now. She made her father come into the kitchen on the pretext of evaluating the greens she had already fried earlier. She put some on his hands and took a small portion, wary of their heat.

'Sabitha,' Yuva said loudly, opening the topic. His mother was chopping onions very slowly now. 'Is getting married,' he added.

Ratha's attention turned towards Yuva.

'Oh, has she come to her senses?' Janaki asked, pausing her chopping. Geetha closed her eyes. She did not want to react. She opened her eyes again and continued to maintain focus on the chicken in front of her.

'No, probably not in the way you expect her to,' he said. 'She's getting married to a woman. Her partner,' he said. Geetha breathed a sigh of relief. 'She wanted to invite you to come for the wedding, but she did not know how to ask you or even start talking to you. So, she has asked us to help ask you and nana,' he added, turning around and looking at Ratha. Ratha looked like he did not want to make a decision on the matter.

Janaki stood up from the chair in a hurry. 'What shit is this? What law allows two women to get married? Has she decided to drag the family's dignity through the mud? Is it not bad enough that she had to come out; now she has to get married and let everyone know that she is lesbian? Can you all not think from our perspective?' she shrieked.

Geetha had never seen her mother like that. Her eyes opened wide and she actively avoided making eye contact. She wanted to react but again she reminded herself of the promise of not judging her mother. Yuva resumed chopping the onions that his mother had abandoned, hoping the storm would pass.

'Mom, can you tell me what the problem is? Do you have a problem with her being gay, or do you have a problem with her getting married?' Geetha asked, raising her voice over the frying chicken.

'Well, we can't stop you guys from whatever you want to do, apparently, because then we are seen as enemies. But we don't have much to hold on to—all we have is this, our standing in the community, our dignity and honour. If you do something behind closed doors, that is one thing, but when you announce it to the world, do you think about what it will do to the family? What it will do to my sister? Is this why we slogged so hard to send you off the schools, why we saved so much money so that we can make you lawyers, engineers, doctors?' she asked.

'And where is this wedding going to be? Church? Some hall? It sure won't be at the registration department. Why are we needed there? Are we expected to go there and observe all the traditions of giving our family's daughter away to another woman? What is the other woman's side going to do then? Act like they are from the groom's side? Do you guys have common sense?' Janaki was standing smack in the centre of the dining area, directing her questions at both Yuva and Geetha.

'Actually,' he cleared his throat, 'they are getting married in a temple.' His voice was somewhat muffled, as his mom's meltdown had left him trembling and with a dry throat. He looked at his sister for help.

'That's why she wants you there. She wants you and the other family members there, to do all the things you would expect to do during her wedding, the only difference being she is not getting married to a man,' Geetha explained. 'And that other girl, she has no family. She is an orphan. So, in a way, they both want you guys there, to act as elders for both of them, to bless them,' she added.

'What is this, blessing after the fact? The deed has been done. If everything is at liberty and you are doing it your way, why do you need our blessing?' Janaki asked.

'Because we are still family,' Geetha and Yuva said at the same time. They both looked at each other, and in the midst of the tension, exchanged a smile. Geetha felt like she had only recently discovered a brother in her life.

'Which temple said okay to this?' Ratha calmly interjected.

* * *

'Temple? Which temple?' Sabitha's father asked, leaning forward in his chair. He was doing all the questioning. Her mother was quiet, and Sabitha felt like she was sitting in an interrogation room, just waiting for the bad cop to enter once the good cop inevitably leaves.

'Pangkor Temple,' she said. 'One of the priests there is my childhood friend, and he has arranged everything. You used to take me there a lot as a child and in my mind, I always wished I would get married there,' she added.

'You still wished to get married in a temple even after you knew you were . . .' her mother hesitated to use the word; she left her sentence hanging.

'Yes mom, me being lesbian didn't make me any less Indian. It didn't turn me white overnight. I still like idli and I still hate pasta,' she said. She was still mellow and careful with every single one of her sentences, and kept picturing herself driving away from Bagan Datoh in her car in less than an hour from now. At least she had had a good breakfast.

They had asked all the questions they wanted to ask about Karthi. 'Any intention of bringing her here, introducing her to us?' her father suddenly asked, still in his stern, seemingly displeased tone.

'No, I do not want to make things worse than they already are,' she said.

'Then? What do you expect us to say without even meeting her or knowing the kind of person she is?' he said. 'People would normally introduce partners before a decision about marriage is taken, before a temple is chosen, but you seem to have decided everything without our help,' he added.

Sabitha looked at her father enquiringly. He was not reacting the way she had expected him to react. This was not going the way she had expected it to go. 'I am sorry,' was all she could muster. 'But I did not know if you guys would even speak to me after what happened the last time,' she said.

Her father got up from his chair, took his hand towel and gently swatted away the dust on the chair he was sitting on.

'Well, bring her here then, and then we shall see what can be done next,' he said. 'And I think you can start cooking lunch. It will be late otherwise. Make something that she likes,' he said to his wife, pointing at his daughter. Sabitha's mother merely nodded. Sabitha cupped her mouth and fought back tears. Her mother stood up, walked to her, and held her head against her stomach.

'I saw the bags packed in your room earlier,' she said. She caressed her daughter's hair, and Sabitha started crying uncontrollably into her mother's oversized t-shirt, which reeked of curry and spices. 'Your choice is not easy for us, but you are the only child we have. We still have to learn, but you will always be our only daughter.'

Minutes later, with her eyes dried and her mom in the kitchen, Sabitha picked up the phone and called Karthi, who was at work. 'How did it go?' Karthi asked, without wasting any time. Sabitha was still not confident enough to speak loudly to her girlfriend on the phone while in her parents' house, so she whispered a little.

'You won't believe it,' Sabitha she said slowly.

'Babe, I would love to hear all about it, but I am at work I can only spare five minutes for you right now,' Karthi said.

'You don't have to spare five minutes. Can you, instead, drive down here for me?' Sabitha asked.

'Is it that bad? You need me to drive you back?'

'No, I want you to come meet my parents.'

There was silence on the other end of the line. Karthi took a while before she said anything. 'Are you serious?' she asked. 'How?'

'Five minutes is not enough for that story. Just come as soon as you can, before they change their minds,' Sabitha chuckled. She could almost hear Karthi's smile from the other end of the line.

'Okay, love you,' Karthi hung up.

Just as Sabitha ended her phone call with Karthi, her phone pinged—it was a message from Geetha. 'I'm sorry, I couldn't convince my mom to come. She reacted badly and hasn't really calmed down. Yuva tried as well,' the message read. Sabitha was surprised by the last sentence—the cousin she resented the most had tried to get his mother to come for her lesbian temple wedding. She could not invent words to describe how surreal the day had been for her. Her aunt's refusal to attend didn't faze her. 'Are you on the road already?' Geetha asked. Sabitha realized Geetha had fully expected the former's parents to react just as badly as her own mother did. In fact, Geetha expected that convincing her own mother to come would be an easier task—it's always easier to convince the aunt rather than the mother, because the stakes are not just as high.

'Thanks for trying,' Sabitha typed back. 'Actually, they want to meet Karthi. I think mom and dad will be involved in the wedding,' she added.

Geetha sent a shocked reaction. Sabitha chuckled, and took a tissue to wipe off the sniffle from her nose. She breathed the sea breeze in the air. This was going to be her home for a while longer. The goodbyes were not necessary, yet.

Geetha was watching her mom pacing the house, doing unnecessary tidying up, seemingly avoiding conversation with anyone. The former was sitting at the front porch, on a small wooden chair, under an awning protected by the afternoon heat. She worried looking at her mother—what would her reaction be when she got to know about Anand?

But that was a question for another day. She breathed in the west coast breeze, and closed her eyes. Home.

Chapter Twenty

MANGALYAM

February 2020.

For decades, Malaysian Indians thronged a spot in the island of Pangkor, located some three kilometers off the coast of Perak, at a particular time every year for a festival at a Hindu temple that seemed to open its path out into the sea. It housed what many of them believed to be a powerful goddess, and the crowd on this island of 25,000 grew exponentially once a year for this temple's festival. Located right by the sea, the steps at the end of this temple joined the sea effortlessly, flanked on either side by fishing boats and fishermen's huts, built on stilts.

This was also the island where the British dominance over the Malay Peninsula started, with the signing of Pangkor Treaty of 1874.

Sabitha had come here every year throughout her childhood, mainly because her parents had prayed to this goddess for a daughter after being without a child for the first four years of their marriage. She was seen in her family as the goddess' gift, and coming back here felt like a natural destination for something as important as her wedding. Sabitha and the rest of the family members all got down at the ferry pier on an early weekday morning, just as the rest of the people of Pangkor were going in the opposite direction—many of the residents here worked in the mainland, and made that thirty-minute ferry trip every morning and evening in order to make a living. The island was lined with extremely narrow, winding roads, which could only accommodate one car at a time. Small stalls serving broth-based food and selling dried seafood products lined up most of the street, before the road started becoming a series of winding uphill and downhill battles, with nothing but the voices of trees and winds for accompaniment. This fifteen-minute walk from the pier to the temple past this quiet road, punctuated by the odd motorbike or tourist van had characterized every visit Sabitha had made to this temple, and she was glad to realize that even though the ferries had gotten more modern and expensive, this part of the journey had never changed.

She was wearing a salwar kameez, as was Karthi; accompanied by her parents, Geetha, Yuva, Anu, Anand, Kasturi and Lakshmi. Between them, they were carrying clothes, and a small pot of rice, and packets of cooked food, as much as they could fit among the small group. They didn't look like a regular wedding entourage. They headed to the temple entrance and got down the slope that led to the temple grounds, and Sabitha found her friend Rajan sitting by the side of the temple and smiling, waiting for them, with the temple keys in his hands. Rajan was dusky, thin, had a stutter, and was a native of the island. His family was settled and reasonably well-to-do on the island, and Rajan's own journey had been one involving a search of identity. Sabitha had known for years that he was gay, but he had never come out to his family—mainly because he was not highly educated and never had the chance to explore his sexuality in a small coastal island where fishing and agriculture were the main economic drivers. He had admitted his sexuality privately to her, but never publicly professed it to them. He was more religious than his family since his childhood, and had come to this temple without fail every year, before opting to pursue a religious path by becoming an apprentice of the temple priest. Rajan would go into a trance and speak in the voice of goddess during festivals, but had never shown interest in any other female form aside from the goddess at this temple.

'Where is your boss?' Sabitha asked, approaching him.

'He went back to his hometown in India, that is why I have arranged for this to be today,' he said, winking at her. Sabitha looked around the temple. 'Don't worry, very few people come here this early in the morning. Most of the everyday morning crowd has come and left for the morning ferry. This will be like a private event,' he added, standing up and stretching his skin-and-bones frame. Sabitha's father stepped forward and handed him a tray with silk sarees, which the priest swiftly brought into the temple for prayers, before giving it to the two brides.

'I think you can go get changed now,' he said, and handed the sarees over to Sabitha and Karthi. They both walked into the adjoining changing room near the temple's hall, and came out decked in heavy sarees that instantly melted their moderate make-up under the heat. Geetha and Anu stood outside the changing rooms, and respectively tended to the two brides to fix their make-up and adjust their clothes. Karthi was in a brimming red saree, while Sabitha was in a yellow saree with golden borders. Rajan had arranged the space in the centre of the temple accordingly, and both the women walked gingerly to the centre and were made to sit next to each other, struggling under the weight of their attires.

Slowly, the regular morning heat gave way to a gust of coastal wind, and everyone in the temple felt some relief from the heat.

'What if someone comes?' Sabitha's mother asked, worried, looking at her husband. But he did not answer her. He did not need to. Within a couple of minutes since the winds started, the clouds unleashed a deluge of rain on the temple, trapping them inside, and definitely trapping anyone else intending to come to the temple. There was no shaded walkaway in Pangkor and the only means of public transportation was a big nine-seater van that seemed to hold the entire breadth of Pangkor's minuscule roads. Rajan, who was already without a shirt, as part of his priestly duties, started chanting his prayers. The strong winds, which were making the sea even more choppy, were threatening to blow out the fire he had started using dried cow dung cakes, so the wedding party, for their own worth, huddled in a circle around the two girls and Rajan, hence protecting the fire in their own little way. Rajan constantly took a break from chanting to shade the fire, and the two brides helped him as well, although it came at the expense of them sweating even more.

Rajan chanted louder, refusing to let his voice be drowned by the rain, the wind, the lightning, the storm, and the sound of the water crashing against the temple's floors. Sabitha looked at her parents with a smile that was difficult to erase. Her mother smiled back at her, albeit a little subtly, while her father continued being as stoic as he had been since she had broken the news to him. He was exceptionally kind towards Karthi, however, and she was convinced that he had another side to his affection that he had is not expressing to his own daughter ever since she came out. Or, maybe, he didn't know how to express it, Karthi thought. Karthi was more than happy with their presence; it meant at least one of them had a set of parents present at the wedding.

Karthi brimmed looking at her sisters, Kasturi and Lakshmi, who looked decked up for the first time in their lives. They acted as Karthi's bridesmaids for the wedding, while Anu acted as Sabitha's bridesmaid.

Rajan took around thirty minutes to finish most of his prayers, before he started chanting faster, while non verbally waving his hands and urging the rest of the wedding party in the temple to bring the wedding mangalsutra. Sabitha's father kneeled forward and put a tray with a mangalsutra in front of Rajan and between the two women. Both Karthi and Sabitha looked at it and each other, confused.

'Who's going to tie it?' Rajan asked, with a smile, having paused his chants momentarily. In a traditional wedding, the man would tie the mangalsutra on the woman's neck, but this was a wedding without traditional gender roles, and both of them wondered who will be acting as the man of the relationship. Just then, Sabitha's father leaned forward again, and flipped a white cloth on the same tray, revealing that there were two mangalsutras on the same tray. Rajan smiled, and contained his laugh, wanting to keep his poise for his role as a priest.

'Looks like both of you will,' he said, and picked one of it and handed it to Karthi. 'You do it first,' he instructed. Rajan chanted the wedding mantra twice as both of them took turns to get up on their knees, crawl a step to the other person, and tie the mangasutra around their neck with the help of the bridesmaid and elders, who made sure the knots were tight at the back. In between making sure the mangalsutra was tied properly, the single-digit wedding party also tossed handfuls of uncooked rice on the bride and bride. Karthi and Sabitha also exchanged garlands before they stood up and walked around the fire seven times as strong winds continued to threaten to diminish the fire. Geetha knelt down and tied the ends of their sarees to each other after the first round, and the whole group shared a laugh together. When the couple finished going around the fire, the marriage was finalized with a few more prayers, and Rajan allowed both of them to leave the altar. As Rajan stood up, having finished his prayers, the wind finally got better of the fire, putting it out before he could react. Karthi and Sabitha, now giggling like school children, removed the garlands, and tried to remove as much rice as possible from each other's hairs, bodies and attires.

Geetha walked to the edge of the temple, took a plastic bag filled with dried banana leaves, took them out and sprinkled some rain water on them to get them moist. She then placed the banana leaves in a small circle at the edge of the temple, but far enough from the rain. Anu carried a pot of rice, and served a little bit of rice in each of the banana leaf that was laid out. Sabitha's mother collected another, smaller pot, and put out small amounts of thick, green vegetable gravy onto each dish, before Kasturi and Lakshmi decked them with sweets and savoury snacks.

'Please, everyone, come and eat. Something simple,' Sabitha's mother said. The entire wedding party took their seats. Sabitha and Karthi struggled to sit cross-legged and contemplated changing back into more comfortable clothes. 'No, please eat a little while being dressed like that, first,' Sabitha's mother insisted. The two women, who were supposed to sit next to each other, smiled, and got up, not wanting to sully their expensive attires with curry. Sabitha walked over to the other end and kneeled in front of Anand, who was sitting next to Geetha. Anand chuckled, and fed the woman he had loved in so many different ways for the past seven years. Karthi, meanwhile, kneeled in front of Kasturi and Lakshmi, and they took turns to feed her. Satisfied after taking five mouthfuls, both of them walked back to the changing room and get into more comfortable clothes. Rajan sat down for his meal on the floor, cross legged, having cleaned up most of the prayer area.

'What is this?' he asked, slowly mashing the curry with the rice.

'That is gongura,' Sabitha's mother said, referring to roselle leaves that are very much a staple of the Telugu diet in India. The curry was sour, but beautifully tempered with all the savoury snacks that came with the served dish.

'They go best with fish, but . . .' Sabitha's mother said, 'but since we are in a temple,' she added, referring to the tradition of only serving vegetarian food in temples.

Having changed into more comfortable clothes, Sabitha and Karthi took their seats next to Rajan.

'Won't you be in trouble for doing this?' Sabitha asked, as she sat down beside Rajan.

'When have I not been in trouble? I am always doing things that put me in trouble. In fact, me just being myself already puts me in trouble. How much worse can it get from that?' he asked, before taking a mouthful of the rice mixed with gongura, with a satisfied smile on his face. Sabitha chuckled.

After Sabitha and Karthi finished their second serving of meals, Sabitha's father and Geetha separately paid Rajan money for his troubles, after thirty minutes of the entourage collectively observing the rain from the within the temple.

When the rain finally subsided, the family hiked up the same road they had come in from and made their way back to the pier. All of them stood on the viewing deck of the ferry as it negotiated the choppy post-storm sea, leaving the small island where everything started—for the British and also for Sabitha's family.

The ferry's engine gave a low grumble and a sputter as it pulled up to the pier at Lumut, the seaside town which serves the Pangkor ferry route. They walked out of the jetty and slowly separated into their respective cars. The siblings walked in a group with Anu and Anand, and slowly, Yuva retreated and walked besides Anu.

'Hi,' he said.

'Finally, you acknowledge me,' she said, walking slowly.

'Well, I did not know what or how to say anything to you at the temple,' he said.

'How about starting with an apology?' she said, with a smile.

He smiled. 'Yes, I am sorry. Though, I do not think just saying sorry quite covers it,' he added.

'Then what does cover it?'

'I don't think anything in particular can cover it, but I can start attempting to make it up to you. Maybe, coffee,' he said. Yuva did not have a calculation for what he was doing. He was changing his life and he had to ask all the questions he felt like asking in order to know what might work and what not. He was groping in the dark, he was not sure what or who he could hold on to.

'Look, before you say anything, this is not an attempt to win you back. Just coffee as acquaintances, or friends; just no labels. Let's see,' he said.

Anu smiled and stopped walking. 'Yuva, I don't want to have coffee with you and tell you the same thing I want to say to you now. Something happened that day—both during the day when we took a break, and that day at your office. On both those days, I lost something. And I've never got back what I lost on those days. And you can't give those things to me,' she said. 'I won't lie. I am not immune to you. You still have some effect on me. That is why we can't have coffee together. Because we are not good for each other. When I see you, I still get reminded of a lot of bitterness and hurt. Your bitterness and my hurt,' she added. 'Maybe one day I will be able to get over it and we can have coffee, but as friends. Because I don't want to wait until then. I have to move on. So do you,' she said.

'You are rejecting me, wow,' Yuva said with a sigh.

Anu tried to disagree with his assessment, but stopped short of saying it. 'Actually, I think yes. I think I have to, for both our sakes,' she added. Anu continued walking towards her car. 'Send my regards to your parents,' she said as she unlocked the car. Then, she changed her mind, and walked really close to him. 'Yuva, I am glad to see how you are today. Continue being this person. And don't hold someone's past against them. Accept. Like how you did at the temple today,' she said, leaning in to give a warm hug, which he knew was a final, goodbye hug. He felt sadness swelling up in his heart again, but he resolved not to show his emotions in front of her. He nodded to her, mildly reciprocating her hug. Anu got into her car and took a box of tissue and immediately dabbed her eyes, fighting her own tears. She looked at him, still standing by her car, and waved goodbye to him, before driving off. Yuva jogged to his sister's car, with Geetha and Anand both waiting for him. Geetha gestured inquiringly at him, and he merely shook his head. As he walked past her to get into the back seat, she patted him on the shoulder, before pulling his hands and hugging him.

'She just hugged me like that to say goodbye,' he said.

'And I am hugging you like this to say I'm here for the rest of your life. You can choose which hug you want to remember,' she said. Anand smiled, and got into the passenger seat of the car. The three of them drove to Janaki and Ratha's house, and pulled up in the porch. Geetha looked on nervously. She had informed her parents that she was going to introduce someone to them, and now it was her turn to feel what Sabitha had felt at the hands of her parents for so long. The trepidation built up inside her. Yuva stirred from his melancholy and tapped her shoulder. 'Come, you should guide the guest, you can't be afraid. That's your father and mother,' he said. She and Anand had gotten down from the car, but Yuva led the way.

Janaki came out to the porch and greeted them. She initially seemed oblivious to Anand, and went straight for her son. 'How did it go?' she asked, looking at Yuva.

'Wonderful. You missed it. It's your loss,' Yuva said, before immediately going to his room to remove his long, uncomfortable kurta, and changing into a simpler shirt.

He came back into the living room a couple of minutes later and saw his sister and Anand awkwardly sitting on the sofa. Janaki and Ratha were in the kitchen, chattering with each other. Yuva sat next to his sister, before his mother showed up with a cup of hot tea for Anand. Anand thanked Janaki, and she calmly took a seat. By now, her attention had completely turned towards him.

'What are you doing, ya?' Janaki asked, looking at Anand, who was sipping a cup of hot tea.

'I am just about to finish my medicine,' he said.

'Why? Did you start late?' she asked.

Geetha was fearing the worst. Ratha, who had just showed up to the living room, could already sense what was coming. He looked at Yuva instead, and they exchanged a look of solidarity, sensing that heightened tension was going to take place in the house yet again.

'Why?' he heard his father mutter haplessly. Yuva was trying to contain the laughter on his face.

'No, aunty. As usual, after school and all,' he said.

'Just tell them your age before she asks you another ten indirect questions about it,' Yuva interjected.

'I am twenty-three, aunty,' Anand said. He had a small smile on his face—one that acknowledged the awkwardness that information was going to create. Janaki was completely silent. She looked at her daughter. She looked at her husband. She looked at her son.

'I am actually Sabitha's classmate,' he added. Geetha lifted her fingers and stopped him from giving any more elaboration about how he was connected to Geetha. In the process of stopping him, she held his hands and did not remove her hands thereafter.

Janaki stood up and walked into the kitchen. Geetha tapped Anand's hands and excused herself. Both siblings followed their mother into the kitchen.

'If you hear some shouting, just close your ears or don't pay attention to the words,' Ratha said to Anand. Anand was still mildly amused by the whole situation.

'Mom,' Yuva reached his mom first and put his hands around her shoulder. She was standing by the kitchen top, her back to her children, breathing heavily. He was afraid she was going to have a heart attack. 'Are you okay?' he asked.

Geetha, who didn't want to come too close, and stood behind Yuva, forming a mini-queue behind her mother, looked a little concerned as well. 'Do you need any medicines?' Geetha asked. Janaki turned around and shot a long, angry look at her daughter, before she shook her head calmly.

Yuva decided to try his luck in explaining the situation to her. 'When I had a Malayalam girlfriend, you asked me to bring her to the house. If you treat Geetha's choice differently, then it would be a double standard,' he said, his hands still on her.

'What happened to her by the way? You never gave an update,' she said, as if she needed a distraction in topic. She turned around and faced him.

'Oh, she just broke up with me,' he added, and shot a small glance at Geetha. Geetha shot him a look—it was the story of their family dynamics. She was introducing her partner to her parents and yet her mother remained more inquisitive about her son's love life.

'I told you, those people are like that. I never warmed up to her,' Janaki said. Yuva nodded, not wanting to add another argument on top of the one that his mother was clearly avoiding.

'Yes mom, Malayalam people are all bad,' he contained his own chuckle as he said that,

'Now let's focus on the issue presently at hand.'

Janaki looked at Geetha. 'I want to yell at you; make no mistake,' Janaki said, and paused for a while. 'But I don't want you staying away from home for so long again. I know you blame me for a lot of things that have happened in your life; I am not stupid. I do sense it. And I don't want you to blame me for any opinion I would have about this as well,' Janaki said.

'Akka, I think it's time you hold mom,' Yuva said, stepping away from his mother, so that he no longer stood between Geetha and his mother. Geetha leaned in and offered an awkward hug to her mother—there was no hugging culture in her family—which she accepted immediately.

'Do you want to marry him now?' Janaki asked. Geetha and Yuva chuckled a little.

'No mom. We only just started. And he is not even working yet,' she said.

'Then why are you introducing him to us? We are getting old. Please only introduce people when you are ready to get married to them, so we can get used to it and stick with it. I don't want what happened with your brother to happen to you. All that effort over a weekend, and now it is all wasted,' Janaki said, turning around and cleaning the kitchen, even though it didn't need cleaning.

Geetha smiled. 'Okay mom, in that case, you just treat him as a house guest. Don't see him as potential son-in-law. Be normal about it,' she said.

Her mother had reacted badly when she was told about Sabitha's marriage, and Geetha had fully expected an equally strong reaction, if not a stronger one, to the choice she had made in her love life. But as Geetha was finding out, mothers were different than aunts.

* * *

August 2020.

Geetha dragged in the mid-sized sofa pillows into her house and tossed them on the light blue sofas in the centre of the house. She turned around and noticed the mirror hanging on the wall, and took a good look at herself. Strands of white hair had started to appear on her head, and she plucked them out, looking at the mirror. She was disheveled and tired, and more things were streaming into the condominium unit. It was just over a 1,000 square feet; half the size of her previous home. Yet, this time she was doing most things by herself, without a deluge of helpers and movers. It wasn't a question of cost—but rather one concerning health. After months in a lockdown due a raging pandemic, she didn't want to be exposed to more strangers if she could help it. She sighed, and sat on the sofa.

'I am sorry, I am done,' she said, looking at Karthi and Sabitha, who had just come into the house. They were panting as well, with several home appliances in their hands. 'I can't any more. I am old. You lot are young,' she said. She was thirty-three years old, had handled two pro-bono cases, and gotten a far smaller apartment for her needs. Geetha decided she was not going to live alone, but would instead live with people who would know how to give her the privacy she wanted in life. She signed up for not one, but four housemates.

A screeching sound and loud chatter came through her front door, and Geetha immediately knew the source of the sound. Lakshmi and Kasturi walked in, the sisters busy arguing with each other. Geetha looked to her left and noticed that the married couple were busy arguing about the placement of things in their room, while the two sisters in front of her were having an argument about who was going to hold the front end of the tea table that they had carried up the stairs.

Geetha smiled, and just about then, the doorbell rang. She was not expecting any other visitors—there was enough cacophony in her house by now. She skipped over the things that were strewn across the house and saw Anu holding a bottle of wine and a packet of cheese.

'As promised, to celebrate the new house!' Anu said, helping herself inside. 'And also, to celebrate coming out of a lockdown.'

'Wow, you are early. I said tonight,' Geetha said.

'Well, I came to see if I might be of any help,' Anu said.

'Well, then, have a look, and roll up your sleeves,' Geetha said. Her phone pinged—it was her boyfriend. 'Are you sure you can't use some male strength?' he had asked in a text message, after she moaned to him about being old and tired.

She looked around her house again.

'No, I am sure six women have enough strength,' she wrote back.

Anand had decided not to pursue medicine right after graduating from medical school—mainly because he simply couldn't get a placement in the public healthcare system to do his housemanship. He placed the blame squarely on the Malaysian Indian obsession with producing doctors, which had led to an oversupply of them. He instead chose entrepreneurship—expanding his father's clinic brand to other areas.

'How does it feel to be an activist and a lawyer nowadays?' Anu asked, having pried open the bottle of wine, handing a glass to her. She wanted to refuse, saying it was too early to be drinking, but Geetha felt she had earned the right to enjoy a glass while the sun was still out.

'Not easy. In fact, terribly difficult,' she said. 'Sometimes, you go up against the establishment because you feel the people, or at least a majority of them, are on your side. And then you realize that is not the case. You don't win popular opinion, and the state sees you as a thorn. All you get are white hair,' she said, smiling. 'But I feel like I am finally someone I am meant to be. I feel like I am learning law all over again,' she added.

Despite losing the constitutional challenge which attracted much media attention, she was still acting as Karthi's lawyer for a less glamorous case—a suit at the Industrial Court seeking compensation and damages for unlawful termination from the government. The Industrial Court would not be interested in listening to an argument about Karthi's rights as a sexual minority, but it would definitely be interested to hear an argument about Karthi's rights as a working class person.

Geetha was cautiously optimistic that Karthi would get some monetary compensation out of this process.

'All revolutionary and evolutionary ideas started with minorities. If humanity always listened to majorities, we would have been stuck in perennial inertia,' Anu said, taking a sip of her wine after toasting it with Geetha.

'Man, I missed talking to you,' Geetha said. Her doorbell rang again, and this time, it was a delivery man. She picked up her delivery and unpacked the box, failing to remember the exact details of things she had ordered in the last few weeks. The rest of the housemates—who had come to the door to head for another round of picking up stuff from their cars and rented vans parked below the apartment—stood around her, curious.

It took her a few minutes before she managed to pry open the box. It was a sign, something that she had ordered absentmindedly at an online marketplace a week ago. The sign was supposed to be fixed on the front of the door.

'What does it say?' Kasturi asked, her view being obstructed by all the other women who were standing in front of her, closer to Geetha.

Geetha walked to the front grill, and positioned the small signboard where it was supposed to hang. She gestured the housemates to step outside and have a look at the sign for themselves. She held it up with her hands, against the wall, just below the plate displaying the apartment unit number. 'How does it look?' she asked.

No one said anything. All of them nodded in approval. They didn't need to give an approval, because Geetha knew she wanted to bring a piece of home to her new home.

The board read, 'Muhibah'.

ENDS.